Understanding the Christian Life

Understanding the Christian Life

E L M E R   T O W N S

Academx
Publishing Services

Editor: Joann Manos
Cover Designer: Krista Pierson

Understanding the Christian Life
Copyright © 2005 by Elmer Towns

Requests for permission to make copies of any part of the
work should be mailed to:

Permissions Department
Academx Publishing Services, Inc.
P.O. Box 56527
Virginia Beach, VA 23456
http://www.academx.com

Printed in the United States of America

ISBN: 1-932768-33-5

— CONTENTS —

— PREFACE —

MY INTRODUCTION
TO THE CHRISTIAN LIFE

Since my conversion experience on July 25, 1950, I have never once doubted my salvation. I have had a presence of Christ in my life that I can only explain by the phrase ". . . Christ lives in me . . ." (Galatians 2:20 NKJV).

However, Easter Sunday following my conversion, I experienced a special communion with God that I had not previously felt. At the time I was discouraged, even though I knew I was saved and I knew Christ lived within me. At about 9:00 A.M. I was waiting for my ride to Sunday school. At the time I taught in a small Presbyterian mission called Capital View Community Chapel, outside Columbia, South Carolina. My ride was approximately thirty minutes late that morning. During that time I meditated on the meaning of Galatians 2:20, especially the phrase ". . . Christ lives in me. . . ."

Another phrase in that verse, " . . . I live by the faith of the Son of God . . ." challenged me. For the first time I realized that Christ rose on the first Easter of history, but that morning He lived in my heart. I experienced His fullness, and for the first time I experienced His faith working within me. As I stood in the warm sun, waiting for my ride, I volitionally yielded anew to God. I asked Jesus Christ to give me victory by living His faith through me. Jesus Christ had never gotten discouraged, and I wanted to live above discouragement. I wanted not only faith that could trust God for money, but also faith that would not worry about anything. I wanted to trust completely in Him.

What I experienced was inward reality. I did not kneel in

7

prayer, nor did I close my eyes. I simply talked to Jesus and yielded everything to Him. I asked Jesus Christ to live His life through me. That morning, for the first time in my Christian life, I fully experienced the meaning of the resurrection life. The previous year, when I was still unsaved, Easter had simply been a historical fact. Now I had come to know personally the One who was raised from the dead; and He was not only at the right hand of God in heaven. Christ was alive in my heart. Little did I know that the inner presence of Jesus Christ in me would be tested. But that morning I did not have a care in the world, because I had the faith of Christ.

Later, Dr. R. C. McQuilkin, president of Columbia Bible College, explained in a class that he too had sought victory that comes by Jesus Christ. He explained that each year he went to a youth conference and got his spiritual bucket filled, but during the ensuing months the bucket went dry. Then one year he completely surrendered to Jesus Christ and accepted the Word of God by faith and "sank a well of his own." That Easter Sunday morning I experienced what Dr. McQuilkin and thousands of others experienced. Jesus promised, "But whoever drinks of the water that I shall give him will never thirst. But the water that I shall give him will become in him a fountain of water springing up into everlasting life" (John 4:14 NKJV).

— INTRODUCTION —

I believe: These words represent the very heart and core of the Christian faith. Latin expresses it in one word, *credo*, from which we get the word *creed*.

Too often we think of Christianity in terms of a creed written on a piece of paper, like the Apostles' Creed. But belief takes more than that. Though some teach belief in Christ is only a matter of head knowledge, recognizing that He lived and died and lived again, and others teach it is a personal response to God's invitation to be saved, in reality it requires both. The convert receives Jesus Christ into his life (John 1:12), based on knowledge of the objective promises of Scripture. Conversion that saves also involves a person's mental awareness, emotional response, and volitional acceptance of God's offer. When he expresses saving belief, a person receives Jesus Christ into his life. In this experience, the Son of God comes to live in his life.

The entrance of Jesus Christ into a life is more than an idea or concept about a new life-style entering his thoughts. It is more than the teachings about Jesus or the "spirit" of Jesus capturing his ideas, as some might be influenced by the ideas and life of George Washington or Julius Caesar. In a nonphysical experience called the new birth, Jesus Christ actually enters the life of the convert.

Though Christ cannot be seen, touched, smelled, tasted, or heard, in response to the objective Word of God, a convert experiences the reality of meeting Him. It may involve the five senses: hearing, seeing, touching (which relate to the Scripture); tasting and smell (which are involved in the Lord's Table). These five senses also form an objective basis for the sixth sense—the spiritual experience—and they prompt it. As a result of conversion, "the Spirit Himself bears witness with our spirit . . ." (Romans 8:16 NKJV); God directly communicates with the believer's spirit, apart from the five senses.

The Christian lives in two worlds. First, he lives in the everyday world and is subjected to this world. But he also lives with God. He experiences those things common only to born-again Christians. He lives in a spiritual world.

Conversion leads to a changed life. The new Christian walks with God, talks with God (in prayer), and God speaks to him. Because of this, some say the Christian is mystic, that is, he communes with God apart from the five senses.

When he becomes a Christian, a person experiences God in new ways and hungers to experience as much of Him as possible. Some ways Christians have attempted to experience God are false—even dangerous. I do not mean to give them credibility. Other ways are true.

In this book I attempt to describe and analyze various systems by which Christians have attempted to enjoy a deeper experience of God. By describing all experience (true and false), I hope to shed light on what is genuine.

I have written two books on theology, in which I have tried to place the facts about Christianity into a comprehensive system of Christian experience. Here I want to present a comprehensive system of Christian experience.

I will follow this pattern:

1. I gather data about Christian experience from revelation in the Bible and the created world.
2. I suggest a principle by which we may interpret and understand experience.
3. The principle is tested to see if it is consistent with Scripture or if it corresponds to reality.
4. The results are presented.
5. The results are communicated and defended against error.

The believer must not blindly accept every claim or even believe everything others say about an alleged experience with God. Not only must he "try the spirits," he must also "search the Scriptures" to discern a fuller understanding of a deeper walk with God. The pages that follow are devoted to an analysis of the valid place of biblical experience and a consideration of theological principles that show how a person can live in two worlds.

To gain credibility, I have not based my conclusions upon anyone's experience. As an illustration, Billy Graham argued, "I know God is real because I talked with Him this morning." He was not just describing communication with God by interacting with the written message; he was also describing an experience of communing with God in daily devotions. I will not try to argue that you can have a deeper walk with God because someone else had that experience. You must base your experience with Him on objective Scripture.

There are numerous illustrations in this volume of individuals who had deeper experiences with God. Some are very real. Another group might be biblical in nature, but described in nonbiblical terms. Others may have been manufactured so that the person could claim spirituality he did not have, or he may have honestly attempted to seek an experience he desired. Some tell of pseudoexperiences that are more psychological than spiritual in nature. I use the term *the deeper Christian life* in a positive sense, to describe those who base their experiences of walking with God on His objective Word. As you read, use the scale in the Appendix to evaluate the credibility of each testimony.

I must give many people credit for their contribution to this book. Two months after I was converted I went to Columbia Bible College. As a freshman, I took an introductory course on the Christian life from the president, Dr. Robert C. McQuilkin. His theme of the victorious Christian life challenged me and motivated me to live for God. My college experience taught me much about the deeper walk with God, although I quickly add I was not a very good example, with my selfish desires, breaking rules, and inflated ego. But there I got a thirst for God. Later, my experience as president of Winnipeg Bible College refined the principles by which I lived. I had some Christian mysticism that was not based on the Bible. I was tested and found wanting. (I prayed all night on several occasions for money but did not get it. The problem was I *only* prayed.) I learned that my walk with God must be based on biblical principles, not feelings. (The college prospered when I not only prayed for money, but organized a financial outreach campaign. God honors both faith and works.)

I want to recognize my wife, Ruth, for her willingness to live with me by faith. It would have been difficult to walk with God without her support and her shared life, because she is "one flesh" with me.

Others gave me insight into walking with God. Hence, every person I have known who exemplified walking with God contributed to this book. The same could be said for every sermon and lesson I heard on the deeper Christian life.

Mr. Douglas Porter, a former graduate assistant at Liberty Baptist Theological Seminary, was involved in researching footnotes, illustrations, and primary sources. Doug lived in our home while going through seminary. Almost every morning, when I got up before dawn to pray, I could see the light under his door. Early he sought the face of God. As we shared insight into the Word of God, I came to the conclusion I should write this book to help others attempting to walk with God. It was only natural to get him to help in the research. As we discussed this volume, he helped clarify the issues and express them simply. I am greatly indebted to him.

I do not take the credit for this volume, but share it with all who contributed to my life. Any honors go to the Lord Jesus Christ, who is the source of the deeper Christian life. However, I do take complete responsibility for all the opinions, mistakes, and any wrong emphasis. May God continually forgive me for my shortcomings and failures and in spite of them all, use the message of the book.

May the great number of contributions that have been invested in this book produce its intended aim—that you live a deeper Christian life.

PART ONE

DESCRIPTION
OF EXPERIENCES

Christians' postconversion experiences vary. How can
we classify the basic types of experience, and what do they
mean? How do they relate to a Christian's faith or doubts?
What kind of outlook on signs and wonders reflects faith?

— 1 —
TYPES OF CHRISTIAN EXPERIENCES

Christianity means more than a mental agreement with a doctrinal creed. When a person accepts Jesus Christ into his life, he has a conversion experience that identifies him with God. The conversion experience can be divided into three time sequences: preconversion experience (conviction of the Holy Spirit, desire, seeking, and so on); the conversion experience (repentance, praying, regenerating, happiness, and so forth), and postconversion experience (joy in Christ, relief from guilt, peace from tumult, confidence, and so on).

Christians have claimed a variety of postconversion (deeper-life) experiences. Many are genuine biblical experiences of victory over sin, optimism, peace, and insight into the Scriptures. The child of God can live his life with the awareness of the indwelling Christ. He can inwardly know he is redeemed and that at death he will go into the presence of God.

One alcoholic can break his addiction. Others, whose drinking habits are not dried up instantaneously at conversion, can slowly overcome the problem with time. What is the source of both transformations? Jesus Christ! Whether the deliverance comes gradually or instantaneously, it does not come from fear of losing a family because of addiction or from training that has "conditioned" the taste buds. The new believer is not bribing God to give him eternal life by changing his life-style. He quits drinking because of an inner compulsion—because of love for Christ, because he has new motives—but most of all, he quits because

Christ convicts him that it is wrong and then gives him a new power to overcome his old ways. That *power* is the secret of the Christian experience, but many Christians have not experienced it.

Some people meet Christ, then lapse back into a habit of sin. But enough Christians experience the power of deliverance to tell us the child of God can have victory. The testimony of those who get the monkey of narcotics off their backs or those who break other enslaving habits testify that a new experience or new power awaits those who come to Christ.

A Christian postconversion experience exists, but just as there seems to be a substitute for everything that is real, so there are many nonbiblical expressions for walking with God. The descriptions included in this volume should help the reader classify the different experiences that people claim. Based on an analysis of experiences, the reader should be able to interpret the various claims that individuals make about postconversion experiences and determine those that are fraudulent, those that are self-induced, and those that are real. In chart 1 Ex = Experience. Experiences are ranked from Ex–8, with extreme experiential claims, to Ex–1, a largely nonexperiential Christian life.

CHART 1

CATEGORIES OF CHRISTIAN EXPERIENCE
Ex–1 *doctrinal experience*
Ex–1a non-supernatural experience
Ex–1b orthodox experience
Ex–2 *the deeper-life experience*
Ex–2a Christological deeper-life experience
Ex–2b Holy Spirit deeper-life experience
Ex–2c soteriological deeper-life experience
Ex–3 *revival*
Ex–4 *experiential power for service or life*
Ex–5 *victorious experience*
Ex–6 *sinless experience*
Ex–7 *intuitive communication with God*
Ex–8 *absorption mystics*
Ex–8a trances, visions, or hearing voices
Ex–8b physical manifestations
Ex–8c asceticism

The categories outlined in chart 1 are not a hierarchical relationship to God, so that Ex–1 is the most spiritual, or ranking the list from the opposite order, Ex–8 is closest to God. The list is not a qualitative assessment, but a quantitative analysis. It measures the amount of experience, which means the intensity or extremity of experience. Ex–1 is objective Christianity, with a complete rejection of any forms of mysticism. Ex–8 is the ultimate mystical experience in which, according to the claims of mystics, the person is absorbed into God and loses his identity in the divine.

Ex–1: Doctrinal Experience

Some Christians express their faith through what might be classified as creedal Christianity. They deny all modern signs and wonders, the experiential intervention of the Holy Spirit, and the empirical deeper Christian life. Their "Christian" experiences are probably just as satisfying to them as any other experience. But they base it on what they intellectually know of God through revelation in Scripture. Their experience is not directly from God to their hearts but indirect, from God, through the Bible, to them. God uses the means of His Word to produce an experience. Therefore, Ex–1 describes this objective Christian, because he has ordinary life experiences that center on God, but do not directly come from God. To him, the Christian experience is not unique in its feeling, but only in its source. Objective knowledge about God produces inner feelings. This person's experience with God is not different from that of a Muslim to Allah or a Hindu to his gods. The Ex–1, doctrinal Christian, does not believe a living God indwells his life, gives him victory over sin, gives him positive emotions, or actually guides his life. There seem to be two categories of Ex–1, doctrinal experience: those who deny the supernatural nature of Christianity and those who accept the supernatural, but believe it is nonoperative in today's world (*see* chart 2).

CHART 2

EX-1: DOCTRINAL EXPERIENCE
Ex-1a Nonsupernatural
Ex-1b Orthodox

Ex-1a: Nonsupernatural Experience. Several groups believe in God but teach the absence of God in their life or experience. In his book *Honest to God*, John A. T. Robinson wrote that there was an absence of God in his life. He felt he did not feel the shining of God's face in his life. Yet he did not deny the existence of God or of Christianity. His book became the basis of the "Death of God" movement in America in the sixties. This group did not teach that God actually died, but that in the experience of man, the presence of God was absent. In a debate on the "Death of God," an antagonist asked, "Is God close to those who have warm chatty prayers?" Then another question was asked, "Can I be close when I don't feel good about suffering and problems?"

Also, a group of Christians accepts Christianity as their creed, but they deny its supernatural experience because they deny the supernatural source of Christianity. They deny the verbal-plenary inspiration of Scripture, the virgin birth, and the physical resurrection. But they accept the general teachings of Christ and give allegiance to the historical Jesus. They believe in a "Christian" experience as any person may have various sources of experience in normal life. Therefore, the person is nonsupernatural in his orientation to the Scriptures, prayer, or the intervention of God in his life. As such, he does not expect or claim to experience a deeper walk with God. His "Christian" experience may be psychologically satisfying as any other experience. He has an experience but not a "Christ produced" spiritual experience. For the Ex-1a person, "Jesus is [only] the universal Conscience of mankind."[1] Christianity is a principle or moral life-style but does not recognize the uniqueness of Christ. Representative of this view of Christian experience, William Barclay wrote:

So then for me the supreme truth of Christianity is that in Jesus I see God. When I see Jesus feeding the hungry, comforting the sorrowing, befriending men and women with whom no one else would have anything to do, I can say: "This is God." It is not that Jesus is God. . . . But in Jesus I see perfectly and completely and finally, and once and for all revealed and demonstrated, the attitude of God to men, the attitude of God to me.[2]

The Ex-1a person believes that Christianity is expressed only in the evolutionary hypothesis, the inevitability of progress, the dignity of human rights, and the equality of men. He attempts to reconstruct his life around an evolving center that is progressive, relevant, meaningful, and functional. He is committed to the life-style of the Ten Commandments, but denies the historic fundamentals of Christianity and the modern experience of a personal God living within the life of man. This element is characterized by liberal theology and a liberalized life-style.

Ex-1b: Orthodox Experience. A large group of Christians accept the historical aspect of supernatural Christianity but deny the present active intervention of God into contemporary lives. They are not deists, for they probably would not deny that God is in the world or in believers, but they tend to be nonexperiential in both their life-styles and beliefs. They believe the day of miracles is past but will one day reoccur when Christ returns.

They have joy or peace that comes from knowing God's Word, and their victory over sin comes from applying the principles of Scripture to daily life. They do not expect the reality of a spiritual enablement to overcome sin beyond their normal life. Some are dedicated Bible students, while others are relatively ignorant of biblical content, but neither expects nor acts upon promises of the deeper Christian life. The satisfaction they get from Christianity comes from psychological or phenomenological sources.

Ex–2: The Deeper-Life Experience

Beyond objective Christianity, there appears to be a real experience from God that influences the believer. The Bible describes both the fleshly (carnal) Christian and the Spirit-led believer. The fleshly Christian lives in sin and feels defeated. The Spirit-led believer overcomes temptation and enjoys the presence of God in his daily life. Both have an experience that the Christian who has objective Christianity lacks. The fleshly Christian experiences life at a level of struggles, depression, and defeats because he follows his natural desires in religious things. When he surrenders to Jesus Christ and allows the Holy Spirit to work through him, he experiences a level of joy and victory (1 Corinthians 2:14–3:4).

Not everyone who becomes a Christian goes on to live for God, so not every Christian experiences a Spirit-filled walk with Christ. It is an experience that is potential but not claimed.

Ex-2 experience is better than the non-Christian and better than just creedal Christianity. Ex-2 is joyful Christianity. This type of Christian life is called many things by different teachers: the abiding life, the victorious life, the crucified life, the normal Christian life, the transformed life, the Spirit-filled life, the abundant life, the overcoming life, and the life of union and communion. Ex-2 is an affirming experience available to all Christians so that they:

1. Realize Jesus Christ dwells within them.
2. Enjoy positive emotions of love, joy, and peace.
3. Live victoriously over sin.
4. Constantly control their lives and grow in grace.
5. Are inwardly assured of salvation and guidance.
6. Have communion with God.
7. Are able to obey the commands of Scripture regarding character and service.

The Ex-2 is not based on one's subjective feelings or desires but on the objective Word of God that produces the deeper life experience. The Ex-2 deeper-life Christian does not lose awareness of his personality, his limitations, or his sinful tendencies. He continues to experience temptations, struggles, and failures; yet he usually knows Christ will forgive him and restore him when necessary. He believes it is possible to experience assurance, patience, and productivity. The Ex–2 deeper-life Christian can have inward happiness, both in times of outward reverses and outward victories. He usually knows how to live in two worlds (spiritual and physical) without losing the reality of the other. He usually knows how to live with two natures (sinful and new desires) without denying the existence of either.

The Ex–2 deeper-life experience is available to Christians who:

1. Yield to Christ.
2. Identify with Christ.
3. Recognize Christ's indwelling.
4. Learn and apply the principles of Christian living from Scriptures.
5. Express faith.
6. Seek to know and grow in Christ.

Basically deeper-life teachers emphasize three general areas:

1. Some teach that a Christian experiences a deeper life with Christ by entering it through abiding with Christ (Christological).
2. Some teach they get it by the fullness of the Holy Spirit (pneumological).
3. Others teach that the Christian enters the deeper-life experience through an experience of the cross or in the crucified life (soteriological).

CHART 3

EX–2: DEEPER-LIFE EXPERIENCE
Ex–2a Christ-centered deeper life Ex–2b Holy-Spirit-centered deeper life Ex–2c Cross-centered deeper life

The deeper-life experience answers the deepest longings of the human heart. Augustine once cried out, "Who will give me what it takes to rest in you? Who will make it so you come into my heart and captivate it, so I can forget my rottenness and take hold of you, the one good thing in my life?"[3] Later, Lady Julian of Norwich prayed, "God, of your goodness give me yourself, for you are enough for me. If I ask anything less I know I shall continue to want. Only in you I have everything."[4] More recently, Norman P. Grubb confessed, "My soul thirsteth for God, for the *living* God. Not for a doctrine, not for a theory, not for a philosophy, but for a Person."[5]

For many people today, the "deeper life" teaching concerning the Christian life is a fairly recent emphasis, usually attributed to holiness or charismatic churches and the Keswick movement. But throughout history, there has been a continuous testimony to some kind of deeper-life experience with God. Years before the existence of a Keswick conference or holiness and charismatic churches, a Puritan preacher named Thomas Hooker told his congregation at Hartford, Connecticut, "The soul was made for an end, and good, and therefore for a better than it self, therefore for God, therefore to enjoy union with him, and communion with those blessed excellencies of his. . . ."[6]

Ex–2a: Christological Deeper-Life Experience. In this experience deeper-life Christians emphasize indentification with Christ, "Abide in Me, and I in you . . ." (John 15:4 NKJV). They stress a vital, spiritual, inscrutable union between Christ and the believer. Emphasis is placed on separation from the influence of sin and lust. The believer has communion with Christ through the Scriptures and tends to isolate himself from contacts with the world that interrupt his walk with God. The Ex–2a Christological deeper life is usually identified with the Keswick movement, early Plymouth Brethren, and the early American Bible Institute/College movement.

The Christological deeper-life experience is usually based on the verse ". . . I have come that they may have life, and that they may have it more abundantly" (John 10:10 NKJV). The distinction is between the first life (salvation) and the second life (deeper life). The key is that Christ gives this life.

This deeper life comes from the indwelling of Jesus Christ, "Ye in me, and I in you" (John 14:20). When the believer allows

Jesus Christ to fill his life with His divine presence, he experiences the ultimate satisfaction available to him.

Donald Grey Barnhouse summarized the theological foundation of this position when he told those gathered at a Keswick convention:

> On the contrary, the life that God has given us is the life of His son. All whom He has called He has also justified, and all whom He has justified He counts as already glorified. God never begins anything that He does not bring to an end. The world may start that which it cannot finish, but God says: "He that hath begun a good work in you, will keep on perfecting it until the day of Jesus Christ" (Phil.i. 6, Gk.). Here are all three of the great doctrines of God's work within us. He which hath begun a good work in you—that is justification—will keep on perfecting it—that is sanctification—until the day of Jesus Christ—that is glorification. There is no change in God, and there will be no change in His work in us.[7]

In what is probably the best known of the books coming out of the Keswick movement, Watchman Nee declares:

> The apostle Paul gives us his own definition of the Christian life in Galatians 2:20. It is no longer "I, but Christ." Here he is not stating something special or peculiar—a high level of Christianity. He is, we believe, presenting God's normal role for a Christian, which can be summarized in the words: I live no longer, but Christ lives His life in me.
>
> God makes it quite clear in His Word that He has only one answer to every human need—His Son, Jesus Christ. In all His dealings with us He works by taking *us* out of the way and substituting Christ in our place. The Son of God died instead of us for our forgiveness: He lives instead of us for our deliverance. . . . It will help us greatly, and save us from much confusion, if we keep constantly before us this fact, that God will answer all our questions in one way and one way only, namely, by showing us more of His son.[8]

Ex–2b: Holy Spirit Deeper-Life Experience. In this experience the deeper-life Christian emphasizes the role of the Holy Spirit.

This is a postconversion work of the Holy Spirit in indwelling, filling, and guiding the believer. They base their experience on verses like, ". . . Out of his [the believer's] heart will flow rivers of living water. . . . this He spoke concerning the Holy Spirit . . ." (John 7:38, 39 NKJV) and "Be filled with the Spirit" (Ephesians 5:18). They tend toward exclusiveness surrounding the Holy Spirit's ministry. The Ex–2b Holy Spirit deeper life is found among Independent Baptists, Bible churches, and certain charismatics not identified with Ex–6 sinless experience or Ex–5 victorious experience.

Oswald J. Smith believed a deeper Christian life was tied to what he referred to as the anointing of the Holy Spirit. He affirmed, "It is an undeniable fact that all down the centuries God has anointed men with the Holy Ghost."[9] With similar conviction, A. W. Tozer wrote:

> I want here boldly to assert that it is my happy belief that every Christian can have a copious outpouring of the Holy Spirit in a measure far beyond that received at conversion, and I might also say, far beyond that enjoyed by the rank and file of orthodox believers today. It is important that we get this straight, for until doubts are removed faith is impossible. God will not surprise a doubting heart with an effusion of the Holy Spirit, nor will He fill anyone who has doctrinal questions about the possibility of being filled.[10]

This was also the conclusion of John R. Rice. In his book on the subject, he wrote:

> The fullness of power is the heritage of every Christian! It may be an unclaimed heritage, but the power of God which enables a Christian to witness for Christ and win souls is the right of every Christian. Not to be filled with the Holy Spirit, not to be endued with power from on high, is to miss the highest good, and fail to claim the highest blessing, offered to every child of God. . . . That the power of Pentecost is for every Christian is made clear; first, by the promises which are to all alike; second, by the New Testament examples; third,

the indwelling of the Holy Spirit in every Christian makes the enduement for service logical for every Christian; fourth, by the fact that the soulwinning task demands supernatural power; and, fifth, because the Word of God clearly commands Christians to be filled with the Holy Spirit.[11]

Ex–2c: Soteriological Deeper-Life Experience. In this experience Christians rely on the results of Calvary for the sources of their deeper life. They emphasize ". . . crucified with Christ . . ." (Galatians 2:20) and identifying with His death and resurrection (Romans 6:4–6). Some are positive: They want to appropriate the benefits of Calvary. Others are negative in orientation: They want to "crucify" their flesh or fleshly desires. This means denying the normal bodily functions or blocking immoral desires. At times they become confused about what is pleasurable and what is sinful, so they tend to separate from the things perceived as sinful. Their "crucifixion" of their selfish desires leads to self-denial as a virtue or expression of the deeper Christian life. For some it is not denial but disciplining their priorities. The Ex–2c soteriological deeper Christian life tends to identify with Watchman Nee and the Little Flock, Faith Missions, and some Bible institutes/colleges.

Addressing the congregation at the 1980 Keswick Convention, Dr. Alan Redpath addressed this aspect of the deeper Christian life. In his message, "The Price of Christian Service," he noted:

'I have been crucified with Christ,' says Paul. What does this mean? In principle, it means that my right to myself is annihilated, as His concern and love for others is expressed through me. Identification, that's the first thing. Not simply to die to myself, but to live in Him. Bless your hearts, evangelism isn't a 'project', it's a way of life! 'Feed My sheep. Identify yourself with My interests in other people,' says Jesus. Oh, to be so satisfied, identified with Jesus that my life is spoiled for everything but His will! Am I more concerned with my right to live, than with my daily dying to Him? Which are you more concerned about? Paul says, 'I die daily'—do you? Do I? Is that my major passion?[12]

A similar emphasis is found in the writings of Oswald Chambers. According to his biographer, D. W. Lambert, Chambers believed, "The Cross is then not only the secret of salvation, but the place where we deny ourselves and [to use a favourite phrase of Oswald Chambers'] 'give up our right to ourselves'."[13] Chambers himself gives evidence of holding this conviction in a meditation on Romans 6:6.

> It takes a long time to come to a moral decision about sin, but it is the great moment in my life when I do decide that just as Jesus Christ died for the sin of the world, so sin must die out in me, not be curbed or suppressed or counteracted, but crucified. No one can bring anyone else to this decision. We may be earnestly convinced, and religiously convinced, but what we need to do is come to the decision which Paul forces here. . . . I cannot reckon myself "dead indeed unto sin" unless I have been through this radical issue of will before God. Have I entered into the glorious privilege of being crucified with Christ until all that is left is the life of Christ in my flesh and blood?[14]

Ex–3: Revival

Revival is an experience that is taught in Scripture and has a historical precedent in the Christian church. It is a state of spiritual enthusiasm or excitement for Christ. Yet the experience of revival is not a continuing one. Revival is not a normal experience, but comes in certain seasons. The normal church, no matter how spiritual, seems to need a revival of interest, a revival of soul winning, or a revival of believers. Revival is a return to one's original Christian experience or a return to original Christianity as found in the book of Acts.

Since revival is not the normal Christian experience, it is more than normal. It is more than Ex–2 the deeper Christian life. Hence, revival is a deeper experience described as Ex–3. It is more intense than what Watchman Nee has described as *The Normal Christian Life*.

Four Greek and Hebrew verbs are translated "revive" in biblical and extrabiblical writings, and they illustrate the emphasis of revival as a renewal of life or well-being. The Hebrew verb *chayah*, meaning "to live" or "to cause to live," is used in the Old Testament to describe the restoration of life (Genesis 45:27; Judges 15:19), the rebuilding of the walls of Jerusalem (Nehemiah 4:2), and the restoration of a state of well-being (Psalms 85:6; 138:7; Isaiah 57:15; Hosea 6:2; 14:7). A second Hebrew term, *michyah*, "preservation" or "means of life," is translated "revive" in Ezra 9:8, 9.

In the New Testament, the Greek word *anazao*, meaning "to live again," is twice used of the resurrection of Christ (Romans 7:9; 14:9). A second Greek verb, *anazopereo*, "to stir or kindle as a fire" occurs in 2 Timothy 1:6. Although the verb is not there translated "revive," the same word occurring in 1 Maccabees 13:7 is translated in the expression, "and the spirit of the people revived" ("was rekindled" according to the Revised Standard Version).

Revival is an outpouring of God on His people in which Christians:

1. Repent of sin.
2. Renew their love for God.
3. Recommit themselves to God's purposes.
4. Experience positive emotions of love, joy, and peace.
5. Invest extended time in prayer, communion with God, and meditation.
6. Experience blessings in Christian service.

The biblical expression of the Ex–3 experience is transhuman and apparently cannot be initiated by human means. It does not seem to be an evenly experienced phenomenon, for some seem to benefit more from the revival experience than others. But in any case, the experience of revival is a supernatural experience or display from God. The Second Great Awakening (Charles Finney) was an American expression of Ex–3 revival. The Evangelical Awakening (John Wesley) and the Welsh Revival (Christmas Evans and Evan Roberts) were British expressions.

Ex–3 revivals can be a national experience or just express themselves in one city or part of a city. Revival can affect certain

churches within a region and not others in the same region. It
can affect certain churches within a nation or area and not other
denominations in the same nation. Those who study revivals
describe them as ". . . times of refreshing . . . from the presence of the Lord" (Acts 3:19). They teach that the conditions of
revival are found in 2 Chronicles 7:14 and come when God's
people humble themselves, pray, seek God, and repent.

Those who testify to experiencing revival usually claim other
accompanying phenomena that support their theological position. Some Ex–4 claim to experience revival with signs and
wonders. Some Ex–5 and Ex–6 claim to experience revival without signs and wonders. Because of men's hunger to know God,
all those who have had religious experience have attributed
their vitality as a cause or effect of revivals. As an illustration,
when Pentecostals testify of revivals, they include claims of
signs and wonders. Wesleyans (Ex–5) leave them out but include their unique holiness experience. Independent Baptists
(Ex–3) may attribute a revival to those who pray and work for
power, while the late Dr. J. Edwin Orr, formerly the Fuller
Theological Seminary professor of awakenings, claims the opposite, that is, that man can do nothing to produce a revival but
that it is a sovereignly bestowed blessing by God.

There is a distinct difference of opinion concerning the nature
and origin of revival, even among those who would describe
themselves as advocates of this dimension of Christian experience. Over a hundred years ago, a Baptist minister described
revival in terms of the work of the Holy Spirit. In an opinion
typical not only of that time but of revivalists today, he wrote:

> By a revival of religion we understand such a work of the
> Spirit of God as results in the simultaneous conversion of a
> multitude of men. When the gracious influence rests on a
> community, not only is the range of conversion widened, but
> the different elements of the Christian character are cultivated
> and invigorated, the aspects of society are spiritualized and
> beautified; and saint and sinner are alike led to rejoice in the
> common salvation.[15]

Charles Grandison Finney, himself a noted revivalist, agreed that revival was a work of the Spirit of God but objected to what he viewed as an undue emphasis on the sovereignty of God in initiating revival. In his lectures on the subject, he suggested:

Revivals have been greatly hindered by mistaken notions concerning the Sovereignty of God. Many people have supposed God's Sovereignty to be something very different from what it is. They have supposed it to be such an arbitrary disposal of events, and particularly of the gift of His Spirit, as precluded a rational employment of means for promoting a revival. But there is no evidence from the Bible that God exercises any such sovereignty. There are no facts to prove it, but everything goes to show that God has connected means with the end, through all the departments of His government, in nature and in grace.[16]

Although many link revival primarily to a special work of the Holy Spirit, others prefer to describe this experience in Christological terms. Norman P. Grubb testified:

For long I had regarded revival only from the angle of some longed-for, but very rare, sudden outpouring of the Spirit on a company of people. I felt that there was a missing link somewhere. Knowing of the continuing revival on a certain mission field, and because it was continuing, and not merely sudden and passing, I long felt that they had a further secret we needed to learn. Then the chance came for heart-to-heart fellowship with them, first through one of our own missionary leaders whose life and ministry had been transformed by a visit to that field, and then through conferences with some of their missionaries on furlough, and finally through the privilege of having two of the national brethren living for six months at our headquarters. From them I learned and saw that revival is first personal and immediate. It is the constant experience of any simplest Christian who "walks in the light," but I saw that walking in the light means an altogether new sensitiveness to sin, a calling things by their proper name of sin, such as pride, hardness, doubt, fear, self-pity, which are often passed over as merely human reaction. It means a readiness to "break" and confess at the feet of Him who was broken for us, for the Blood does not cleanse excuses, but always cleanses sin, confessed as sin; then revival is just the daily experience of a soul full of Jesus and running over.[17]

Ex–4: Experiential Power

Certain Christians seem to focus their Christian experience on power, strength, or an ability outside themselves. Experiential power is more than the Ex–2 indwelling strength that the believer gets from Jesus Christ as he lives a deeper Christian life. One is from a person, the other power seems inherent in a system, and when the believer plugs into it, like plugging a toaster into an outlet, the power will flow.

C. Peter Wagner, professor of church growth at Fuller Theological Seminary, explains their power in his book *On the Crest of the Wave*, and his friend John Wimber elaborates further in his book *Power Healing* and calls it "power encounter theology." The supernatural—especially healing—is the focus of this power. It also includes signs, wonders, casting out demons, raising the dead, but especially miraculous healings.

It sounds like Pentecostalism, but it is not. Wagner explains the first wave was Pentecostalism that was ushered in at the beginning of this century, especially the movement growing out of the Azusa Street Revival, Los Angeles. This movement was tied to Pentecostal theology. In the late fifties a charismatic renewal began to sweep through mainline denominational churches, Catholic churches, and other groups. This movement focused on tongues as a prayer language and was not associated with Pentecostal theology or their view of the "second work of grace." Wagner called that the second wave. Now he calls the third wave an emphasis on power theology. It is related to evangelism, because the supernatural: opens people's hearts to the gospel, makes the power of God visible, and reveals God's love and power to the world. As a result, many get saved.

The next two positions are more intense experiences, inasmuch as Ex–5 victorious experience may include Ex–4 power experience and Ex–6 eradication of sin may also include the display of power.

Pat Robertson, host of "The 700 Club," describes this power experience in his book *The Secret Kingdom*. He identifies two kingdoms, the visible world we see and an invisible kingdom that has power for the believers. While many Christians have believed in the kingdom of God as being under the rule of Jesus as king of their lives, Robertson seems to be saying more. He states, "Both Nicodemus and Paul discovered that the kingdom of heaven is based on an invisible, spiritual reality, capable of visible physical effects."[18] While Christians have assigned power to the person of Christ, Robertson sees power in an invisible world that surrounds the believer. It is almost as if he is surrounded by an invisible "bubble world" that appears to be charged with electrical power, but it is charged with spiritual power.

Robertson claims that power is available to the believer who will exercise a "word of faith" to give him the riches of victory that is already his. Also he says negativism blocks the kingdom. In chapter 13 he advocates miracles to release the benefits of the kingdom. While much of Robertson's book is aimed at Christian character revealing the kingdom, he does lay a foundation for "power fixation."

But Ex–4 experiential power also is attributed to those who are not charismatic or inclined toward Pentecostalism. They would believe the "sign miracles" are past, but they do accept or seek the experience of power. In religious revivals of the past this has resulted in people shaking (Shakers) or rolling. Their experience is external and physically manifested.

Another nonpentecostal aspect of Ex–4 experiential power for service is characterized by R. A. Torrey, Jack Hyles, and John R. Rice. It is usually tied to Christian work and is evidenced in powerful convicting preaching, souls saved, people delivered from habits, or young people surrendering for full-time service. This experience of power is not usually tied primarily to Christian character or to the indwelling of Jesus Christ or the Holy Spirit. Rather power is related to fasting, agonizing prayer, or communion with God. It is experiential power that is tied to their unique view of the baptism of the Holy Spirit for exceptional service that is more than the filling of the Spirit (Ex–2) for a personal walk with God.

R. A. Torrey described the baptism of the Holy Spirit as the "one condition of success in bringing men to Christ." Stressing its importance, he further argues:

> If the apostles with their unparalleled fitting for service, were not permitted to enter that service until all their other training had been supplemented by the Baptism of the Holy Spirit, what daring presumption it is for any of us with our inferior training to dare to do it. But this is not all, even Jesus Himself did not enter upon His ministry until specially anointed with the Holy Spirit and with power. (Acts x. 38, comp. Luke iii. 22 and iv. 1, 14.) This baptism is an absolutely essential preparation for Christian work. It is either ignorance of the plain requirements of God's word or the most daring presumption on our part when we try to do work for Christ until we know we have been Baptized with the Holy Spirit.[19]

Ex–5: Victorious Experience

This experience of suppression of sin is similar to the next (Ex–6) in that it involves a second work of the Holy Spirit or a second experience; but in the Ex–5 experience the sin nature is not eradicated but only subdued. This group claims the Christian can have a perfect walk with God, as does the next level of Ex–6 sinless experience. But the next level claims an eradication of the sin nature, in which one is "not able to sin," whereas this group usually testifies they are "victorious over sin," but their sin nature (potential) remains. The Ex–5 victorious experience usually comes to the believer in a second experience or a second blessing.

If this second experience does not include signs, wonders, or outward authentication, it is usually characterized as a "holiness," "Wesleyan," or "entire sanctification" experience. The believer experiences a crisis in which:

1. He draws closer to God.
2. He is able not to sin.

3. He is filled with supernatural love.
4. He has new power from the Holy Spirit.

The believer has power to do things he could not do before the experience. The "old" Methodist, Wesleyans, and Church of God (Anderson) are characterized by this level. However, many not of this theological system believe they can come to a place of living without sin. The Presbyterian Horatio Bonar taught Ex–5 in his book *God's Way of Holiness*.

Some Ex–5 victorious experiences are Pentecostal in theology or practice. When they have a second work of grace, they get victory over sin. This may be accompanied by tongues, being slain in the Spirit, or other miraculous gifts.

Andrew Murray emphasized the possibility of this kind of victorious life-style in a sermon on the carnal and spiritual. The key to this experience, according to Murray, was the ability of Christ to keep him. He writes:

> Yes, it is not a mere view, it is not a consecration in any sense of its being in our power, it is not a surrender by the strength of our will. No. These are elements that may be present, but the great thing is, that we must look to Christ to keep us to-morrow, and next day, and always; we must get the life of God within us. We want a life that will stand against any temptation, a life that will last not only till another "Keswick," but till death. We want, by the grace of God to experience what the almighty indwelling and saving power of Christ can do, and all that God can do for us.[20]

What happens to the experience in the Ex–5 Christian when he sins? Inasmuch as sin is an experience, as well as a fact, he experiences disequilibrium. If he is Arminian or Wesleyan, he experiences "lostness" and claims to have lost his salvation. He becomes distraught and torn apart. This is called conviction of sin. Usually he will seek God and salvation and be "resaved."

Some Ex–5 Christians believe they cannot lose their salvation, yet they believe they can live without sin. But when they sin (either willfully or by circumstance) they suffer emotional damage. Their experience is inconsistent with their perception, so they also suffer a disequilibrium and inconsistent self-image. They experience the conviction of sin and repent, seeking renewed fellowship with God.

Ex–6: Sinless Experience

Certain Christians claim they have had an experience after salvation in which their sinful nature is eliminated or they gain a level of spirituality so that they no longer experience sin. Most say they no longer desire sin and they no longer actually sin. This experience is introduced by a "second work of grace," "the baptism of the Holy Spirit," "complete sanctification," or "the second blessing." This experience of eradication begins after the Christian has been:

1. Seeking or tarrying.
2. Searching his soul for sin.
3. Making total submission to God.
4. Praying through until he experiences it.
5. Exercising extraordinary faith to secure the experience.

In response, God gives him unique power and eradicates his sinful nature. This is called the holiness experience. Sometimes the Ex–6 Christian has an experience that eradicates his sin nature, and it is accompanied by signs and wonders and sets him aside for special purposes. This is usually called the "Pentecostal experience" and is associated with Pentecostal doctrine.

Not all at the Ex–6 sinless-experience level experience outward signs and wonders. Some claim their ability to sin is eradicated, but it is not accompanied by outward phenomena. Certain "Wesleyan" groups believe in the second experience after conversion that enables them to experience a perfect lifestyle, but they are not Pentecostal in doctrine, nor do they accept the evidence of miraculous signs.

Describing the character of the Ex–6 sinless experience, Nazarene preacher "Uncle Bud" Robinson wrote:

The man that is led by the Holy Spirit will never pass through a day that we used to call "blue days," lonesome and sad and downcast, although he may have many trials and hardships and many battles with the devil. But if his heart is filled with the Spirit and he is led by the Spirit, he will have a joyous, victorious life. In fact he will be more than conqueror, because when a man is led by the Spirit it proves that he is willing to be led. No man can make a leader until he is willing to be led himself; no man can make a teacher until he is willing to be taught; and no man can make a commander until he himself is willing to obey. . . . And for thirty years I have gone no place that the Holy Ghost didn't lead me, and, thank God, I never will.[21]

The Ex–6 Pentecostal experience can be authenticated by miraculous signs and wonders, such as speaking in tongues, being slain in the Spirit, miracles, the gift of revelation (predicting or proclaiming what is happening elsewhere), or other outward manifestations. David Wilkerson argues the "Baptism of the Holy Spirit" as evidenced in speaking in tongues is the key to his success in the rehabilitation of drug addicts.[22]

The Ex–6 experience is usually associated with Pentecostals, mystic Roman Catholics, some holiness groups, and various sects. Ex–6 may or may not involve true Christians. The Ex–6 experience may be the same experience the Ex–2 Christian has when he surrenders to be filled with the Holy Spirit. In reality because they both desire a deeper walk with Christ, both may be actually filled with the Spirit (Ex–2b) so that they become victorious over sin. The problem may be terminology and different interpretations of the same experience. But one is deceived or self-deceived concerning his sin nature or his practice of sin. The Ex–6 mistakenly thinks his sin nature is eradicated because he is experiencing victory over sin. He wrongly thinks sin is only cognitive disobedience, whereas sin involves ignorantly breaking God's law, intentionally breaking God's law, and omission of doing all the good that is required.

Ex–6 practices may actually be Ex–2 deeper-life experience

walks with Christ, or the person may be deceived, deceptive, or experiencing a pseudomiracle that is inspired by Satan (SW–7).

Ex–7: Intuitive Communication With God

The next level involves those who gave or received messages, communications, or revelations from God. They believe they experience direct communication with God in periods of "quietism," or meditation. Obviously the Christian communes with God through the Word and prayer, but the Ex–7 mystic believes in experiences whereby God gives a message to him apart from Scripture or apart from the five senses. They claim to hear actual voices or see visions or other extraphysical phenomena. They receive messages from God that are more than an urge or feeling.

During her lifetime, Ann Preston claimed to have such communications from God, earning for herself the nickname "Holy Ann." Her biographer insists she often received instantaneous directives from God in answer to her simple prayers. According to an account of her life:

> That she received special answers, those who lived with her have no doubt. Even the children in their play would run to Ann for a solution of the little difficulties that arose. . . . The children would come to her when their toys were lost, and invariably after Ann had prayed she would at once go to where the missing article was lying.[23]

The Christian believes God speaks through the Bible, and any message that is beyond revelation or contradicts revelation is wrong. Ex–7 mystics are found among Catholics, Protestants, and the cults. Certain groups among the Quakers believe God speaks directly to them. (Even among Quakers you will find varying beliefs in degrees of communication.) They may or may not share the message with others (subjectivism).

At times Pentecostals, charismatics, or those who practice power theology, Ex–4, may actually belong to this intense expression of communication with God. The Ex–7 may get or give a "word of knowledge" or "word of revelation," whereby he gets a "content" revelation from God. Some who get a "word of knowledge" or "word of revelation" do not actually receive new content, but they get an impression or "burden" concerning a message already revealed in Scripture.

The same experience could be related to speaking in tongues. The content of the message one gives while exercising tongues would determine if he should be placed at Ex–4 or Ex–7. The historic Christian position is that the revelation (message) of God was completed in canon and extrabiblical messages from God are rejected. Hence, the Ex–7 might be rejected by the Pentecostal and charismatic because of their allegiance to the revelation of God, and their realization that their experience of tongues or "word of knowledge" is not a new message.

Ex–7 mystics express their experience differently. Some give a high priority to meditation, chanting, fasting, denying the flesh, praying, or seeking God, while others only seek an inner voice or inner light. Even though some Protestants may practice Ex–7 experiences, they may not fall within the historic Christian position, because they seek or accept revelations apart from Scripture (the final seat of authority).

Ex–8: Absorption Mystics

Some claim the ultimate experience of being united with God in the spirit or flesh so that they lose their personal existence. They are absorbed into God. These usually lose their sense of reality and/or personal identity to some degree. They would use the phrase "union with God" or "one with God" differently than the historic Christian. They are caught up into their experience and lose their sense of the world around them and their sinful nature within them. These lose the I-Thou relationship to God. The Christian must always be "I" and never lose his personal identity or consciousness of his own personality. God must always be the "wholly other" One. God must be "Thou." Some lose this distinction of the "I-Thou" relationship through a wrong understanding of union with God (see chapter 6). The ultimate mystic in the traditional sense of the word has lost touch with reality, because of a confusion of the "I-Thou" relationship to God. The Ex–8 absorption mystic can be a harmless person who is kept in a monastery, convent, or a member of any church. It is also possible that some will end up in mental asylums or have mental disorders and never live healthy lives. We should not glorify such people, canonize them, or respect them for their spiritual state. Their sincerity is misplaced, and it is questionable that they please or influence God with their experience.

CHART 4

EX–8: ABSORPTION MYSTICS
Ex–8a trances, visions, hearing voices Ex–8b physical manifestations Ex–8c asceticism

Ex–8a: Trances, Visions, or Hearing Voices. These mystics have arrived at a place in their experience where they have given up control of their lives and focus largely on visions (such as the Virgin Mary, Christ, Paul, and so on) or miraculous feats.

Ex–8b: Physical Manifestations. Saint Francis of Assisi apparently meditated on Christ (identified with Christ) until there was a physical manifestation of the crucifixion wounds in his hands. Called the *stigmata*, the appearance of these wounds were apparently the result of meditation. Kenneth Scott LaTourette writes of Saint Francis of Assisi, "His ardent devotion to Christ and his meditation of Christ's passion were crowned by the appearance of the *stigmata*, the wounds of his Master, on his own body."[24] Some claim the wounds were the work of God, others said they were psychosomatic, while still others said they were contrived.

Ex–8c: Asceticism. Many Catholic mystics went to extremes to subdue the flesh so that their physical life was controlled by the spiritual. While this may be a valid principle, the Ex–8c mystic tries to "beat" the flesh into submission with bodily punishment, denials (extreme fasting), physical flagellation, and even to cutting off the hand that offended them. Asceticism is usually attached to meditation with God and/or Ex–8a or Ex–8b.

Guidelines to Experiences

1. *People representing different categories may have the same experience but explain it by different terminology.* Those from different theological schools tend to define terms differently. As a result, what appears to be differences between some groups or churches may be only semantic in nature. The Calvinist and Arminian tend to define certain aspects of sin differently. When the holiness Christian says he is living victoriously over sin, the Calvinist sees him with a sin nature (potential lust) and falling short of God's righteousness (positionally). When the Pentecostal gets angry, he may label his frailty a weakness; his dispensational brother calls it iniquity. One brother claims to get the "baptism of the Spirit" and bubbles with excitement, calling it the second work of grace. The next brother yields to the filling of the Holy Spirit and gets excited about soul winning. Both have the same experience but use different terms to explain their feelings.

The problem with the categories in this chapter is not understanding the differences between terms, but separating the experiences. I am a Calvinist, not a Pentecostal, nor am I a Wesleyan in doctrine. Yet I have spoken in many Sunday-school conferences in denominations representing those who believe in eradication as a second work of grace. Even though we are different in doctrine, I am comfortable in their groups because we both have a similar desire to live a holy life, avoid the appearance of evil, and surrender to the control of the Holy Spirit. We know our differences, but need to emphasize our similar experience.

2. *The experiences in these categories are not hierarchical but a range of expression.* Hierarchical implies an organization of rank, each subordinate to the one above. In such a case one rank would be better than the other, with Ex–1 best and Ex–8 poorest. This would place a quality judgment on each expression of experience. If I did that, I would tend to say that Ex–2 is best, because

it represents my point of view or it agrees with my understanding of Scripture. But I don't mean to imply that Ex–2 Christians
have the best spiritual life. I know many who represent Ex–2,
but they may not have the blessing of God in their life as some
Ex–5 or Ex–6. I don't believe God blesses a person just because
his doctrine is correct or because he can explain his spiritual
experience with proper biblical terminology. Experience and
doctrine may be inconsistent. The person of Jesus Christ can be
just as real to a person in Ex–2 as He can be to a mystic at Ex–7.
The hierarchical question is not doctrinal purity, but the experiential indwelling presence of Jesus Christ.

However, doctrinal elasticity has its limit. There is a point of
no return beyond which God cannot bless and beyond which
the person of Christ will not bless a person with wrong doctrine. Each must examine his doctrine and experience in light of
Scripture.

The question becomes one of personal perspective. I should
not measure others to determine how close they are to me or
how close I think they are to God. I should be concerned with
my own spiritual growth. Is Christ real to me? Can I get closer
to Him?

3. *Some aspects of each category are found in most believers.* A
person may believe in Ex–2, yet some conditions or expressions
found in Ex–7 may characterize his life. As an example, the
favorite expression of Christianity by the Ex–7 may be meditation, but all other descriptions classify him as an Ex–2 deeper-
life Christian. One aspect is not the final factor to categorize an
experience, but rather a Christian is characterized by the dominant cluster of descriptive qualities that will be the ultimate
factors in describing what category controls him.

4. *Various aspects of different categories may be characteristic of
different times in a person's life.* We all go through phases of life
when we express our Christianity differently, according to the
needs that drive us at the time. That is, because when we have
changing needs, we claim different ministries from God to help
us. At times we need objective study of the Word of God (Ex–1),
at other times we pray for power (Ex–4) or God sends us the
excitement of revival (Ex–3).

Let's be careful about telling others their experience is wrong because it is different from ours. It may be that God is using a certain experience to minister to a person at a certain time in his life. Later, he may have a different need and express his Christian experience differently.

Perhaps one reason for the different types of experience is that leaders try to perpetuate in others a ministry that God used in their lives. Or a leader may even push his ministry on everyone else and try to make his "experience" the standard of the church.

5. *The standardization of experiences is the result of people with similar needs who colonize together.* Larry Gilbert describes the colonization of spiritual gifts, so that those with similar spiritual gifts attend a church where gifts similar to theirs are honored and exercised. Those with the gift of teaching go to a Bible church, and those with the gift of evangelization go to Fundamentalist soul-winning churches. The same thing happens with experience. Those who have a great thirst for holiness attend an Ex–5 or Ex–6 church that emphasizes separation from sin or the "holiness experience." Those who need excitement go where they find revival and become Ex–3 Christians.

This does not mean one church is better than another; it means a church has a different ministry to the different needs of individuals, perhaps at different phases in the lives of believers. However, this does not mean that experience is everything and doctrine is secondary. Many times, those in a church with the same experience tend to support one another and seek to verify their experience by Scripture. Then their doctrine becomes predominant and they claim that doctrine is foundational to experience. But many times, the opposite is true.

6. *There is a correlation between experience and doctrine.* Over the years, there has been a relationship between what a church taught and what it practiced in experience, for all there is the exception of the "Pentecostal" church that was more like a Presbyterian church than like its revivalistic sister churches. Then there is the Ex–1 Episcopal church that suddenly moves into Ex–4 power evangelism. The Episcopal church is characterized by healing lives and revivalistic life-style.

But generally, there is a correlation (not always a cause and effect) between life-style and doctrine. Generally speaking the lower numbers, Ex–1 to Ex–3, historically have a deeper commitment to doctrine than the higher numbers, Ex–7 and Ex–8. As the experience becomes more intense, there is less emphasis on objective belief and more on feelings, sensibility, and intuitive experience. When this happens, it is difficult to determine if Scripture is more important than experience or if experience is verified by Scripture; then both become foundational to the position.

7. *Some believers begin at Ex–1 and progress through the categories.* While this is not taught in Scripture, nor is it normative, it may represent some who are caught up in experientialism or experimentation. This is not a growth in grace, but a growth in experience. It is probably not healthy for a person to continually change his expression of experience, but when the experience becomes more important than Christ, it is easy to see how it happens. As the person seeks deeper experiences of love, rather than the one he loves, it is easy for him to go from Ex–1, objective belief, to Ex–8, mystical absorption into God. Actually, the Bible calls him immature as ". . . children, tossed to and fro . . ." (Ephesians 4:14).

While we may criticize such a person, his love for God may not be spurned by Him. Christ may become very real to him, even though his experience reflects emotional immaturity. No doubt, some in mental institutions, with delusions of God, are there because they lost the objectivity of their faith, Ex–1. But is not their love for God real, and can we say God has turned His back on them?

8. *Some believers are converted within one category and remain there throughout their lives.* Those who are open to God and the teaching of their church usually have the type of conversion experience that is suggested or expected by their church. Because of their yieldedness to their denomination, they do not seek alternate experiences from other churches or other sources. They remain within the framework of their home denomination (should they change churches) and remain within one typology of experience for their Christian life on earth. This is probably

the history of experience for most believers. When they find any internal yearning to change, they may interpret it as a temptation and reject it. They remain true to the doctrine and life-style of their church. They have a relatively solid experiential foundation for the Christian life.

— 2 —
TYPES OF
FAITH
AND DOUBT

According to his biographies, George Mueller seemed to have had the greatest faith of any person since the Apostle Paul. There are enough eyewitnesses to give credibility to such stories as that Mueller prayed for food for his orphanage, and someone immediately knocked on the door, with the food. Once he prayed with the captain of an ocean liner, and fog immediately lifted so that Mueller arrived on time for a speaking engagement. According to Mueller's son-in-law and biographer Arthur T. Pierson:

> If George Mueller could still speak to us, he would again repeat the warning so frequently found in his journal and reports, that his fellow disciples must not regard him as a *miracle-worker*, as though his experience were to be accounted so exceptional as to have little application in our ordinary spheres of life and service. . . . Every child of God, he maintained, is first to get into the sphere appointed of God, and therein to exercise full trust, and live by faith upon God's sure word of promise.[1]

I have witnessed the faith of Jerry Falwell as he prayed for millions of dollars for Liberty University, Lynchburg, Virginia. He has faith that most believers do not possess. I've tried to analyze the nature of his faith and how he developed it. Falwell seems to be so in tune with the will of God that when he makes a "faith expression," God grants the answer.

I first encountered his faith when we were beginning Liberty University (originally called Lynchburg Baptist College). I asked Jim Moon, the associate pastor of Thomas Road Baptist Church, how many new students would begin the college.

"How many did Dr. Falwell say we'd have?" Moon asked.

"He said one hundred," I replied, "but if we have fifty, we'll be lucky." Because I had been a college president, I knew how hard it was to recruit students. I also knew we had only three months to recruit them. But I was looking at the problem through the eyes of natural man.

Jerry Falwell was launching out on faith, and after he had prayed, he had stated a goal of 100 new freshmen.

There were 153 freshman that first year, and I learned something about the experience of faith. From that first encounter with Jerry Falwell, I determined to learn the principles of faith that got results from God.

Categories of Faith

Chart 5 suggests how a Christian grows from initial faith to a deeper life of faith so that he can move mountains in his life. (*Fa* stands for "faith," and the increase in number is not a hierarchy of growing to better faith, but represents different functions of faith.)

CHART 5

CATEGORIES OF FAITH
Fa–1 knowing the statement of faith
Fa–2 experiencing saving faith
Fa–3 justifying faith
Fa–4 indwelling faith
Fa–5 living by faith
Fa–6 the spiritual gift of faith

Fa–1: Knowing the Statement of Faith. The first step in deepening one's faith is to know the content of faith. When the Bible uses the definite article *the* with the word *faith*, it means a statement of faith or the doctrinal content of faith. According to James I. Packer, " 'the faith' denotes the body of truths believed (e. g., Jude 3; Rom. 1:5; Gal. 1:23; 1 Tim. 4:1, 6). This became standard usage in the second century."[2] The deeper Christian life of faith is not a purely mystical expression, such as someone taking a drug-related trip on narcotics or some Eastern-religion guru searching for an experience. There is objectivity in Christianity, and the deeper Christian life is based on the objective Word of God. The basis of walking the deeper Christian life is to know the content and principles of Scripture, and the more you know, the better you can live by faith.

Fa–2: Saving Faith. Before a person can walk with God, he must experience conversion, also called saving faith. "For by grace are ye saved through faith . . ." (Ephesians 2:8). Personal salvation is an experience that involves the response of the total person (personality: intellect, emotions, and will) to God. Note how the total personality is involved in a conversion experience. First, a person's mind must know the gospel (1 Corinthians 15:1–3); he must know he is a sinner (Romans 3:23); and he must know the punishment awaiting sin (Romans 6:23). Second, the positive emotions are involved in love for God (Matthew 22:37), and negative emotions are involved in remorse for sin, "For godly sorrow worketh repentance to salvation not to be repented of . . ." (2 Corinthians 7:10). Third, the person's will must respond to God in receiving Christ (John 1:12), repentance (Acts 3:36), and yielding himself unto God (Romans 6:13).

Saving faith is both passive and active, according to Augustus Hopkins Strong. In his standard theology text he writes:

> We need to emphasize this active element in saving faith, lest men get the notion that mere indolent acquiescence in Christ's plan will save them. Faith is not simple receptiveness. It gives itself, as well as receives Christ. It is not mere passivity,—it is also self-committal. As all reception of knowledge is active, and there must be attention if we would learn,

so all reception of Christ is active, and there must be intelligent giving as well as taking.[3]

Fa–3: Justifying Faith. Paul uses an unusual expression, primarily in the book of Romans, that reveals God justifies or "declares us righteous" because of our faith. The phrase, "being justified by faith" (Romans 5:1), means that out of our faith God declares the record of the believer perfect in heaven. The believer is not *made* perfect, because he still has a sinful nature and will not stop sinning until he arrives in heaven. God stamps perfection on the believer's record. This is a nonexperiential action that is not felt in the believer's daily life. But when the believer realizes the truth of justifying faith, he should respond by changing his life-style. According to Martyn Lloyd-Jones, being justified by faith "does three things for us at once. It gives us peace with God; it puts us firmly in the place of all blessings; and it enables us to exult at the prospect of our future final glorification."[4] While there is no inherent power or experience in Fa–3 justifying faith it becomes the knowledge basis of the next type of faith.

Fa–4: Indwelling Faith. Jesus challenged His disciples to have greater faith. He offered them the power to cast mountains in the sea when He declared, "Have the faith of God" (*see* Mark 11:22, 23). While the King James Version translates it, "Have faith in God," the original is *pistiou theou*, genitive, which is "Have God's faith." This indwelling faith gives the believer the power of God to solve problems or remove barriers (mountains) in his life. Sometimes I have called this deeper-life faith, for it gives the believer power beyond himself.

Despite his reputation as a great man of faith, George Mueller denied he had the gift of faith but rather explained his faith was "the self-same faith which is found in *every believer*, and the growth of which I am most sensible of to myself; for by little and little it has been increasing for the last sixty-nine years."[5]

The power of indwelling faith is gained by yielding the problem to God, following biblical principles in solving the problem, expressing faith in God's solution, not doubting, and praying for a solution.

The experience of Fa–4 indwelling faith grows as the believer trusts God for greater things. However, there is not perfection in any human, so not everything the deeper-life believer claims will come about, and not everything the great men of faith like Falwell and Mueller say will come about. Nevertheless, those who experience deeper-life faith (Fa–4) know that they are walking with God and are assured that God will operate through them in the future because He did it in the past. Those who experience deeper-life faith are keenly aware that: There is no power in themselves, they are evidently human, their strength is in the Bible, but their fellowship with Christ is real.

Fa–5 Living by Faith. The Bible admonishes "the just shall live by faith" (Romans 1:17; Habakkuk 2:4; Galatians 3:11; Hebrews 10:38). To this command, Paul adds, "For we walk by faith, not by sight" (2 Corinthians 5:7). The experience and testimony of some faith missions boards and faith Bible institutes leads certain people in the Keswick circles to interpret living by faith as trusting God for money. What they did was exercise Fa–4 indwelling faith, let Christ's faith answer their needs, and exercise Fa–6 the spiritual gift of faith; they used their spiritual gift of faith to solve their money problem. The person who works for money can live by faith as well as the person who is supported by Social Security or the child who doesn't work for money. The experience Fa–5 living by faith is simply living by the principles of Scripture (the faith). As one writer expressed his view of the importance of living by faith:

> Faith, I realized, isn't just another of the good activities in the Christian life. It is the basis—the one essential—for hearing God's "Well done!" God had been trying to tell me through all those faith experiences that Christian activity was good, but the one thing He wanted me to do was to trust *Him*. Faith in Christ isn't just an additive for an extra-good Christian life—it *is* the Christian life.[6]

Technically speaking, living by faith doesn't give the believer power to live the deeper Christian life, nor does it give him the experience of fellowship with God. But when he orders his life by the principles of Scripture, he has a basis for the experience of the deeper Christian life and a basis for getting things by faith from God.

Since there are different levels of knowing Scripture, there are different levels of Fa–5 living by faith. The new Christian can immediately begin to live by faith, no matter how elementary his life. The mature believer who has controlled his long life by Scripture can also continue to grow in faith. Fa–5 living by faith is a cognitive experience that is the objective basis for an inner deeper-life experience.

Fa–6: The Spiritual Gift of Faith. The ultimate expression of faith is an ability to solve problems or move mountains by faith. Called a spiritual gift (Romans 12:3, 6; 1 Corinthians 12:9; 13:2), it seems to be given to some and not all Christians (1 Corinthians 12:11), as are all spiritual gifts. It seems to be greater in some than in others. But like all spiritual gifts, we can seek it (1 Corinthians 12:31), and it can grow in its manifestation. Donald Gee defines this spiritual gift, noting:

> The spiritual gift of faith is a special quality of faith, sometimes called by our older theologians the "faith of miracles." It would seem to come upon certain of God's servants in times of special crisis or opportunity in such mighty power that they are lifted right out of the realm of even natural and ordinary faith in God—and have a divine certainty put within their soul that triumphs over everything. It is a magnificent gift and is probably exercised frequently with far-reaching results.[7]

The spiritual gift of faith (Fa–6) is an experience of complete trust in God for His blessing in their Christian service. Those who experience this ability probably have met the criteria of the previous five categories of faith. The spiritual gift of faith of a person will grow with his knowledge of Scripture (Fa–1), with his awareness of his new position before God (Fa–3), with his experience of the deeper life of indwelling faith (Fa–4), and with his application of the principles of Scripture to his life (Fa–5).

Categories of Unbelief

There also seem to be descending steps away from faith. It is possible for the Christian who experiences salvation, through saving faith, to then grow as he experiences fellowship with Christ and walks by faith. But there is also a possible downward spiral away from trust in God. Like a person who experiences sickness in the body, so a Christian can suffer the disease of unbelief. This experience is the pathology of faith. (UF = the unbelief of faith, and the numbers represent different functions of unbelief.) These expressions of unbelief are not a hierarchy of descent from God. Each, like a disease, may weaken one's faith, or they may attack the person in cluster.

CHART 6

CATEGORIES OF UNBELIEF
UF–1 weak faith UF–2 little faith UF–3 faithlessness UF–4 doubt UF–5 unbelief

UF–1: Weak Faith. The first step away from confidence in God is the weakened faith of a believer. This phrase described the early faith of Abraham (Romans 4:19) and the new believer who was still wrapped up in doubtful questions of whether or not he could eat meat (Romans 14:1ff), "i.e., not fully established, or not with so clear and enlarged views about Christian liberty as others might have."[8] Willoughby Allen describes this condition in terms of "an inadequate grasp of the great principle of salvation by faith in Christ; the consequence of which will be an anxious desire to make this salvation more certain by the scrupulous fulfilment of formal rules."[9] A person with UF–1 weak faith gets his eyes off Jesus Christ and becomes more concerned with legalism (what to eat, wear, and do). Hence, those who claim the experience of walking with God, yet base it on self-denials, special diets, and clothes do not have strong faith (Romans 14:20) but are weak in faith. If the deeper Christian life is the norm for believers, the UF–1 weak faith is the first step away from that experience.

Two different Greek words are translated "weak in faith" in the New Testament, and each reveals an aspect to this area of unbelief. The first word, *adunatos*, means "without power." The other word, *asthenes*, means "without strength." The person who is weak in faith lacks the spiritual power to accomplish what he attempts for God and also lacks the strength to endure in the trial of faith. Concerning this expression, John Gill suggests:

> By *him that is weak in faith*, is meant, either one that is weak in the exercise of the grace of faith, who has but a glimmering sight of Christ; who comes to him in a very feeble and trembling manner; who believes his ability to save him, but hesitates about his willingness; who casts himself with a peradventure on him; and who is attended with many misgivings of heart, faintings of spirit, and fluctuation of mind, about his interest in him: or one that is weak in the doctrine of faith; has but little light and knowledge in the truths of the Gospel; is a child in understanding; has more affection than judgment; very little able to distinguish truth from error; can't digest the greater and more sublime doctrines of grace; stands in need of milk, and can't bear strong meat; is very fluctuating and unsettled in his principles, and like children tossed to and fro with every wind of doctrine: or rather one that is weak in his knowledge of that branch of the doctrine of faith, which concerns Christian liberty; and that part of it particularly, which respects freedom from the ceremonial law.[10]

UF–2: Little Faith. On several occasions, Jesus described His disciples as having "little faith," especially when they were not able to serve God the way they wanted. "They lacked in moments of anxiety the courage which leads men to rely implicitly on the love and wisdom of their father."[11] A person did not need a great amount of faith, only the faith as a grain of mustard seed (Matthew 17:20). Because of little faith, the disciples could not cast the demon out of the boy (Matthew 17:19) or walk on water (Matthew 14:31) and they worried about food (Matthew 6:31). This second declension of faith is trying to serve God with one's ability and not in the power of Christ. The believer who has UF–2 little faith eroded his deeper-life experience when he failed in his service for God. Perhaps he served with the wrong motivation, wrong tools, or he was trying to serve God out of ignorance. His UF–2 little faith causes him to fail.

Although the expression "little faith" is used only by Jesus in the New Testament, it was a common rabbinical expression of the time, used to identify believers who at times doubted. Little faith is therefore a mix of faith and doubt. As one commentator has noted concerning the disciples:

> They were of *little* faith, in that they were afraid of perishing while they had on board the slumbering Saviour: they were not *faithless*, for they had recourse to that Saviour to help them. Therefore He acknowledges the faith which they had; answers the prayer of faith, by working a perfect calm: but rebukes them for not having the stronger, firmer faith, to trust Him even when He seemed insensible to their danger.[12]

UF–3: Faithlessness. This third descent of faith is a person's unwillingness to trust God, even in the face of evidence. The disciples tried to heal (Matthew 17:14–19), apparently in their own strength, but could not (v. 19). Jesus described them as "faithless" and asked, ". . . How long shall I be with you? . . ." (v. 17). The word "faithless" is *apistis* in the original language, which is also translated "unbelief" and "infidel." The Greek word *pistis*, means "faith," and the prefix *a* could be translated as a means of negating or neutralizing the rest of the word. *Faithlessness* means "neutral faith" or "no faith." It refers to "being without faith"[13] or to a "want of an energetic faith."[14] The person has not plunged into a negative distrust of God but simply does not believe God or disbelieve God. The UF–3 faithless believer ignores the presence of Jesus Christ in his life and refuses to be responsive to the Word of God. Thomas the Doubter expressed UF–3 faithlessness when he refused to believe the testimony of others that they had seen Jesus. A Christian who experiences UF-3 faithlessness has denied the experience of walking with God. Just as Thomas had to recognize Jesus' claims on his life and renew his fellowship, so the UF-3 faithless Christian has sinned in denying Christ and must return to the deeper Christian life.

UF-4: Doubt. When a Christian refuses to walk forward in fellowship with Christ, he will inevitably fall backwards into doubt. The word *dialogia,* translated "doubt," means "to reason through." According to Heinrich Meyer:

> The primary idea of *dialogismos* is a *thinking through* or *over* as with one's self, or in one's mind. Hence it comes to mean, in the plural, *speculations* or *reasonings.* This primary idea is apparently suggested directly or indirectly in most, if not indeed all, of the N. T. passages where it occurs. It is thus adapted to express that mental state which, in connection with questions such as are here under consideration, is described by our word *scruples.*[15]

Instead of living by faith, which is obeying the Word of God, the doubting believer begins to think through the nonscriptural options. He allows his reason to be controlled by his unbelief, not the Word of God. This Christian no longer experiences fellowship with Christ, but UF-4 doubt controls his thought processes. UF-4 doubt is a slow erosion of faith, because it probably does not include outward sin. However, it leads ultimately to the experience of life-corrupting sin.

UF-5: Unbelief. This is the negative expression of rejection by the Christian of the existence of God, the Word of God, and/or the claims of God on his life. The Christian has so deteriorated that he passes beyond a passive relationship to God and now actively refuses to believe. According to R. C. H. Lenski, "The trouble of unbelief is always in the heart, the seat of the will."[16] The UF-5 unbelief usually manifests itself when a Christian refuses to do the commands of God (read Scripture, pray, give financially, and so on) and/or he deliberately sins. The UF-5 unbelieving Christian does not lose his salvation, if he truly is converted, but loses his fellowship with God. Hence, the believer in UF-5 unbelief is not experiencing the deeper Christian

life, but probably has opened himself to all the emotional experiences that accompany backsliding and sin. Usually, he has
the opposite experience of the deeper Christian life.

The experience of Ex–2 the deeper Christian life is a constant
motivation to the believer, whether he is enjoying prosperity or
trials. His inner assurance keeps him going. As he begins to
drift away from his unbroken faith in God, his outward life may
not evidence change. Initially he continues to practice all the
outward forms of fellowship with Christ. Drifting usually
causes little immediate outward change. A person does not go
from one emotional extreme to the other. He usually continues
in the same emotional state, not realizing he is losing his faith
walk with Christ. Just as it is difficult to tell a pot of water is
getting hotter, so some people cannot tell they are losing their
deeper Christian life until the situation becomes a dangerously
hot, scalding pot.

— 3 —

TYPES OF
SIGNS AND
WONDERS

In 1952 I was the weekend pastor of Westminster Presbyterian Church, Savannah, Georgia, as a nineteen-year-old sophomore at Columbia Bible College. One day a group of men from a Pentecostal-type church came to pray with me. I did not want to have anything to do with their little church, because the shouting from this small church's Friday-night prayer meeting could be heard a block away. Their negative testimony made it hard to win souls in the neighborhood. My church was growing and winning souls.

"We have come to pray with you so you can be baptized with the Holy Ghost," the men told me.

I would not pray with them and could not give them a reason why not. As a nineteen-year-old I had never faced this problem. I did not have an answer.

"Have you ever spoken in tongues?" they asked.

I said I had not, but could not give a reason why I did not speak in tongues or did not want to.

"Don't you want everything God has for you?" That was a hard question. I wanted the joy of Christ and wanted a deeper walk with God. I wanted power in my ministry. I wanted everything God had for me. Today, many Christians seek tongues or a "second-blessing experience" because they have the same yearnings that I had. They want more fellowship with Christ and respond with sincerity to search for a special experience that might or might not be legitimate.

For every truth in life, there is a substitute. For the reality of a deeper walk with Christ, there is the pseudoexperience. One must always test the experience against Scripture.

The men from the Pentecostal-type church had met me on the front steps of the church. They pointed inside to the church altar. One of them said, "If you won't pray for the Holy Spirit, will you at least go to the altar and pray with us?" I was uneasy, and therefore I could not have prayed with an open heart to God. I refused. After a brief conversation, they left. I did not feel guilty for not being hospitable to them, nor did I feel intimidated. But I determined that I would find out everything I could about the Holy Spirit and be able to answer any who questioned me in the future about these issues.

Just because I do not believe or practice certain expressions of signs does not mean I do not believe God works today. About the same time I met the men at the front door of Westminster Presbyterian Church, I had another experience in which God apparently healed in answer to prayer.

Mrs. VanBrackle, an elderly lady in the little Presbyterian church, was losing her sight because of cataracts. She had been taken to a healing tent meeting in Charleston, South Carolina, over 100 miles away. The well-known evangelist laid hands on her and prayed three times. When asked if she could see, she responded, "No." Finally in exasperation the evangelist said, "It is your lack of faith."

Mrs. VanBrackle came home crushed in spirit. It was past midnight when she phoned me. I dressed and rode my bicycle to her home. I expected her to ask me to heal her. I knew I did not have the gift of healing, so I was afraid when I walked into the room. Her sons, who had taken her to the meeting, were there. They were not Christians, but had taken Mrs. VanBrackle at her request. I knew they were "sizing me up," so that intensified my fear.

"The evangelist told me I did not have faith," she said rising up in bed. "How can I get more faith?" she asked.

I explained that faith comes by the Word of God (Romans 10:17) and that she needed to hear, read, study, memorize, and meditate on the Word of God. Before leaving her room, I asked if I could pray for her.

First I prayed and confessed my unbelief and asked God to give us faith to believe for greater things. Next, I prayed for God to heal Mrs. VanBrackle, if it were His will. It was not a command to be healed, nor was it a victorious prayer of confidence. If anything, it was a prayer of fear, as though I were praying with my fingers crossed. But I knew I was talking to God, and I knew He heard me.

A few days later Mrs. VanBrackle sent word for me to visit her. She astonished me by picking up her Bible and reading a complete Psalm. She credited her healing to my prayer. Even though people in the neighborhood talked about it, I refused to announce it from the pulpit or take any credit. I was too young a Christian to understand all that was happening. I did not want people to think that my church was like the "Pentecostal church" down the street.

The problem I experienced with Pentecostals has been faced by others. Most Pentecostals teach that in the experience of the "second work of grace" God usually gives an outward sign such as speaking in tongues. Charismatic author Dan Basham claims that if tongues are not necessary, at least they are affirming.

"With God all things are possible" (Matt. 19:26), therefore the answer to this question is yes. However, it is a qualified yes! I personally know two people who received the baptism of the Holy Spirit in English rather than with unknown tongues. Both were exceptionally sensitive, prophetic men, true spiritual giants of our time. . . . So we must admit that the baptism in the Holy Spirit can be received without the manifestation of tongues, but we encourage no one to seek the baptism without expecting tongues. Both our understanding of spiritual gifts and our willingness to receive them affect what gifts and manifestations will appear. SOMETHING IS MISSING IN YOUR SPIRITUAL LIFE IF YOU HAVE RECEIVED THE HOLY SPIRIT YET HAVE NOT SPOKEN IN TONGUES. Those Spirit-filled Christians who have not yet spoken in tongues will receive a precious added assurance of God's presence and power when they do.[1]

In addition to tongues, other signs might be viewed as an evidence of spirituality or some aspect of spirituality: shouting, taking up rattlesnakes, performing miracles, being healed, drinking poison, being slain in the Spirit, receiving a word of prophecy, lifting the arms in prayer, and so on. Outside North American culture, there have also been reported cases of miraculous phenomena associated with the ministry of the Holy Spirit, including claims of raising the dead. Together with the Catholic mystics who claimed visions and stigmata as evidence of the deeper life, contemporary charismatics agree that the deeper life is to some degree characterized by miraculous signs. In fairness to those involved in this movement, it should be noted that many who believe in speaking in tongues would not engage in snake handling or certain other claims of miraculous signs. Indeed, it might be more accurate to conclude that for a variety of reasons most charismatic Christians would oppose the more extreme practices of the smaller sects. Because of the confusion about signs and wonders, this chapter attempts to classify them.

Not every observer of the charismatic phenomena has been impressed by their "evidences." Sir Robert Anderson, a writer many times quoted both within and outside the charismatic movement for his insight into prophecy, viewed the revival of Pentecostalism as an evidence of spiritism within the church. In a book on the subject he observes:

> The days we live in are intensely solemn. The stupid materialism of the science of yesterday has been exploded by the facts of spiritism, vouched for by some of our leading scientists of today. And the blind infidelity of the past has thus given place to a craving to get into touch with the realities of the unseen world. This morbid influence has invaded the sphere of religious thought and life, and spiritual Christians, even, are being corrupted by it. It creates a tendency to make the great facts and truths of the divine revelation of Christianity subordinate to subjective spiritual manifestations, and to the emotions and experiences which such manifestations are

fitted to produce. Among the many phases of this movement none is more striking than that of which the distinctive characteristic is what is termed "the gift of tongues."[2]

It is widely held that the contemporary Pentecostal movement began as a sectarian expression of the holiness movement at the turn of the century. George Dollar and others cite the glossolalia experience of Agnes Ozum at the Bethel Bible Institute in Topeka, Kansas, December 31, 1900, as the first instance of a baptism of the Holy Spirit being evidenced by speaking in unknown tongues.[3] Others, however, imply that the charismatic experience has historic succession reaching back to the apostolic era and including church fathers in both the Eastern and Western church and sectarian movements like the Montanists, medieval mystics, Huguenots, Jonsenites, Quakers, Irvingites, Shakers, and Mormons prior to the Topeka, Kansas, incident.[4] Those involved in what is generally called the charismatic or neopentecostal movement generally point to the rise of the Full Gospel Business Men's Fellowship International and the popularity of Oral Roberts in the 1950s, together with the charismatic experience of Episcopalian minister Dennis J. Bennett in 1960 as the beginnings of "interdenominational pentecostalism."[5] Today this is generally called the charismatic movement.

The fundamental difference between Pentecostalism and other expressions of the holiness movement is their belief that the evidence of the "baptism" or "fullness" of the Holy Spirit is speaking in tongues. Article Eight of the *Statement of Fundamental Truths of the Assemblies of God,* says in part, "The Baptism of believers in the Holy Ghost is witnessed by the initial physical sign of speaking with other tongues. . . ."[6] Tongues and other sign gifts are not emphasized by Pentecostals alone. Joseph Smith, founder of the Church of Jesus Christ of Latter-day Saints (Mormons), included in his original statement of faith, "We believe in the gift of tongues, prophecy, revelation, visions, healing, interpretations of tongues, etc."[7]

Categories of Signs and Wonders

We believe there is a reality in the deeper Christian life that is more than the experience that grows out of doctrinal agreement with Christianity. There is a deeper walk with Christ that is promised in John 14:20 (NKJV), "and you in Me, and I in you." Those who experience the presence of Christ know the reality of the deeper life, just as those who jump in a river know they are wet.

However, different groups make various claims concerning signs and wonders that accompany His presence in one's life. The following categories, SW–1 to SW–8 (SW stands for signs and wonders), reflect an attempt to systematize the reported experiences associated with signs and wonders. The following categories are not hierarchical but represent different expressions of miracles or the supernatural.

CHART 7

CATEGORIES OF SIGNS AND WONDERS
SW–1 biblical miracles
SW–2 counterfeit miracles
SW–3 psychosomatic miracles
SW–4 holistic-healing miracles
SW–5 confession-oriented miracles
SW–6 stimulated miracles
SW–7 pseudomiracles
SW–8 deceptive miracles

The following consideration of signs and wonders is necessary because some have indiscriminately accepted and promoted every testimonial of miraculous occurrences. Others have gone to the opposite extreme of slandering these signs, from their antisupernatural bias. If we are careful in our analysis of miracles and we assume the possibility of both natural and supernatural explanations, the reported signs and wonders can be explained in at least eight ways. The following categories of signs and wonders recognize that every reported phenomenon may not be genuine, and every genuine case may not necessarily be a direct act of God. God works indirectly by giving or providing a natural means to answer prayer, rather than providing a supernatural answer; that is, God sends a doctor to give a correct diagnosis and prescribe the correct medicine, rather than directly and supernaturally healing without a doctor or medicine. The following suggestion of eight types of signs and wonders makes no attempt to suggest the universal application of any one type to any specific situation.

SW–1: Biblical Miracles. The first explanation of the signs and wonders is seen in those miracles that find their origin in the power of God. These are genuine miracles similar to those of the prophets and apostles. Several evangelical concepts held by noncharismatic groups suggest the real possibility of miracles. If God answers prayer according to His Word, then it is conceivable He will answer the prayer of faith with a miraculous healing. However, He might also choose to heal through the application of medicine and be no less involved in answering the same prayer of faith. Further, in the Scriptures, since the blood of Christ and the Holy Spirit are characteristically described in terms of power, it is reasonable to anticipate periodic manifestations of that power in signs and wonders. In his discussion of the interpretation of miracles with particular reference to the miracle phenomena of the Timor revival, George W. Peters suggests the following principles concerning the possibility of miracles:

1. The Gospel of God is supernatural in nature, dynamics and results. It may be so in manifestations.
2. It could be possible that such miracle manifestations are a reenactment—a recapitulation—of the miracles of the Book of Acts. . . .
3. In the study of miracles it is wise to make a distinction between miracles that relate to man—healing, resuscitation—and miracles that relate to nature. . . .
4. In evaluating miracles it behooves the Christian to remain sober and vigilant on the one hand, and open and humble on the other.[8]

SW–2: Counterfeit Miracles. The second type of sign and wonder is a genuine miracle, but has a supernatural source outside of God. This type of miracle recognizes the ministry of Satan as

". . . an angel of light" (2 Corinthians 11:14). Evangelical fundamentalist writers tend to interpret a miracle by the devil in
terms of his ministry of counterfeiting the works of God. This is
an area often overlooked by writers on mysticism; however, as
Roger Bastide observes:

> Side by side with divine Mysticism is Satanic mysticism. Ac-
> cording to the theologians it allows two degrees. When a
> demon torments a soul from without it is a case of obsession,
> but when he completely masters the soul it is a case of pos-
> session. This demoniac Mysticism presents the same charac-
> teristics of passivity and of violence as the others, but the two
> are distinguished by their efforts. While divine Mysticism
> brings joy, consolation and moral progress, demoniac Mysti-
> cism induces nervous disorders, spiritual torture and the dis-
> position for sin.[9]

The question might legitimately be asked if such an explanation for signs and wonders can realistically be applied to an
evangelical experience described by its participants in terms of
biblical phraseology. For some observers of such movements,
the answer is undoubtedly yes. Sir Robert Anderson cites the
writings of Robert Baker, historian of the Catholic Apostolic
Church, and adds his own comments concerning the nature of
the "charismatic" experience of that group, noting:

> I have been much confounded by the fact occurring in this
> instance, as also in most others of the public testimonies of
> preaching; that Christ was preached in such power, and with
> such clearness, and the exhortations to repentance so energetic
> and arousing, that it is hard to believe the person delivering it
> could be under the delusion of Satan. Yet so it was, and the fact
> stands before us as a proof that the most fearful errors may be
> propounded under the guise of greater light and zeal for God's
> truth. "As an angel of light" is an array of truth, as well as
> holiness and love, which nevertheless Satan is permitted to put
> on, to accomplish and sustain his delusions. It is yet more
> mysterious, and yet not less true, that the truth so spoken was
> carried to the hearts of several who, on this day, hear it, and

these services were made the means of awakening them, so far as the change of conduct and earnest longing after Christ from that day forward can be an evidence of it.

As an angel of light. These words recur as a refrain throughout the "Narrative." Many a one will exclaim: "How could a movement which denounces the devil and all his works, and which promotes piety and honors Christ be Satanic?" But this ignores the solemn warning of our Divine Lord, "They shall deceive, if it were possible, the very elect." A moment's thought might satisfy us that the false could never deceive the elect if it did not simulate all the characteristics of the true—honor paid to Christ, a high tone of spirituality, and a beautiful code of morals.[10]

How can a believer tell a counterfeit miracle? Moses dealt with the issue of counterfeit supernaturalism in Deuteronomy 18:20–22; 13:1–5. A miracle from God will:

1. Be in the Lord's name (18:22).
2. Not recognize false gods (13:2, 3).
3. Stimulate love for the Lord (13:3).
4. Be consistent with the Word of God (13:4).

SW–3: Psychosomatic Miracles. An area of the nonmiraculous signs and wonders finds its explanation in terms of psychosomatic orientation of the healer or the convert. Dr. S. I. McMillen defines the psychosomatic phenomenon as the power of the mind over the body, noting:

These cases illustrate the most intriguing subject in modern medicine. With every passing year, we obtain a wider comprehension of the ability of the mind (*psyche*) to produce varied disturbances in the body (*soma*), hence the term *psychosomatic*. Invisible emotional tensions in the mind can produce striking visible changes in the body, changes that can become serious and fatal.[11]

Aware of this phenomenon, George W. Peters stresses the need to differentiate between miraculous and psychosomatic healing:

One must distinguish between faith healing and divine healing. Divine healing comes through the gracious intervention
of God. It may come with or without medication; it may come
suddenly or gradually. Faith healing rests mainly on the individual's psychological make-up and his personal relationships. It is principally a matter of psychology and suggestion.
No doubt, many healings in healing campaigns are of this
nature; they have little to do with the Gospel and divine
intervention.[12]

A psychosomatic healing may be described as nonmiraculous
because God does not intervene directly, but what about an
indirect work of God? If a person has an "illness" that is not real
and is healed of that "illness," do we call it a nonreal miracle or
a nonreal intervention by God? The illness may not be real by
medical definition, but there is a reciprocal influence between
body and mind that gives the same effect in pain where there is
no adequate cause.

The one who is healed psychosomatically is actually healed,
not in a SW–1 fashion, but SW–3.

SW–4: Holistic-Healing Miracles. The area of holistic medicine
may be a consideration in reported signs and wonders. The
fundamental premise of holistic healing is that the body can and
will heal itself of some disease when positive mental health and
corrective action are taken on the part of the sick. This includes
a positive mental attitude toward wanting to be healed. Because
of the radical nature of evangelical conversion, it is to be expected that life-style changes on the part of the new convert will
affect other areas of life, and this could include bodily functions.
The man with an ulcer, who gains the peace of God internally
and for religious reasons abstains from the use of alcohol and
caffeine drinks will also be treating his ulcer, that is, being
healed. The widespread application of this typology of healing
is evidenced in Dr. Carl Jung's conclusion:

> Among all my patients in the second half of life—that is to
> say, over thirty-five—there has not been one whose problem
> in the last resort was not that of finding a religious outlook on
> life.[13]

SW–5: Confession-Oriented Miracles. The fifth type of sign and wonder is also nonmiraculous. This type involves a testimony from a participant who knows the sign is nonexistent but at the same time feels pressure from an evangelist or friend to experience a sign such as tongues, being healed, receiving a revelation, and so on. This creates a major problem, particularly in movements where the desired miracle is particularly internal and pressure is intense for all members of a group to enjoy the full benefits of the experience. This is further complicated by the catch-22 statement of faith. A person must "say" he is healed as a statement of faith so God will heal him. He knows he is not healed, but sincerely claims something he doesn't have so he can get it. Catch-22 usually occurs when a seeker has for some time sought healing without success. If the illness is psychosomatic, he is obviously healed because of a change in the mind-body relationship previously described by Dr. McMillen. But the sad example is the case of the individual who "confesses" a healing from a serious disease but dies shortly thereafter. Many just continue to suffer, while some die.

SW–6: Stimulated Miracles. A sixth type of nonmiraculous sign may be the result of some stimulus, that is, drugs or other physical or psychological stimulus (music, hypnotic suggestion, brainwashing, and so on). Many drug-oriented religious sects use drugs as part of their religious experience and report visions and new revelations while under their influence. While this sort of stimulus and its effects are widely known, the influence of music, physical posture, behavior, and special diets can also result in a physical response. In his study of a revivalistic sect in Jamaica, Joseph Moore noted a direct relationship between the practice of hyperventilation and the entering of a possession trance state.[14] Similarly, Field was able to explain the unique religious experience of at least one sect in Ghana in terms of hypoglycemia caused by prolonged periods of fasting.[15]

SW–7: Pseudomiracles. A pseudomiracle is promoted not for ulterior motives but largely out of ignorance involved in the reported sign and wonder. This is apparently the explanation of one of the more remarkable reports of raising the dead during the widely publicized Indonesian revival. In his conclusions after interviewing those reportedly raised from the dead and those who raised them, George W. Peters writes:

> The reports from Timor that God raised some people from the dead have startled many American Christians. I do not doubt that God is able to raise the dead, but I seriously question that He did so in Timor. In fact, I am convinced that it did not happen. Let me explain:
>
> I visited a man known in the community as having been raised from the dead. I met a woman who reported that her infant daughter of four months had been raised. I talked to the woman who was said to be responsible for having brought back to life two people, and to the man who claimed to have been instrumental in raising two people from the dead, a boy of twelve and a man of forty to forty-five years old.
>
> In my questioning, I kept the sentiments of the people in mind. Their absolutist beliefs will not respond to questions of doubt. I was also aware of the fact that their word for death may mean unconsciousness, coma, or actual death. I also knew of their traditional belief in the journey of the soul after death from the body to the land of the ancestors.
>
> I had to explore the experiences of these people while they were in the state of death, how far they had "traveled," so to speak, between death and resuscitation. It became apparent that death takes place in three stages according to their beliefs. In the first stage, the soul is still in the body; in the second stage, the soul may be in the home or immediate community; and in the third stage, the soul takes its flight to the beyond and the land of the ancestors. Not one of the dead persons believed his soul had completely departed to the region beyond. That is the region of no return.
>
> Those who claimed to have experienced resuscitation and immediate restoration were people who had died suddenly. Several children who had died after suffering prolonged illnesses had more gradual restorations.
>
> I noted several interesting facts regarding the exeriences reported during the state of death. One man told me that his soul had been so near his body during his state of death that he was able to hear people come near his body. However, he

was not able to speak or move. He was able to relate experiences during his state of death. After some questioning, his wife added, "My husband was not absolutely and totally dead." This led to some further probing and lengthy discussions.

The mother whose infant daughter was raised was quite sure that her soul had not left her body, for she had been dead only about half an hour. An older man was able to describe his condition after dying. While dead he had promised God that if he could ever live again he would confess his sins and pay back the money he had stolen from an evangelist. He was sure that this theft had caused his sudden death, and so was the evangelist who brought him back to life. Thus the stories went. Two younger boys, one four and another eight, were not able to recount their experiences while dead. However, they were sure that they had not yet left the earth.

I shall leave any judgments about these miracles to the reader. I went away satisfied that according to their usage of the word death, and their concept of death, they had experienced resuscitation. According to my concept of death, no such miracles happened: I learned again the value of seeing words and concepts from the people's point of view and interpreting them according to their mentality and understanding.[16]

SW-8: Deceptive Miracles. There are some alleged signs and wonders that have been humanly faked or deceptively reported. In any analysis, it must first be determined if the miracle is genuine, and then the source or motive behind the deception must be accounted for. One SW-8 miracle is a pseudomiraculous phenomenon promoted for ulterior motives by the miracle worker and/or his agents. Not every reported miracle is miraculous, and some who report them have been found to have less than pure motives. In the fall of 1971, leaders in the controversial Children of God sect tapped phones at a French Canadian church camp where they were holding a special conference. As new converts to the cult made calls home for money, notes were taken and later became the basis of prophecies given in public meetings. The prophecies were regarded by undiscerning converts as an evidence of God speaking to them through the sect leaders.[17] This is but one of many such abuses and must be considered as a possible explanation in evaluating a particular manifestation of a sign and wonder.

Discerning the Authority of Miracle Workers

The presence of the above eight types of signs and wonders in the contemporary evangelical experience only serves to stress the need to exercise spiritual discernment in evaluating alleged miracles and those who are chiefly involved in their performance. If this is diligently practiced, it will reveal comparatively few if any miracles of the SW–1 type. In a study of the reported healings in the Timor revival, Peters described the type of miracles that are almost universally accepted among Christians today.

In the interpretation of the healing miracles in Timor one must keep in mind the following classifications:

(a) Faith healings that are primarily psychological. These do not require divine intervention because the illness is psychological. Large numbers of healings are of this nature.

(b) Physical healing and restoration as a result of the experience of salvation. Soul sickness affects the whole man. No medicine can cure this illness. The answer lies in the words of the Psalmist: "He restoreth my soul." With such salvation comes liberation from oppression, fear, anxiety, insecurity, and the satisfaction of one's spiritual hunger and thirst. Peace, joy, assurance of the forgiveness of sins, and the hope of eternal life are a "medicine" for millions of people.

(c) Liberation from demonic influences and powers, and direct demon-possession, as a result of salvation in Christ and the indwelling Holy Spirit. He resides in the heart of every true believer. "Greater is he that is in you, than he that is in the world" (1 John 4:4). Occultism is a terrible reality that destroys body and soul. Liberation from it brings restoration.

(d) Direct divine intervention which brings healing and restoration of the body. Christ is the great physician. He is able to heal.

After my investigation of the healings in Timor, I am
convinced that the vast majority of all of them belong to the
first three groups. I cannot say that there were none in the
fourth classification. However, I think there were relatively
few.[18]

The problem of miracle workers performing nonmiraculous
signs and wonders or miracles that have a demonic source of
power is not new but rather was one characteristic of the
history of both Israel and the church. As a result, the Scriptures provide numerous warnings concerning false prophets,
teachers, apostles, and so on, providing numerous specific
instructions concerning the identification of true and false servants of God. A study of the principal passages concerning
false teachers suggests the false prophet will in many respects
look like a true prophet, but in one or more areas he will fail
to measure up. In any attempt to discern a counterfeit from
reality, it is best to understand the character of the genuine.
From the many biblical passages that warn the reader about
false prophets, the following list of seventeen characteristics
of the true servant of God may be compiled.

1. Speaks in the name of the Lord (Deuteronomy 18:22).
2. Prophecy shall come to pass (Deuteronomy 18:22).
3. Does not advocate the worship of false gods (Deuteronomy 13:2, 3).
4. Promotes a deeper love for the Lord (Deuteronomy 13:3).
5. Life and teaching consistent with the Word of God (Deuteronomy 13:4).
6. Promotes a deeper trust in (cleaving to) the Lord (Deuteronomy 13:4).
7. Teaching is not characterized by perverseness, but rather
   truth (Jeremiah 23:25–34; Acts 20:30).
8. Produces spiritual fruit characteristic of the servant of the
   Lord (Matthew 7:15–20).
9. Has a personal experiential knowledge of God (Matthew
   7:21–23).
10. Does not attempt to raise a following to himself but rather
    to the Lord (Acts 20:30).

11. Ministry not characterized by secrecy and ulterior motives (2 Peter 2:1; 1 John 4:2, 3).
12. Adheres to fundamental doctrines of the evangelical faith (2 Peter 2:1; 1 John 4:2, 3).
13. Concerned with helping others rather than using others to attain personal goals (2 Peter 2:3).
14. Practices personal separation to God from the world (1 John 3:6).
15. Remains loyal to the teachings of Christ rather than a more contemporary or "advanced" teaching (2 John 9, 10).
16. Promotes a personal holiness as a consistent response to biblical doctrine (Jude 4).
17. Has a proper respect for authority (Jude 8).

In some cases, a true servant of the Lord may be guilty of inconsistency. If that is the case, he should repent and bring himself back under the authority of the Lord. The refusal of a religious leader to repent of known sin or error is specifically identified by the Lord as characteristic of the false teacher (Revelation 2:21).

Biblical Teaching Regarding Signs and Wonders

Miracle has been generally defined over the years as "something that cannot be explained, apart from God." Among the broadest of these definitions is that of Kathryn Kuhlman, who before her death was a widely known charismatic faith healer. Kuhlman includes everything unexplainable, from electricity to divine healing, under her broad definition. In her testimonial book on the subject, she suggests all healing is miraculous, even if it involves medical treatment. Yet the majority of the book is devoted to the case histories of twenty-one individuals or families that testify to physical healing without the aid of medicine. This emphasis tends to raise questions as to the accuracy of her statement that all healing is miraculous, in that her stories of miracles only include those beyond the hope of medicine.[19]

Among the historic evangelical theologians of various schools of thought, several definitions of *miracles* have been suggested.

Charles Grandison Finney suggested, "A miracle has been generally defined to be a Divine interference, setting aside, or suspending, the laws of nature."[20] Finney's definition is deistic, while Augustus Hopkins Strong's is typically theistic:

> A miracle is an event in nature, so extraordinary in itself and so coinciding with the prophecy or command of a religious teacher or leader, as to fully warrant the conviction, on the part of those who witness it, that God has wrought it with the design of certifying that this teacher or leader has been commissioned by him.[21]

More recent writers tend to emphasize the effect of the miracle, rather than the authentification of the miracle worker or the act itself. Henry Theissen states, "A genuine miracle is an unusual event, accomplishing some useful work, and revealing the presence and power of God."[22] In so defining a miracle, Theissen differentiates genuine miracles from spurious miracles and natural phenomena. Perhaps the most comprehensive definition of miracles is that developed by George W. Peters in connection with his research into the miraculous phenomenon associated with the Indonesian revival:

> A miracle is a historical event resulting from divine interposition. Such interposition may (1) *supersede* and *transcend* all natural laws as they are known to man, and as they are inherent in the universe—for example, creation, revelation, the incarnation. Or, (2) it may *supersede* and *counter* natural laws as are known to man and are manifested in nature—for example, the departure of Enoch, of Elijah, the resurrection and ascension of Christ, the rapture of the saints. (3) It may mean the *suspension* of natural laws—Christ walking on the sea, Christ stilling the storm and waves, Peter walking on the Sea of Galilee, the apostles set free from bondage in prison, Paul's deliverance from the poison of the serpent. (4) It may involve the *intensification* of natural laws—turning water into wine, feeding the five thousand, catching fish, as reported several times in the gospels. (5) The *redirection* of natural laws—

dividing the Red Sea and Jordan River to permit Israel to go through; Elijah on Mount Carmel; the dispersion of clouds and rain when they seem natural; the sending of manna and quails to Israel in the desert. (6) The *neutralization* and *counter* of the consequences of sin—physical healing, exorcism, resuscitation. Miracles may be the result of direct or indirect interpositions. God may intervene with or without the use of man or means. Miracles may be instantaneous or gradual.[23]

The reality of miracles is verified, not by documented cases but by biblical teaching on the subject. Unless the evangelical believer is convinced of the possibility of miracles today, so-called documented cases can be reinterpreted by the observer and explained outside of the miraculous realm. C. S. Lewis illustrates this principle in his book on miracles:

> In all my life I have met only one person who claims to have seen a ghost. And the interesting thing about the story is that that person disbelieved in the immortal soul before she saw the ghost and still disbelieves after seeing it. She says that what she saw must have been an illusion or a trick of the nerves. And obviously she may be right. Seeing is not believing.
> For this reason, the question whether miracles occur can never be answered simply by experience. Every event which might claim to be a miracle is, in the last resort, something presented to our senses, something seen, heard, touched, smelled, or tasted. And our senses are not infallible—if anything extraordinary seems to have happened, we can always say that we have been victims of an illusion. If we hold a philosophy which excludes the supernatural, this is what we always shall say. What we learn from experience depends on the kind of philosophy we bring to experience. It is therefore useless to appeal to experience before we have settled, as well as we can, the philosophical questions.[24]

Five Greek words are used in the New Testament to describe miracles, including *terata* ("wonders"), *erga* ("works"), *thaumasin* ("wonderful thing"), *dunameis* ("powers") and *semeion* ("signs"). A miracle is a spectacular (*terata*) thing (*thaumasin*) or work (*erga*) expressing the power of God (*dunameis*) for some signal purpose (*semeion*). While the synoptic gospels prefer the word *dunameis*, "power," to describe the miracles of Jesus, emphasizing their source in the power of God, John employs the term "sign," *semeion*, seventeen times in his gospel, emphasizing the spiritual significance of eight particular miracles.

The debate over whether miracles can happen today centers around one's understanding of the purpose of miracles. The word *semeion* is used in the Septuagent to convey the idea of a heavenly symbol (Genesis 1:14), a protective mark (Genesis 4:15), a pledge (Genesis 17:11), a miracle (Exodus 7:3, 9), a memorial (Exodus 13:9), a sample of divine power (Isaiah 7:11), and a signal (Jeremiah 6:1). In the New Testament, the term was used by John of the miracles of Christ and by Paul of speaking in tongues (1 Corinthians 14:22). A sign usually points to the message from God and gives the message credibility. Concerning the meaning of *signs* and its use in the New Testament, W. E. Vine writes:

A sign, mark, indication, token, is used (*a*) of that which distinguished a person or thing for others, e.g., Matt. 26:48; Luke 2:12; Rom. 4:11; 2 Cor. 12:12 (1st part); 2 Thess. 3:17, "token," i.e., his autograph attesting the authenticity of his letters; (*b*) of a sign as a warning or admonition, e.g., Matt. 12:39, "the sign of (i.e., consisting of) the prophet Jonas;" 16:34; Luke 2:34; 11:29,30; (*c*) of miraculous acts (1) as tokens of Divine authority and power, e.g., Matt. 12:38, 39 (1st part); John 2:11, R. V., . . . indicates that the Apostles were met with the same demand from Jews as Christ had been: "signs were vouchsafed in plenty, signs of God's power and love, but these were not the signs which they sought. . . . They wanted signs of an outward Messianic Kingdom, of temporal triumph, of material greatness for the chosen people. . . . With such cravings the gospel of a 'crucified Messiah' was to them a stumblingblock indeed" (Lightfoot); 1 Cor. 14:22; (2) by demons, Rev. 16:14; (3) by false teachers or prophets, indications of assumed authority, e.g., Matt. 24:24; Mark 13:22; (4) by Satan through his special agents, 2 Thess. 2:9; Rev. 13:13, 14; 19:20; (*d*) of tokens portending future events, e.g., Matt. 24:3, where "the sign of the Son of Man" signifies, subjectively, that the Son of Man is Himself the sign of what He is about to do: Mark 13:4; Luke 21:7, 11, 25; Acts 2:19; Rev. 12:1, R.V.; 12:3, R.V.; 15:1.

Signs confirmatory of what God had accomplished in the atoning sacrifice of Christ, His resurrection and ascension, and of the sending of the Holy Spirit, were given to the Jews for their recognition, as at Pentecost, and supernatural acts by apostolic ministry, as well as by the supernatural operations in the churches, such as the gift of tongues and prophesyings; there is no record of the continuance of these latter after the circumstances recorded in Acts 19:1–20.[25]

Traditionally, dispensationalists have defined signs largely in terms of revelatory signs authenticating the ministry or message of the apostles or prophets. By this statement they imply there are no longer signs because there are no gifts of apostles and prophets today, and the message of God (Scripture) is complete.

I have used the term "scaffolding principle" to explain the miraculous purpose of signs. Just as workers will construct a temporary scaffold for the purpose of constructing a permanent building, so God produced "signs" temporarily in epochs of Scripture that gave credibility and acceptance to His message, that is, the Word of God. Just as a sign points to something or gives a message, so the miracles pointed to the message of God to men. However, when the Word of God (the message) was established, like a building is completed, the scaffold is taken down, or the signs cease. Just because I explain signs as a scaffold does not mean I reject the miraculous intervention of God in today's world.

The bulk of all recorded biblical miracles occurred chronologically in one of three periods (epochs), that is, when most of the Scriptures were being written, during the ministries of Moses and Joshua, later during the ministries of Elijah and Elisha, and still later under the ministry of Christ and the apostles. Miracles, of course, occurred at times other than those mentioned above, but the above three epochs were times abundant in miraculous phenomena. To a large extent, the miracles were signs, in that they authenticated or were sent to authenticate the messenger and his message.

According to George W. Peters, professor of world missions at Dallas Theological Seminary:

> Miracles are a possibility whenever and wherever the power of the Gospel breaks through in new ways and places. The New Testament does not explicitly close the door on such possibilities. We have no right to deny they happen today, nor to expect and demand them. The Bible remains silent and open in this matter. It should not surprise us, however, if miracles do accompany the introduction of the Gospel in new areas and among people held in bondage by occultism, spiritism, and demonism.[26]

Today's Miracles

God works in today's world. He is not an absentee landlord. Since, extremely broadly speaking, everything that is an intervention by God or a contemporary intentional work of God (beyond His execution of His laws), we can expect God's miraculous hand in our world. We might even suggest a breakdown of SW–1 biblical miracles, into the following categories.

SW–1a: Regeneration. The work of God in the salvation of an individual is the application of God's laws to the salvation of man. But in the work of salvation: the Trinity indwells the convert; he is given a new nature; he has access to God; and he has the inner witness of assurance of salvation.

SW–1b: Internal-Intellectual. The new believer is illuminated to understand Scriptures that he was previously blind to. Supernaturally he can be guided to do God's will and has a new awareness of God in his life.

SW–1c: Internal-Emotional. The believer can experience positive emotional experiences such as the peace of God, joy, love, or the fruit of the Spirit. These are supernatural results of conversion. Also the new convert can feel a negative experience such as conviction or guilt for sin.

SW–1d: Internal-Will. The believer can be led by God to do the will of God (Romans 8:14; Galatians 5:26). This may function through the intellect (SW–1b) or internal emotion (SW–1c).

SW–1e: God Working Through His Laws. God works through His laws to control His universe, but in answer to prayer, He may redirect circumstances, control the situation, or intervene.

SW–1f: The Deeper Life. The believer experiences the filling of the Spirit (Ephesians 5:18), the indwelling Christ (Galatians 2:20), and victory over sin (1 John 5). These experiences are beyond the natural unsaved person or the carnal Christian. These are biblical experiences that are for all believers (*see* chapters 4–10).

SW–1g: The Second Work of Grace. The believer experiences something and claims one or more of the following: the eradication of the old nature, the power of the Holy Spirit, signs and wonders, the ability to refrain from sin, or the baptism of the Holy Spirit. I believe this is a step beyond the biblical promise to believers and would say they are experiencing the SW–1f level of the deeper Christian life.

SW–1h: God's Transcending His Laws. This involves the miracles of the Bible, such as raising the dead, the Ascension, and so on. This level involves both miracles related to people (healing, adding extra life to Hezekiah, and so on) or miracles in nature (such as God's prohibiting rain, or the crossing of the Red Sea).

SW–1i: God Initiates His Laws. This involves creation, the Incarnation, the inspiration of Scripture, and so on; while these miracles are not operative today, the results may be applied to the life of Christians and are the basis of the deeper life.

As a result of this study of signs and wonders, the Christian must conclude that God is at work in the modern world. But not everything that is reported as a miracle is miraculous. Perhaps we devalue Christianity by our claims of "miracle offerings" and "miracle-attendance crowds." If it is from God, let us be slow to call it a miracle and let the evident work of God provide its own credibility.

PART TWO

THEOLOGICAL FOUNDATIONS FOR EXPERIENCE

How the Christian looks at theological questions will influence his experience in Christ. Here we consider issues in theology that are key to our subject.

— 4 —
THE FOUNDATION FOR CHRISTIAN EXPERIENCE

The standard histories of the church have usually described a struggle between two groups on the opposite ends of the theological spectrum. It has been a struggle of doctrine or ideas. Thus one learns of apostolic Christianity's struggle against the Gnostics and Judaizers of that day; the orthodox church Fathers' struggle against heretical Arians, Montanists, and Origen. The evangelical sects of the Dark Ages struggled against the Roman Catholic Church; the Protestant Reformers struggled against an increasingly corrupt Roman church; the revivalistic free-church movement struggled against the decaying state churches; and modern evangelical fundamentalism struggled against German rationalism. Yet beyond these ideological distinctions, sometimes a third, virtually unknown, struggle was going on, more often a reaction against both movements. This third group was an expression of Christianity concerned with Christian experience. Sometimes biblical in its expression and blessed of God, at other times this group's passion for mystical experience drove it to nonbiblical extremes. It is made up of those who desired to experience God in their lives. They wanted more than creeds; they wanted to personally know Christ. Sometimes they were biblical mystics, at other times they were nonbiblical mystics who wanted absorption into God or the experience of the pseudomiracle of God.

The introspective and individualistic nature of these movements is perhaps the best explanation why their adherents did

not for the most part aggressively seek converts to their movement and why in many cases no attempt was made even to
organize a movement. What writings they did produce are
largely devotional in nature and can only be viewed as tractarian
in the sense of all testimonial writing. But even in this, their
works were largely a call to a deeper experience and/or fellowship
with God, or in some cases, saints and angels. Much of their
writings were in-house manuals of discipline, records of experiences, apologetics for their position, but not the sort of thing
easily understood by someone not familiar with the distinctive
subculture of their movement.

These movements, whether evangelical or Catholic, orthodox
or heretical, have little in common apart from the fact they were
all sectarian in nature. They were often the following of an
obscure charismatic leader who claimed his followers could
have a deeper experience or power outside themselves, if they
would to some degree separate themselves from a perceived
evil world and adopt a specifically prescribed program of piety.
At times this involved a total abandonment of the world and a
primitive monastic life-style. More often, piety was identified in
terms of attending meetings or practicing ordinances. Those
who experienced these results were involved in holy-club ses-
sions, believer's baptism, the breaking of bread, the sharing of
the "body life" in visions, singing, testimonies, and so on.

Because experiential Christianity has crossed the usual lines
of demarcation, because the movements often identified themselves as a reformed movement within a larger group, because
the followings of the charismatic leaders were generally small
and/or locally defined, because the various subcultures of the
different experiential groups even of the same era were so dis-
similar, historians have largely neglected their significance, and
theologians have generally failed to systematize their distinctive
concepts and ideals.

When experiential Christianity has been studied, it has been
hard for historians, concerned about records, and theologians,
concerned with orthodoxy and systematic creeds, to be objective in evaluating a movement that cares for none of the above.
Those who understand experiential Christianity must go be-

yond the rational, and they cannot describe the experience until they have had the same experience. All Christian experience seems to have been confused with mysticism, and hence, all has been excluded. Granted, we must reject one aspect of mysticism. However, this book attempts to separate biblical experiences from those we must reject.

The following authorities give ample explanation for the rejection of certain mystics. Theologian Augustus Hopkins Strong observes:

> Mysticism, however, as the term is commonly used, errs in holding to the attainment of religious knowledge by direct communication from God, and by passive absorption of human activities into the divine. It either partially or wholly loses sight of (a) the outward organs of revelation, nature and the Scriptures; (b) the activity of the human powers in the reception of all religious knowledge; (c) the personality of man, and, by consequence, the personality of God. . . . Note the mystical tendency in Francis de Sales, Thomas à Kempis, Madame Guyon, Thomas C. Upham. These writers seem at times to advocate an unwarrantable abnegation of our reason and will, and a "swallowing up of man in God."[1]

Concerning the response of Reformation theologians to mysticism, Roland H. Bainton notes, "Such mystical tendencies did not commend themselves to Luther, who could not conceive how weak and impure man could be merged in the purity of the All-Holy, and to Calvin the very notion of the deification of man was blasphemous."[2]

Historian Earle E. Cairns summarizes a view of mysticism as a reactionary movement:

> The recurrence of mysticism in the eras when the Church lapses into formalism testifies to the desire of the human heart to have direct contact with God in the act of worship instead of passively participating in the cold formal acts of worship performed by the clergyman. The mystic desires direct contact with God by immediate intuition or contempla-

tion. If the emphasis is on the union of the essence of the mystic with the essence of deity in the experience of ecstacy, which is the crown of mystical experience, then mysticism is philosophical. If the emphasis is on an emotional union with deity by intuition, then mysticism is psychological. The main objective in either case is immediate apprehension of God in an extra rational fashion as the mystic waits before Him in a passive receptive mood.[3]

Whatever might be said of the failings or abuses of mystics, it is generally agreed that they act out of a sincerity of heart and a sense of divine necessity. Concerning the fourteenth-century mystic Meister Eckhart, Kenneth Scott Latourette notes:

Eckhart had what he believed to be direct experience with God. His preaching grew out of his own profound religious life and he wished to help others to share it. He did not prize ecstatic emotion, but calmness and quiet. Yet he lived an active life and believed that to have peace in a life of pain was far better than to have a life of rest and peace in God.[4]

This sincerity of heart and sense of divine necessity in one's task is evidenced in the writings of a more contemporary evangelical mystic, A. W. Tozer, an experiential Christian and a leader in the deeper-life movement. In an apparent attempt to justify the writing and publication of one of his books, A. W. Tozer wrote:

The only book that should ever be written is one that flows up from the heart, forced out by the inward pressure. When such a work has gestated within a man it is almost certain it will be written. The man who is thus charged with a message will not be turned back by any blase considerations. His book will be to him not only imperative, it will be inevitable. This little book of the spiritual way has not been "made" in any mechanical sense; it has been born out of inward necessity.[5]

Because mysticism is so subjective and individualistic in expression by a genuine experiential Christian, it is difficult to define in terms of specific identifying features. It is colored by individual personalities and theological subcultures and often differs to some degree even within the same movement. William Ralph Enge perhaps comes closest to a workable definition when he identifies mysticism as:

> The attempt to realize in thought and feeling the imminence of the temporal in the eternal, and of the eternal in the temporal. It implies (1) that the soul can see and perceive spiritual truth; (2) that man, in order to know God, must be a partaker of the divine nature; (3) that without holiness no man can see the Lord; (4) that the true hierophant of the mysteries of God is love. The 'scala perfectionis' is (a) the purgative life; (b) the illuminative life; (c) the unitive life.[6]

Within the broad yet limited spectrum of Christendom, mystical union with God is the sincere expression of experiential Christianity among persons of various temperaments, theological backgrounds, and cultural contexts. Broadly it includes the asceticism of the Anabaptist, the revivalism of the holiness sects, the monasticism of medieval Catholicism, the charismatic baptism of the Holy Spirit of Pentecostals, the deeper life of the Keswick movement, and the fullness or anointing of the Holy Spirit as preached by evangelicals and fundamentalists. In an attempt to analyze various mystical expressions within Christendom, Earle E. Cairns suggests they essentially fall into three categories:

> There may be an *epistemological* type of mysticism in which the emphasis is upon how man comes to know God. Those devoted to this type of mysticism think that all our knowledge of God is immediate and comes directly to us by intuition or spiritual illumination. Reason and, in some cases, even the Bible are subordinated to the inner light. Most medieval mystics, the Roman Catholic Quietists of the seventeenth century and the Quakers held to this view. Others emphasize a *metaphysical* type of mysticism in which the spirit of man is thought to be absorbed mystically into the divine being in occasional

experiences here and now. Following the extinction of his
separate personality by death, man's spirit becomes a part of
the divine being. The Neoplatonists, some of the more extreme mystics of the Middle Ages, and Buddhists held to this
type of mysticism. The Bible in contrast emphasizes an *ethical
and spiritual* type of mysticism in which the individual is
related to God through his identification with Christ and the
indwelling Holy Spirit.[7]

There are several different expressions of mystical Christianity, each with an essential theology of its own. According to this
view, it is not a matter of a biblical versus a nonbiblical view, but
rather a recognition of certain strengths and weaknesses within
each of the views. The theological emphasis and conclusions of
each expression refer to the dominant themes in the relevant
literature and are not intended to deny that other views are held
to a lesser degree within the groups.

The assumption of this book is that there is a legitimate place
for experience in the Christian life. But it must be biblical, not
just an emotional experience. Indeed, the evangelical concept of
conversion to some degree demands an acceptance of experiential Christianity. The man who comes to a God he cannot
physically see, hear, touch, smell, or taste and surrenders his
life to that God engages in a nonphysical act. When the same
man later assumes a humiliating posture of bowing his head to
ask God for certain specific things and rises believing his God
has heard and will answer that prayer, he is in practice a mystic.
When he communes with God through the Bible, he experiences communication with God. This aspect of Christianity is
acknowledged even by those who might otherwise oppose the
concept of mysticism. In more of a denial than an affirmation,
Strong argues:

> We have seen there is an illumination of the minds of all
> believers by the Holy Spirit. The Spirit, however, makes no
> new revelation of truth, but uses for his instrument the truth
> already revealed by Christ in nature and in the Scriptures.
> The illuminating work of the Spirit is therefore an opening of

men's minds to understand Christ's previous revelations. As one initiated into the mysteries of Christianity, every true believer may be called a mystic. True mysticism is that higher knowledge and fellowship which the Holy Spirit gives through the use of nature and Scripture as subordinate and principle means.[8]

There is an uneasy tension with which the theologian struggles in this area of experience. On the one hand, he cannot in his integrity deny the reality of Christian experience. On the other hand, his systematic and analytical approach to theology has enabled him to make objective conclusions that seem at times diametrically opposed to experience. To further complicate matters, in defense of their experience, many, if not all, have erred in opposing and denying the legitimate place of theology in Christian experience. The line must be drawn somewhere to distinguish between the acceptable and unacceptable expressions of experience. The theologian has largely chosen to draw the line excluding experience that insists upon a uniting of human and divine natures. As Roland H. Bainton explains:

If mysticism means simply warm personal religion, then plainly no vital Christianty can be without it. But if mysticism be taken in the more technical sense as that type of religion which sees as its end the union of the human with the divine, then alike reinforcement and peril are implicit for Christianity. The notion that man may partake in the divine nature is found in the Second Epistle of Peter, and the Apostle Paul could quote with favor the heathen who said of God that in Him we live and move and have our being. Pursuing this idea the theologians of the early church appropriated the Greek concept of attainment by moral man of a blessed immortality through the discarding of humanity and the acquisition of divinity. Through union with God, man becomes divine and immortal. So long as man remains man and God remains God these tendencies are entirely compatible with Christianity. But if the devotee is believed to be completely merged in the abyss of the Godhead, then the subject-object relationship, the polarity of the I and Thou, so characteristic of the Hebrew-Christian tradition, is destroyed.[9]

The theologian who proposes a compromise along these lines, in the hope that the evangelical can in good conscience agree to such an artificial limitation, fails to understand the experiential nature of Christianity. Apart from the belief of a potential union of the believer with deity, there might be no mysticism. This is a theme common to Christianity of every age and culture. A. J. Gordon taught:

> It is possible that one may experience a great crisis in his spiritual life, in which there is such a total surrender of self to God and such an infilling of the Holy Spirit, that he is freed from the bondage of sinful appetites and habits, and enabled to have constant victory over self instead of suffering constant defeat. . . . If the doctrine of sinless perfection is a heresy, the doctrine of contentment with sinful imperfection is a greater heresy. . . . It is not an edifying spectacle to see a Christian worldling throwing stones at a Christian perfectionist.[10]

Andrew Murray came to a similar conclusion:

> But let me now add, that *if this absolute surrender is to be maintained and lived out, it must be by having Christ coming into our life in new power.* It is only in Christ that we can draw nigh to God, and it is only in Christ that God can draw nigh to us. We need to have "Christ our life." . . . *Christ in us as our life and strength.* That is the crown of all. The young convert ordinarily understands very little of that. Many a believer has lived long in some experience of Christ with Him as Guide and Helper, but has never yet come to realize what this other means: Christ in me, my very life and my very strength.[11]

In the introduction to her classic *Short and Very Easy Method of Prayer: Which All Can Practice With the Greatest Facility, And Arrive in a Short Time, By Its Means, At a High Degree of Perfection,* the French Catholic mystic Madame Jeanne Guyon wrote:

I have stated that *perfection* can easily be attained, and this is true. Jesus Christ is *perfection*, and when we seek Him within ourselves, He is easily found. . . . Beloved reader, read this little book with a sincere and honest spirit. Read it in lowliness of mind without the inclination to criticize. If you do, you will not fail to reap profit from it. *I have written this book with a desire that you might wholly give yourself to God.* Please receive this book with that same desire in your own heart.[12]

In an evangelistic letter to a friend, Henry Scougal sought to distinguish between true religion and the forms of religions with which his friend was familiar:

But certainly religion is quite another thing, and they who are acquainted with it will entertain different thoughts and disdain all those shadows and false imitations of it. They know by experience that true religion is a union of the soul with God, a real participation of the divine nature, the very image of God drawn upon the soul, or in the apostle's phrase, *it is Christ formed within us.* Briefly, I know not how the nature of religion can be more fully expressed than by calling it a *divine life.*[13]

If there is a common theme in the literature of Christianity, it is a sincere belief in the possibility of a union of the believer with God this side of heaven. Often this theme is expressed in terms of a union to be achieved, and the perceived results of such a union usually provide victory over sin and/or self. To some the union results in perfectionism. Concerning this emphasis, Bainton observes: "The union with God which is the goal of the mystic quest must be unconstrained and force is utterly ineffective either to produce or restrain it. The way to God is a way of trial and renunciation, which is more compatible with the sufferings of the martyr than with the torture chamber of the inquisitor."[14]

There is no uniformity among experience-oriented Christians concerning the means whereby they have union with God. More often than not, there is an identification with some particular ministry of the Holy Spirit, and often this involves a significant and specific spiritual experience. The conditions whereby the experience is prompted and the experience in that state vary from account to account, even among close associates. Some might argue that the sensation of an experience was itself an effect of an earlier experience. Even the nomenclature by which the experience is identified varies. But the experience is real to those who have been *baptized, filled, anointed, endued, indwelt, sanctified, blessed, crucified, renewed, revived* or *cleansed.*

According to William Bramwell's own testimony:

> When in the house of a friend at Liverpool, whither I had gone to settle some temporal affairs, previous to my going out to travel, while I was sitting, as it might be, on this chair, with my mind engaged in various meditations concerning my present affairs and future prospects, my heart now and then lifted up to God, but not particularly about this blessing, *heaven came down to earth;* it came to my soul. The Lord, for whom I had waited, came suddenly to the temple of my heart; and I had an immediate evidence that this was the blessing I had for some time been seeking. My soul was then all wonder, love and praise.[15]

R. A. Torrey described his experience with God in terms of a baptism with the Holy Spirit:

> I recall the exact spot where I was kneeling in prayer in my study. . . . It was a very quiet moment, one of the most quiet moments I ever knew. . . . Then God simply said to me, not in any audible voice, but in my heart, "It is yours. Now go and preach." . . . He had already said it to me in His Word in 1 John 5:14, 15; but I did not then know my Bible as I know it now, and God had pity on my ignorance and said it directly to my soul. . . . I went and preached, and I have been a new minister from that day to this. . . . Some time after this experience (I do not recall just how long after), while sitting in my room one day . . . suddenly . . . I found myself shouting

(I was not brought up to shout and I am not of a shouting temperament, but I shouted like the loudest shouting Methodist) "glory to God, glory to God, glory to God", and I could not stop. . . . But that was not when I was baptized with the Holy Spirit. I was baptized with the Holy Spirit when I took Him by simple faith in the naked Word of God.[16]

In contrast with his friend and ministerial associate, D. L. Moody identified his experience with the Holy Spirit in terms of a deeply moving emotional sensation:

I was crying all the time that God would fill me with His Spirit. Well, one day, in the city of New York—oh, what a day!—I cannot describe it, I seldom refer to it; it is almost too sacred an experience to name. Paul had an experience of which he never spoke for fourteen years. I can only say that God revealed Himself to me, and I had such an experience of His love that I had to ask Him to stay His hand. I went preaching again. The sermons were not different; I did not present any new truths; yet hundreds were converted. I would not now be placed back where I was before that blessed experience if you should give all the world—it would be as the small dust of the balance.[17]

Missionary-statesman Oswald J. Smith preferred to define his experience in terms of the anointing of the Spirit or the enduement of power. In a sermon on that subject, he related the following personal testimony:

It was in Tampa, Florida, February 10th, 1927. I had delivered a message on the Highest Form of Christian Service; viz., Intercessory Prayer. At the close I called for a season of prayer, and knelt beside the pulpit in the Alliance Tabernacle. Now I am handicapped for words. How am I going to describe it? What can I say? Nothing was farther from my mind. Not a moment had I expected anything unusual that morning. But as the people prayed, I was conscious of an unusual Presence. God seemed to hover over the meeting. Presently the blessing began to fall. I was melted, broken, awed, my heart filled with unutterable love; and as my soul rose to meet Him, the tears began to come. I would do nothing but weep and praise my precious, precious Lord. It seemed as though my whole body was bathed in the Holy Ghost until I was lost in wonder, love and praise. It seemed to me as though I wanted to love everybody. The world and all its troubles faded from my sight. My trials appeared, oh, so insignificant, as God, God Himself, filled my whole vision. Oh, it was glorious![18]

Charles Finney's own testimony was similar to Smith's in that he also spoke of a penetrating of the Holy Spirit and an abundance of love, joy, and tears. In his autobiography, he recorded:

. . . I received a mighty baptism of the Holy Ghost. Without any expectation of it, without ever having the thought in my mind that there was any such thing for me, without any recollection that I had ever heard the thing mentioned by any person in the world, the Holy Spirit descended upon me in a manner that seemed to go through me, body and soul. . . . No words can express the wonderful love that was shed abroad in my heart. I wept aloud with joy and love. . . .[19]

Welsh Revivalist leader Evan Roberts recorded a similar experience, not as Finney, on the day of his conversion, but rather after some thirteen years of tarrying for a specific blessing:

I felt a living force coming into my bosom. This grew and grew, and I was almost bursting. My bosom was boiling. What boiled in me was that verse: 'God commending His love.' I fell on my knees with my arms over the seat in front of me; tears and perspiration flowed freely. I thought blood was gushing forth. . . . After I was bent, a wave of peace came over me, and the audience sang, 'I hear Thy welcome voice.' As they sang I thought about the bending at the Judgment Day, and I was filled with compassion for those that would have to bend on that day, and I wept. Henceforth, the salvation of souls became the burden of my heart. From that time, I was on fire with a

desire to go through all Wales, and if it were possible, I was
willing to pay God for the privilege of going.[20]

John Wesley also spoke of his experience as occurring in the
context of a prayer meeting:

> About three in the morning as we were continuing instant in
> prayer, the power of God came mightily upon us, insomuch
> that many cried out for exceeding joy, and many fell to the
> ground. As soon as we recovered a little from the awe and
> amazement at the presence of His majesty, we broke out with
> one voice, "We praise thee, O God, we acknowledge Thee to
> be the Lord."[21]

Christmas Evans spoke of a time when his cold heart was
again warmed by God:

> I was weary of a cold heart towards Christ and His sacrifice,
> and the work of His Spirit—of a cold heart in the pulpit, in
> secret prayer, and in study. Fifteen years previously, I had
> felt my heart burning within, as if going to Emmaus with
> Jesus. On a day ever to be remembered by me, as I was
> climbing up towards Cader Idris, I considered it to be incum-
> bent on me to pray, however hard I felt in my heart, and
> however worldly the frame of my spirit was. Having begun in
> the name of Jesus, I soon felt, as it were, the fetters loosening,
> and the old hardness of heart softening, and, as I thought,
> mountains of frost and snow dissolving and melting within
> me. This engendered confidence in my soul in the promise of
> the Holy Ghost. I felt my whole mind relieved from some
> great bondage; tears flowed copiously, and I was constrained
> to cry out for the gracious visits of God, by restoring to my
> soul the joys of His salvation; and that He would visit the
> churches of the saints, and nearly all the ministers in the
> principality by their names. This struggle lasted for three
> hours; it rose again and again, like one wave after another, or
> a high flowing tide, driven by a strong wind, unlike my
> nature became faint by weeping and crying. Thus I resigned
> myself to Christ, body and soul, gifts and labours—all my

life—every day, every hour that remained for me; and all my cares I committed to Christ. From this time I was made to expect the goodness of God to churches, and to myself. In the first religious meetings after this, I felt as if I had been removed from the cold and sterile regions of spiritual frost, into the verdant fields of Divine promises.[22]

J. Wilbur Chapman, an associate of D. L. Moody who later assisted another young evangelist, "Billy" Sunday, to begin his evangelistic career, also spoke of an experience with God followed by a significant lasting effect. According to A. M. Hills:

Dr. Wilbur Chapman tells us how he went before God and consecrated himself and then said in faith, "My Father, I now claim from Thee the infilling of the Holy Ghost," and he says: "From that moment to this He has been a living reality. I never knew what it was to study the Bible before. And why should I, for had I not just then found the key? I never knew what it was to preach before. 'Old Things have passed away' in my experience. 'Behold all things have become new.' "[23]

There seems to be no typical experience with God, but there appear to be common features to all:

1. The experience often occurred during a time of crisis.
2. The experience was such that the person had full confidence in its reality, even some time after the event.
3. At that time or shortly thereafter the Christian experienced an inner verification of the reality of what had happened and, more often than not, significant ministry results.
4. The experience normally involved a post-conversion yielding to Christ on the part of the believer.
5. The experience was viewed later as the moment when the person rose to a higher spiritual plane and greater awareness of God.
6. The Christian regarded this experience as sacred, in most cases "almost too sacred to tell" or virtually impossible to put into words.
7. A final common feature of these experiences was the belief that they were consistent with the Bible.

An analysis of these experiences also reveals a difference in understanding and explaining the theological nature of these experiences. Some define it as essentially a Christological experience and speak of a closer identification with the person of Christ or a surrendering to His lordship. These writers tend to emphasize the themes of the togetherness of the believer and Christ, the believer's position "in Christ," and the inscrutable union of the believer and God. A second group defines their experience pneumatologically, and although there is some confusion in terms, speaks of the indwelling, fullness, and constant manifestation of the Holy Spirit.[24] A third group are epistemological in their perspective, emphasizing such themes as indwelling faith, victorious expectations, or signs and wonders. In each case, the believer is to some degree ascetic in his teaching and life-style, emphasizing such themes as the crucified life, seeking, tarrying, waiting on God, fasting, and reckoning spiritual truth by applying it to life.[25] Most make constant, positive reference to others who explain their experiences with God.[26] This chapter has analyzed the historical foundations of Christian experience. In the remaining chapters we will consider the biblical foundations for a postconversion experience with God.

— 5 —
LIVING
IN TWO
WORLDS

To understand the deeper Christian life, we must keep two principles separate: union and communion. The first principle is that the believer is united into Jesus Christ in the heavenlies. The second is that Jesus Christ dwells in the believer and has communion with him. This truth was explained by Jesus, ". . . you in Me, and I in you" (John 14:20 NKJV), and again a chapter later, "abide in Me, and I in you . . ." (John 15:4 NKJV). We are united to Christ in salvation (union), and we grow in Christ in sanctification (communion).

The Standing and State of a Christian

Two words have been used to make a distinction between these two works—*standing* and *state*. First a Christian *stands* before God in Jesus Christ (union). In this heavenly standing the believer is perfect (those who teach sinless perfection misunderstand this truth). The second word is *state* (communion). On earth the Christian is still a sinner and struggles with imperfection. In his earthly state Paul looked within his heart and realized, ". . . Christ Jesus came into the world to save sinners; of whom I am chief" (1 Timothy 1:15). Paul knew he was not sinlessly perfect, because he understood the experience of sin. A Christian is perfect because of union, but he is also a sinner who must grow through daily communion. The deeper-life Christian must live in two worlds at the same

94

time. He must realize he is perfect in heaven, because of his *standing* in Jesus Christ. Yet he must struggle against sin in an evil world. While in his sinful *state* on earth, he has the joy of the indwelling Christ to guide and encourage him. Illustration 1 reflects this truth:

ILLUSTRATION 1
THE CHRISTIAN'S STATE AND STANDING

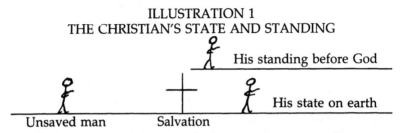

His standing before God

His state on earth

Unsaved man   Salvation

This chapter attempts to explain the standing of the believer before God. Three words or phrases explain the Christian's perfection in heaven: *Together*, used in Scripture, explains that the believer enjoys the things of heaven with Christ. The next two phrases—*partakers* (or *partners with Christ*), and the *fellowship* of the body of Christ—indicate that the believer has joint fellowship with Christ in heaven. These three phrases become the outline of this chapter and will help the reader understand his position before God.

All the truth that applies to the believer's standing in heaven is nonexperiential, in that he does not daily experience the perfection, that is, eradication of his sinful nature. But the new standing should impact his everyday life, hence influencing his experience. Note chart 8.

CHART 8

STANDING BEFORE GOD	STATE ON EARTH
Nonexperiential	Experiential
Perfect in Christ	Sinner in practice
No separation from God	Fellowship can be broken
Joy and peace	Heartache and disappointment
Desire godliness	Temptations and trials
No broken relationship	Broken fellowship

Theologian Augustus Hopkins Strong calls the standing of the believer in heaven "union with Christ." He correctly believes this doctrine should be taught, because it will keep believers from false mysticism, that is, seeking unattainable perfection from sin or seeking through experience a perfect union with God that was not promised in the Bible. According to Strong:

> Dr. J. W. Alexander well calls this doctrine of the Union of the Believer with Christ "the central truth of all theology and of all religion." Yet it receives little of formal recognition, either in dogmatic treatises or in common religious experience. . . . The majority of Christians much more frequently think of Christ as a Savior outside of them, than as a Savior who dwells within. This comparative neglect of the doctrine is doubtless a reaction from the exaggerations of a false mysticism. But there is great need of rescuing the doctrine from neglect. . . . The doctrine of Union with Christ, in like manner, is taught so variously and abundantly, that to deny it is to deny inspiration itself.[1]

The following section shows that the believer has union with Christ in his standing. The word *together* is used to teach that the believer stands with Christ in the heavenlies. Once he is born again, the believer cannot seek this, as he might personal sanctification, by going to the altar to seek and pray for it. Standing "together with Christ" is the believer's new position in heaven. He is to act on his standing and apply it in his life-style.

Five related Greek words or phrases explain this. First the believer is identified together with Christ, *meta* and *sun*; second he has a *metochos* or *koinonos*, partnership with Christ; and third there is *en Christo*, in Christ (*see* chapter 6). These three foundational truths are the basis for understanding the deeper Christian life.

CHART 9

THE BELIEVER'S NONEXPERIENTIAL POSITION
1. Together with Christ—*meta* and *sun* 2. Partnership with Christ—*koin* 3. In Christ—*en Christo*

Together With Christ

The position or standing of the believer in the heavenlies is generally identified by the deeper-life teachers of the early Brethren and Keswick movements. In a paper on this subject, C. H. M. concluded:

Here, then, we have one grand aspect of the Christian's position. It is defined by the position of his Lord. This makes it divinely simple; and, we may add, divinely settled. The Christian is identified with Christ. Amazing fact! "As He is, so *are* we in this world." It is not said, "As He is, so *shall* we be in the world to come." No; this would not come up to the divine idea. It is "so are we *in this world.*" The position of Christ defines the position of the Christian.[2]

The Greek language possesses two prepositions translated "with," *meta* and *sun*. The more general of the terms is *meta;* a more intimate term is *sun*, which suggests a relationship similar to the English prefix *co*, as in co-workers. On at least twenty-five occasions the Apostle Paul used the latter preposition, either independently or as part of a compound verb emphasizing fifteen aspects of the believer's togetherness with Christ. While some of these statements apply to the Second Coming of Christ, there can be little doubt that the majority of these teach that the believer is one with Christ in heaven or together with Christ. This is the foundation upon which the Christian life is possible.

Chart 10 identifies a number of areas in which Paul emphasizes the doctrine of the believer's togetherness with Christ. However, a survey of deeper-life literature suggests they emphasize almost exclusively the crucifixion and death aspects of "togetherness."[3] Perhaps this failure to consider the total perspective of the doctrine of "togetherness" has given rise to the stereotyped deeper-life Christian who seems always dying to self (sin) and never experiencing the abundance of his new life or acting on his new position in heaven. The deeper-life emphasis will not make a believer think he is perfect or drive him into mysticism, but rather make him realize he is responsible to bring his earthly life into conformity with his heavenly life.

The doctrine of "togetherness" teaches that the believer has been crucified together with Christ (Romans 6:6; Galatians 2:20). This is a past act, and we have union with Christ because of it. But some want to crucify the flesh. They want to turn a past nonexperiential truth into a present experience. They want to crucify themselves, so they seek an experience to "put to death" their flesh or lust.

CHART 10

THE TOGETHERNESS OF THE BELIEVER AND CHRIST		
1. United together	*sumphutoi*	Romans 6:5
2. Hidden with Christ in God	*kekruptoi sun*	Colossians 3:3
3. Crucified with Him (Christ)	*sunestaurothe* *sunestauromai*	Romans 6:6 Galatians 2:20
4. Died with Christ	*apethanete sun*	Colossians 2:20
5. Buried with Him	*suntaphentes* *sunetaphenen*	Colossians 2:12 Romans 6:4
6. Made us alive together with Him	*sunezoopoiesen*	Ephesians 2:5 Colossians 2:13
7. Raised us up together (with Christ)	*sunegeiren* *sunegerthete*	Ephesians 2:6 Colossians 2:12; 3:1
8. Made us sit together	*sunekathisen*	Ephesians 2:6
9. To be (may be, being) conformed together	*summorphous* *summorphon* *summorphoumenos*	Romans 8:29 Philippians 3:21 Philippians 3:10
10. Fellow workers, workers together with him	*sunergoi* *sunergountes*	1 Corinthians 3:9 2 Corinthians 6:1
11. We suffer with Him	*sumpaschomen*	Romans 8:17
12. Joint heirs with Christ	*sugkleronomoi*	Romans 8:17 Romans 8:17
13. Glorified together	*sundoxasthomen*	
14. We shall live	*suzesomen* *hama sun autio* *zesomen*	Romans 6:8 2 Timothy 2:11 1 Thessalonians 5:10
15. We shall reign with Him	*sumbasileusomen*	2 Timothy 2:12

Evangelicals still dispute what is meant by the concept of crucifixion with Christ, particularly as it relates to the experience of the believer. Archibald Hodge, representing a more classical reform perspective, suggests the believer's union with Christ begins at conversion and matures through the observance of the ordinance of the Lord's Supper:

> In God's appointed time, with each individual of his chosen, this union is established mutually—1st. By the commencement of the effectual and permanent workings of the Holy Spirit within them (they are quickened together with Christ); in the act of the new birth opening of the eyes and renewing the will, and thus laying in their natures the foundation of the exercise of saving faith. 2d. Which faith is the second bond by which this mutual union is established, by the continued actings of which their fellowship with Christ is sustained, and its blessed consequences developed.—Eph. iii. 17. Thus we "come to him," "receive him," "eat of his flesh and drink of his blood," etc.[4]

In contrast to Hodge, some deeper-life teachers tend toward a postconversion crucifixion experience in the believer. They feel they must "crucify" the old-self man before the new man can give them the abundant life. E. M. Bounds appears to promote this idea when he stresses the need for what he calls "crucified preaching":

> There may be no discount on his orthodoxy, honesty, cleanness, or earnestness; but somehow the man, the inner man, in its secret places has never broken down and surrendered to God, his inner life is not a great highway for the transmission of God's message, God's power. Somehow self and not God rules in the holy of holies. Somewhere, all unconscious to himself, some spiritual nonconductor has touched his inner being, and the divine current has been arrested. His inner being has never felt its thorough spiritual bankruptcy, its utter powerlessness; he has never learned to cry out with an ineffable cry of self-despair and self-helplessness till God's power and God's fire comes in and fills, purifies, empowers. Self-esteem, self-ability in some pernicious shape has de-

formed and violated the temple which should have been held sacred for God. Life-giving preaching costs the preacher much—death to self, crucifixion to the world, the travail of his own soul. Crucified preaching only can give life. Crucified preaching can come only from a crucified man.[5]

The postconversion crucifixion of self to which Bounds alludes is specifically emphasized by A. W. Tozer:

In every Christian's heart there is a cross and a throne, and the Christian is on the throne till he puts himself on the cross; if he refuses the cross he remains on the throne. Perhaps this is at the bottom of the backsliding and worldliness among gospel believers today. We want to be saved but we insist that Christ do all the dying. No cross for us, no dethronement, no dying. We remain king within the little kingdom of Mansoul and wear our tinsel crown with all the pride of Caesar; but we doom ourselves to shadows and weakness and spiritual sterility. If we will not die then we must die, and that death will mean the forfeiture of many of those everlasting treasures which the saints have cherished. Our uncrucified flesh will rob us of purity of heart, Christlikeness of character, spiritual insight, fruitfulness; and more than all, it will hide us from the vision of God's face, that vision which has been the light of earth and will be the completeness of heaven.[6]

The idea of a postconversion crucifixion of self as suggested by Bounds and Tozer is not universally accepted by the deeper-life mystics. Those who oppose do so on the basis of two theological arguments. First, the Bounds/Tozer view suggests an active role on the part of the believer crucifying himself. But it is impossible to crucify oneself. This is true not only physically but spiritually. The second argument against this view is the Pauline tendency to describe this crucifixion of self in terms of a conversion-related experience (Galatians 2:20; Romans 6:4). In the words of L. E. Maxwell, the Christian is "born crucified." This emphasis is also that of Watchman Nee:

So also in historical fact we can say, reverently but with equal accuracy, "I was crucified when Christ was crucified" or "Christ was crucified when I was crucified," for they are not two historical events, but one. My crucifixion was with Him. Has Christ been crucified? Then can I be otherwise? And if He was crucified nearly two thousand years ago, and I with Him, can my crucifixion be said to take place to-morrow? Can His be past and mine present or future? Praise the Lord, when He died on the Cross I died with Him. He not only died in my stead, but He bore me with Him to the Cross, so that when He died I also died. And if I believe in the death of the Lord Jesus, then I can believe in my own death just as surely as I believe in His.[7]

When then is the Christian "crucified with Christ?" The importance of answering this question accurately is evident. Not only does Nee correctly answer the question with his simplistic statement, "I was crucified when Christ was crucified," he also introduces an even more complex issue that few if any of the deeper-life mystics have been prepared to answer. When was the believer cocrucified with Christ?

Upon first consideration, the answer to this question is obvious: on the day of preparation, just prior to the Passover festival about A.D. 30 (see Mark 15:42). Yet John, who alone among the disciples was an eyewitness to the historic crucifixion of Christ as the Lamb of God, also speaks of ". . . the Lamb slain from the foundation of the world" (Revelation 13:8). This is further complicated by Paul's insistence that the believer was placed into Jesus Christ by the baptism of the Holy Spirit, apparently happening on the first Christian Pentecost, when the believer was identified with the body of Christ (1 Corinthians 12:13; compare Acts 2:1–4). Yet in Paul's "togetherness" statements concerning cocrucifixion and death, he appears to make a reference to personal conversion (Galatians 2:20) and baptism (Romans 6:4). These truths need to be reconciled, especially dealing with postconversion aspects of this "together death." Chart 11 attempts to harmonize these thoughts.

CHART 11

WHEN IS THE BELIEVER CRUCIFIED TOGETHER WITH CHRIST?	
THEOLOGICAL PERSPECTIVE	God, who is beyond time and space, views this as happening outside of time, which began with creation, therefore, before the foundation of the world (Revelation 13:8).
HISTORICAL PERSPECTIVE	If I was crucified together with Christ, this could only have occurred historically on Golgotha when Christ was historically crucified (Matthew 27:35; Mark 15:24; Luke 23:33; John 19:18).
ECCLESIASTIC PERSPECTIVE	My togetherness with Christ in His crucifixion, while personal, is also part of the larger corporate identity of the church, which is His body. As I was in a historic sense baptized into that body on the first Christian Pentecost, it was then that the potential benefits of that togetherness were broadly applied (1 Corinthians 12:13; Acts 2:1–4).
SOTERIOLOGICAL PERSPECTIVE	As the benefits of the cross are received by the believer at the moment of conversion, it stands that my crucifixion with Christ is a conversion-related experience (Galatians 2:20).
TESTIMONIAL PERSPECTIVE	In believer's baptism, I give public testimony to having been crucified with Christ (Romans 6:4).
EXPERIENTIAL PERSPECTIVE	In the practice of reckoning myself dead indeed unto sin, I come to experience the reality of my crucifixion with Christ (Romans 6:11).

Viewing the believer's togetherness with Christ from a broad perspective, it is apparent that the believer's union with Christ is a conversion-related experience. This emphasis becomes even more apparent in other aspects of this doctrine to be discussed later. Nevertheless, some deeper-life people claim these truths have drawn them closer to Christ. As we shall see momentarily, it is disputable whether the believer can be drawn closer to Christ than in his initial conversion-related experience of togetherness. But it is reasonable to expect a growing Christian to come to a deeper understanding of his conversion experience as he matures and applies to his life more of the responsibilities of his new life "in Christ." His union with Christ is a conversion-related experience, although in most cases it is realized and appreciated sometime following conversion.

Does this line of argumentation deny the reality of the deeper-life experience? Definitely not. In actuality, the believer is more intimate with Christ than most of the mystics who claim extrabiblical experiences for themselves. The Bible shows us that the believer could not become closer to God than he is when he accepts Christ. From the very beginning, he is close to God because of his position in Christ.

The deeper-life experience is based on conversion, and the truths of "togetherness" are conversion related. It is not only, "I have been crucified with Christ . . ." (Galatians 2:20 NKJV); it is also God " . . . made us alive together with Christ . . . and raised us up together, and made us sit together in the heavenly places in Christ Jesus" (Ephesians 2:5, 6 NKJV). All believers, therefore, have had the basis for the deeper-life experience, and if Strong's observation in a previous generation is accurate today, the vast majority have never come to a full realization of their experience. The difference between the Keswick Christian and other evangelicals is not so much his deeper experience with Christ as it is his deeper understanding and application of a common experience. His emotional and volitional response to such knowledge results in an identifiable point in time, not when he enters into his togetherness or any other aspect of this union, but rather when he comes to more fully appreciate some aspect of his union with Christ.

It is not always easy to distinguish between the believer's togetherness with Christ (his standing in heaven) and his experience of Christ in him (his state on earth). Paul explains the difference in Galatians 2:20 (NKJV), "I have been crucified with Christ [standing]; it is no longer I who live, but Christ lives in me [state]. . . ." Here Paul speaks of a togetherness crucifixion. Yet the reality of his life was "Christ in me," and the practice of his life as he lived "in Christ" was the life of Christ lived out through his own. This emphasis is also apparent in another strangely neglected togetherness statement of Paul.

The apostle uses the term *sumphutoi* in Romans 6:5, which has been variously expressed by English translators as "we have been planted together in his death" or "we have become united with Him in death." According to the anonymous author of a Plymouth Brethren tract:

> The word rendered *planted together* is the adjective *sumphutos*, which occurs nowhere else in the New Testament. In the Septuagint it occurs twice. 1st. In Zach. ii. 2, "the *thickly-planted* forest." Here it represents the Hebrew *batsir*, rendered in the authorised version, "the forest of *the vintage*" (marg. *defenced*). 2ndly., in Amos ix. 13, "the hills shall be *planted*." Here it stands for a hithpahel of *mug*, English translation, "the hills *shall melt*." The idea of *"consolidation in one,"* of what could be looked at as having many component parts, is easily traced in all these renderings. In ordinary Greek (as contrasted with Greek in the Bible) we might give—*Growing together, naturally or necessarily connected together*, as the meaning; as, for instance, *strife* naturally grows up with a contentious character, courage with a manly character, etc. In a secondary sense, it is applied to a closed, healed wound, where the parts have *grown* together in one.[8]

Writing from a different theological perspective, John Murray observes:

> The word used to express our union with Christ in his death and resurrection means, strictly, "grown together"—"if we have become grown together in the likeness of his death". No term could more adequately convey the intimacy of the union involved. It is not that this relationship is conceived of as a

process of growth progressively realized. The terms of the clause in question and the context do not allow for this notion. The death of Christ was not a process and neither is our conformity to his death a process. We are in the condition of having become conformed to his death. But "grown together" points to the closeness of our relation to him in his death. . . . If "grown together" points to the closeness of our relation to him in his death, "likeness" enunciates an important distinction. . . . Our union with Christ in his death and resurrection must not be bereft of its intimacy, but with equal jealousy it must be interpreted in terms of Spiritual and mystical relationship. And the death and resurrection of Christ in their bearing upon us must likewise be construed in such terms. It is to this that "likeness of his death" refers.[9]

Perhaps the most complete statement of the nature of the union of the believer and Christ is the expression, "For we have been united together in the likeness of His death" (Romans 6:5 NKJV). The apostle could not express a greater degree of intimacy than is implied in the term *sumphatoi*. Yet at the same time the individuality of the different personalities is maintained. This mysterious union is not too much unlike the mystery of the Trinity, involving three distinct persons in one. As Strong observes:

. . . The Father and the Son dwell in the believer; for where the Son is, there always the Father must be also. If the union between the believer and Christ in John 14:23 is to be interpreted as one of mere moral influence, then the union of Christ and the Father in John 14:10 must also be interpreted as a union of mere moral influence. . . . The believer has life by partaking of Christ in a way that may not inappropriately be compared with Christ's having life by partaking of the Father. . . . All believers are one in Christ, to whom they are severally and collectively united, as Christ himself is one with God.[10]

Partnership With Christ

Now that we have analyzed the truth of our being together with Christ, we need to analyze the truth of "partnership" with

Christ, which is based on a different Greek expression. The notion of the believer's partaking of the nature of Christ is expressly stated in Scripture on two occasions. First, the word *metochos*, "partakers," is twice used in an argument emphasizing the chastening of God as an evidence of true sonship, "... that we may be partakers of His holiness" (Hebrews 12:10 NKJV). On another occasion, Peter uses the word *koinonos*, "partakers," in the context of the promises of God, concluding "... that through these you may be partakers of the divine nature..." (2 Peter 1:4 NKJV). Both terms were commercial expressions describing a business partnership in Greek culture and are used in the gospels to refer to the fishing business involving Peter, Andrew, James, and John (Luke 5:7, 10). Comparing these two expressions, A. T. Robertson explains:

> This word *metochos*, from *metecho*, to have with, means participation with one in common blessings (Heb. 3:1, 14; 6:4; 12:8). While *koinonos* (verse 10 here of James and John also) has the notion of personal fellowship, partnership. Both terms are here employed of the two pairs of brothers who have a business company under Simon's lead.[11]

As far as the deeper Christian experience is concerned, the believer is in partnership with Jesus Christ. But what does this mean? Note in this relationship the believer does not lose his identity, nor is he absorbed into God. He is in union with God (nonexperiential) but not absorbed into God so that he loses his personality. Albert Barnes explains, when he interprets 2 Peter 1:4:

> This is a very important and a difficult phrase. An expression somewhat similar occurs in Heb. xxi. 10: "that we might be partakers of his holiness." ... It cannot be taken in so literal a sense as to mean that we can even partake of the divine *essence*, or that we shall be *absorbed* into the divine nature so as to lose our individuality. ... The reference then, in this place must be to the *moral* nature of God; and the meaning is, that they who are renewed become participants of the same *moral*

nature; that is, of the same views, feelings, thoughts, purposes, principles of action. Their nature as they are born, is sinful, and prone to evil, (Eph. ii. 3) their nature as they are born again, becomes like that of God. They are made *like* God; and this resemblance will increase more and more for ever, until in a much higher sense than can be true in this world, they may be said to have become "partakers of the divine nature."[12]

It is expected that some mystics would have a different approach to this concept. For them, there is a merging of natures of the believers and Christ implied in Paul's use of *sumphatos* (Romans 6:5). The early Brethren pointed out:

The word *phusis* is from the same root (without the *sun*). It is rendered in Eph. ii. 3, "by *nature* the children of wrath"; and in 2 Pet. i. 4, "made partakers of the divine *nature*." The force of the preposition *sun*, as added to the adjective, would be much that of *co-*, *associated with*, *made participants of this or that*, etc.—*"made of one* nature," co-natured.[13]

Therefore, those who believe in the conature of Christ and the believer would probably teach that the Christian should yield himself to God so that he not only loses his will, but he loses his self-identity or his own personality in God. This is not biblical. The believer has an I-Thou relationship to God. The believer remains an "I" and God remains "Thou." But the believer submits himself to Christ and allows Christ to indwell him for new power and new motives. When the believer becomes a partaker of the divine nature, it means he has a moral nature that is born anew, not that he loses his nature or identity.

The nature of this partnership with Christ and partaking of the nature of God is perhaps illustrated in three of the Pauline illustrations of the believer's union with Christ. The apostle talked of the relation between Christ and the believer in terms of a building and its foundation (Ephesians 2:20–22); the members of the body and its head (1 Corinthians 6:15; 12:12; Ephesians 1:22, 23); and the relationship of a husband and wife

(Romans 7:4; Ephesians 5:31, 32). In each of the above, there is an emphasis upon the relation of two subjects (I-thou), more so than in the other union illustrations in the Scriptures. In understanding the nature of these relationships, we gain a degree of insight in comprehending the nature of our partaking of the divine nature.

In the first of the images, the emphasis appears to be on the believer's attachment to Christ as the cornerstone of the building, which in the architectural context of that day, governed how the rest of the building was constructed. Writing from an ecclesiological perspective, Earl D. Radmacher concludes his study of this symbol:

> By way of summary it has been seen from the building metaphor that Gentile and Jew share equal family privileges in the household of God. Each one is a part of His house which is built upon the foundation of the apostles and prophets of the New Testament, secured by its corner-stone, that corner-stone which gives unity to all the superstructure which is rising from it; so that all such building, being welded into one, is growing into a holy temple as the permanent spiritual dwelling-place of God.[14]

Some would no doubt dispute Radmacher's choice of the phrase "welded into one," on the grounds it assumes the believer is "absorbed into the divine nature." In light of that concern of the critics of mysticism, it is interesting to note the conclusion of Martin Luther, who rejected and opposed the German mystics of his day. According to Luther:

> By faith thou art so glued to Christ that of thee and him there becomes as it were one person, so that with confidence thou canst say: "I am Christ,"—that is, Christ's righteousness, victory, etc., are mine; and Christ in turn can say: "I am that sinner,—that is, his sins, his death, etc., are mine, because he clings to me and I to him, for we have been joined through faith into flesh and bone."[15]

The second illustration of this partnership of Christ and the believer is the mystery of the church, which is His body. In Paul's references to this metaphor, the emphasis is on Christ as the head, individual believers as the members. The relationship between Christ and the believer is likened to the relationship between the head and the other parts of the body. This image appears to emphasize a close connection between the believer and Christ, while maintaining their distinctiveness. As J. Robert Nelson observes:

> As the Head of the Body, then, Christ is both distinct from the Body and inseparable from it. He unites the body in Himself, and is yet not to be identified with it. His Spirit gives the church life and direction, but He is not the soul of the church. Again, the paradoxical relationship of Christ to the church, the head of the Body, becomes manifest. . . . However much Christ may need the church as the instrument of His redemptive work in the world, therefore, it remains subordinate to Him in nature, drawing whatever meaning and value it has from its relation to Him. The Body lives only because it draws power from the head, but it is not identical with the Head.[16]

In this symbolism, Christ is indisputably in control not only of the body but also of the individual members of that body. He, and He alone, is the *kephale*, the "head." J. B. Lightfoot defines this term as "the inspiring, ruling, guiding, combining, sustaining power, the mainspring of its activity, the centre of its unity, and the seat of its life."[17] It was in this image that John Calvin resolved his own view of the union of the believer and Christ, "I attribute the highest importance to the connection between the head and the members; to the inhabitation of Christ in our hearts; in a word, to the mystical union by which we enjoy him, so that, being made ours, he makes us partakers of the blessings with which he is furnished."[18]

The third of the partnership illustrations is by far the most intimate, that of the mystery of the church, which is His Bride. This illustration is often considered by the deeper-life teachers to justify a typical interpretation of Old Testament brides[19] and an allegorical interpretation of the Song of Solomon.[20] Even in the context of the Ephesian epistle there is again an emphasis on an intimate partnership, as reflected in the affection of Christ for the church. Typical of the Keswick interpretations of this symbol, Lehman Strauss argues:

> When the soldiers pierced the side of our Lord "and forth-with came there out blood and water" (John 19:34), the bride of Christ was being taken from His side, for "without shed-ding of blood is no remission" (Heb. 9:22). Beloved, that was the greatest demonstration of love the world has ever seen, or ever will see. When God pierced the side of Adam, He did it to take Adam's bride from his side. Thus she became bone of his bone and flesh of his flesh. Adam "is the figure of Him (Christ) that was to come" (Rom. 5:14). Eve is a type of the church.[21]

The emphasis of this partnership illustration is not the dis-tinctiveness of the partners, but rather their attachment to each other. H. C. G. Moule identifies "joined" as the significant word in Ephesians 5:31, a term "full of importance here."[22] The verb *proskouma* used here is the strongest of the four Greek verbs with which the New Testament identifies the attachment between two objects or two individuals. It is literally translated "glued together with." The Hebrew concept behind the expres-sion "one flesh" means more than a mere physical union; rather it describes a merging of personalities, the oneness of marriage. This is the thought expressed by Paul in another place, "But he who is joined to the Lord is one spirit with Him" (1 Corinthians 6:17 NKJV). It is interesting to note that the initiative and effort involved in this joining appears wholly on the part of Christ. Relating his own experience with Christ in terms of this part-nership illustration, John Bunyan recounted:

> The Lord led me into the knowledge of the mystery of union with Christ, that I was joined to him, that I was bone of his bone and flesh of his flesh. By this also my faith in him as my

righteousness . . . was mine, his merits mine, his victory also mine. Now I could see myself in heaven and on earth at once—in heaven by my Christ, my risen, my righteousness and life, though on earth by my body or person.[23]

This fellowship in heaven is our association with Christ (our standing in heaven), which becomes the basis for participation of fellowship with Christ (our state on earth). As A. R. George observes, "The important thing is that those words (belonging to the *koin*—family) refer primarily, though not invariably, to participation in something rather than to association with others: and there is often a genitive to indicate that in which one participates or shares."[24]

Alexander Archibald Hodge identifies several aspects of fellowship of the believer with Christ. This explanation is perhaps one of the most complete examinations of fellowship.

> 1st. They have a community with him in his covenant standing, and rights. Forensically they are rendered "complete in him." His righteousness and his Father is theirs. They receive the adoption in him, and are accepted as to both their persons and services in the beloved. They are sealed by his Holy Spirit of promise; in him obtain an inheritance; sit with him on his throne and behold his glory.—Rom. viii. 1; Col. ii. 10; Eph. i., 6, 11, 13; Phil. iii. 8, 9. . . .
> 2nd. They have fellowship with him in the transforming, assimilating power of his life, making them like him; every grace of Jesus reproducing itself in them; "of his fulness we have all received, and grace for grace. . . ."
> 3rd. This leads to their fellowship with Christ in their experience, in their labors, sufferings, temptations, and death. . . .
> 4th. Also to Christ's rightful fellowship with them in all they possess.—Prov. xix. 17; Rom. xiv. 8; 1 Cor. vi. 19, 20.
> 5th. Also the consequence that, in the spiritual reception of the holy sacraments, they do really hold fellowship with him. They are "baptised into Christ."—Gal. iii. 27. "The bread we break, is it not the communion of the body of Christ; the cup

of blessing which we bless, is it not the communion of the
blood of Christ." 1 Cor. x. 16; xi. 26; John vi. 51–56.

6th. This leads also to the fellowship of believers with one
another through him, that is, to the communion of saints.[25]

The above listing shows that the believer's individual fellowship with Christ is the source of his fellowship with others
within the family of God. The emphasis of this fellowship is
experiential. What is the *koinonia* of the body of Christ if it is not
an involvement in the life of others? What is true between
individual members within the body is true to an even greater
extent between the member and the Head. As Russell Benjamin
Miller emphasizes:

> From the very beginning the early Christians experienced a
> peculiar sense of unity. Christ is at once the center of this
> unity and the origin of every expression of fellowship. Some-
> times the fellowship is essentially an experience and as such
> it is scarcely susceptible of definition. It may rather be re-
> garded as a mystical union in Christ. In other instances the
> fellowship approaches or includes the idea of intercourse. In
> some passages it is represented as a participation or partner-
> ship. The terms occur most frequently in the writings of Paul
> with whom the idea of Christian unity was a controlling
> principle.[26]

This intimate fellowship with God is paramount. Much of the
perception of the Christian life is defined in terms of coming to
enjoy and striving to maintain this level of fellowship. According to A. W. Tozer, "One of the heaviest problems in the
Christian life is that of sanctification: how to become as pure as
we know we ought to be and must be if we are to enjoy intimate
communion with a holy God."[27] J. Hudson Taylor explains the
same situation:

> Our attention is here drawn to a danger which is preemi-
> nently one of this day: the intense activity of our times may
> lead to zeal in service, *to the neglect of personal communion*. Such

neglect will not only lessen the value of the service, but will also tend to incapacitate us for the highest service. If we are watchful over the souls of others and neglect our own, we shall be disappointed with our powerlessness to help our brethren, while our Master will not be less disappointed in us. Let us never forget that what we are is more important than what we do, and that all fruit borne when not abiding in Christ must be fruit of the flesh and not of the Spirit. As wounds when healed often leave a scar, so the sin of neglected communion may be forgiven and yet the effect remain permanently.[28]

The resolution of this problem in the experience of the believer suggests something of the true nature of the deeper-life experience. The believer should not seek a union; he already has it. However, there *are* aspects of the Christian life to seek (*see* chapters 8–11). When the believer realizes the influence of sin on his life, he usually begins to seek the Lord. Most people who live the deeper Christian life only seek it after there is a great need in their lives. This need could be an extended period of frustration, sin, or defeat in their lives. As A. W. Tozer explains:

If only we would stop lamenting and look up, God is here. Christ is risen. The Spirit has been poured out from on high. All this we know as theological truth. It remains for us to turn it into joyous spiritual experience. And how is this accomplished? There is no new technique; if it is new it is false. The old, old method still works. Conscious fellowship with Christ is by faith, love and obedience. And the humblest believer need not be without these.[29]

Believers must come into a deeper understanding and appreciation of the nature of their conversion experience. Some years after the fact, the believer can come to comprehend the truth of union with Christ and go deeper in his communion with the Lord. This does not mean he discovers new truth that was hitherto unknown or that he enters an experience that is unavailable to others. Neither, however, does a deeper experience with Christ justify attitudes or actions inconsistent with the biblical revelation of Christ. But based on his union with Christ (standing), he can go deeper in fellowship with Christ (state). Based on his salvation (standing in the heavenlies), he can get victory over sin (state). This is not sinless perfection, but the victorious expectation of God for His children.

Human personality is defined in terms of intellect, emotions, and will. If some Christians are at times guilty of responding to God intellectually so as to functionally deemphasize their emotional identity, the deeper-life Christian may also at times be guilty of responding to God emotionally so as to deemphasize the intellectual basis of his faith. It is not without significance that history records all the great scientific discoveries of Pascal before his conversion to Christianity. He was called a mystic because of his emotional relationship to God. In the preface to the second edition of his commentary on the Song of Solomon, Andrew Miller reveals something of the mystical tendency to elevate the emotions over the intellect when he argues, "As the following Meditations were more the expression of my *feelings*, than any attempt at exposition, when they were written, I have not thought it right to alter a single word in a second edition."[30] In contrast, Robert Coleman argues from the example of Christ that a biblical deeper life is not based so much on feelings as the objective Word of God itself:

> Jesus has given us the example. As the incarnate Word, of course, He did not have to refer to the Scriptures to show His authority. In His divine wisdom He could have expressed His mind, as He often did, without recourse to what God had said before. But the fact that He still chose to bind His words by the Scriptures underscores the Bible's importance. If in the plan of God it was deemed necessary for God's Son to measure His life by Holy Writ, surely our need is no less real. Of this we can be sure: The only enduring worth of our witness is that verified in the Word. Nothing else we say or do has any real significance to the Gospel. God disclosed Himself in words—words spoken by His prophets, written in the Scrip-

tures, and finally, personified in His Son. . . . His life is wedded to His Word, so much that His Words given unto the disciples are the means by which the world will come to know Him.[31]

A second negative tendency of deeper-life teachers involves the development of a kind of class structure within Christianity, usually placing one in a closer relationship with God than the average believer. One's experience becomes the basis of his authority and makes other Christians second-class citizens of the kingdom. Of course, this spirit is diametrically opposed to the spirit of the gospel (see Philippians 1:27, 2:2; Galatians 3:26–29). This tendency is evident in J. Hudson Taylor's identification of the daughters of Jerusalem in the Song of Solomon with those Christians who he concludes are not part of the Bride of Christ and therefore not raptured but left to endure the tribulation period. He concludes his otherwise edifying meditation on the Song with the words:

> We wish to place on record our solemn conviction that not all who are called Christians, or think themselves to be such, will attain to the resurrection of which St. Paul speaks in Philippians 3:11, or will thus meet the Lord in the air. Unto those who by lives of consecration manifest that they are not of the world, but are looking for Him, He will appear without sin unto salvation.[32]

However, the basis of the rapture is a person's *relationship* to God, not his *fellowship* with God. Because a person does not understand the distinction between standing and state, he might be confused about the rapture or a number of other items relating to doctrine or ministry. But confusion does not change a person's relationship (standing) with God.

The deeper life is possible. It is based on a believer's union with Christ. The believer is saved, justified, and is perfect before God in heaven (union with Christ or standing in heaven). Therefore, he must seek God in prayer, yield, and rid himself of sin (communion with Christ or state on earth). The problem comes when some believers interpret verses that speak of the truth of salvation as applying to sanctification.

Union with Christ is taught by three truths. First, the Greek words translated "together" (*sun* or *meta*) mean we have been placed with Christ in heaven. Second, the words translated as "partakers" (*metochos* or *koinonos*) mean we have the moral nature of Christ and have His life. Third, the words *en Christo*, "in Christ," describe the believer's position at salvation and throughout his Christian life. The experiential deeper life of the believer is possible because of his nonexperiential standing in heaven.

— 6 —

THE BELIEVER'S POSITION "IN CHRIST"

I was converted on July 25, 1950. From then I spent almost every succeeding night attending a revival meeting at some church. I was swept along in the enthusiasm of my new relationship to Christ. Six weeks after my conversion, I went to Columbia Bible College. There I was caught up in the Christian environment. I did not go back to my old ways, nor did my old habits plague me. I could almost see myself growing in Christ.

After approximately six months, I confided to my roommate, "I haven't sinned since I've been saved." I was dead serious when I said it. I had evaluated my actions and couldn't remember committing an outward sin. Actually I was naive and childish. But just as some children are not aware of their actions and words, as an immature Christian, I had remained unaware of my sins.

My roommate laughed at me. He went next door to the two boys who shared our bathroom. When he told them I said I hadn't sinned, they laughed. Then they began to rehearse my actions. They pointed out the dorm rules I had broken, such as not going to bed on time, eating in the room, visiting in other rooms during study hours, and so on.

I didn't consider these infractions sin, but they did. Next they pointed out other things I did wrong. They chewed on me about my faults until I got mad. Then I wanted to fight them. The angrier I got, the more they laughed.

A few minutes earlier I had claimed to live for six months

without sin. Now I was angry and wanted to hurt brothers in the Lord. They were horsing around and wrestled me to the floor so I couldn't fight. They continued to laugh as only boys can do when teasing a naive youngster.

I don't remember all the details of the wrestling match, but I was broken. I began to cry under the conviction of sin. The Holy Spirit opened my blind eyes to see that I was guilty of the worst sin of all—pride. In my ignorance I thought I was sinless, when actually I was, like Paul, the chief sinner.

As a young Christian I struggled with the standards of sinless perfection. I would try to quit anything I knew was sin. Then I would get frustrated when I saw my imperfections, and I would plead the blood of Jesus Christ.

Who can live in a state of sinless perfection, that is, without sin? How can one eradicate the sinful nature, that is, eliminate the desire (lust) of sin in anyone? Some people claim they *are* sinless, perfect. They claim they can live without sinning. Certain groups claim that God can do a second work of grace in their hearts and eradicate their desire to sin. I disagree with these people, but how do I evaluate them? How can they make such claims?

1. Some are lying to us. They know they sin, but they will not admit they violate their consciences.
2. Some are ignorant of the definition of *sin*. They define *sin* as "major trespasses of moral law." When they do not break their definition of the law, they think they are sinless. They do not realize they have sinful natures, nor do they realize they fall short of God's righteousness.
3. Some deceive themselves. They are blinded to their sinful natures and their sinful actions.

These people go about thinking they are perfect, when actually they are hypocritical or frustrated. Some think they are perfect because they only understand half the biblical expectations for Christians! The Bible seems to teach two extremes for the believer. First, the child of God is told to ". . . Be ye holy . . ." (1 Peter 1:15), which is interpreted "Be ye . . .

perfect . . ." (Matthew 5:48). These commands seem to expect similar perfection.

But there is a second extreme. The Apostle Paul testified, "I am the chief of sinners" (see 1 Timothy 1:15), and John says, "If we say that we have no sin, we deceive ourselves . . ." (1 John 1:8). The believer is told he is a sinner and should not be surprised by that revelation.

The first picture is perfectly white; and the second is utterly black. These two apparently extreme positions drive different Christians in opposite directions. Some think they can live without sinning, which suggests that they think their sinful nature is eradicated. At the opposite end of the pendulum are those who enjoy their sin, indulge in sin, and make no effort to get victory over it.

The believer's *position* of perfection is described in Scripture as "in Christ" or with the words "the believer's standing," "the believer's union," or "in the heavenlies." It is the subject of this chapter.

The believer's position "in Christ" is portrayed as perfect. In recent history the doctrine of "in Christ" has been almost exclusively identified with what is commonly referred to as the Keswick movement. Though the movement is not without its critics, it is generally conceded to have been an asset to evangelical Christianity because it has popularized this doctrine. As James M. Campbell observes:

> In recent years certain groups of Christian students and workers, like the Keswick school in England, have made the doctrine of the believer's union with Christ central in their teaching; and while they may not have been always free from exegetical vagaries and from exaggerated representations of truth, they have done not a little to quicken and edify the lives of Christians. To their gatherings many have repaired to find a spiritual uplift which they have failed to find elsewhere. In the region which they explore, and over which they sometimes seem to claim proprietary rights, lie the treasures of truth by which the spiritual life is enriched. Perhaps the main service which they have rendered to the religious

thought and life of the times has been the emphasizing of the mystical side of the Pauline theology. While preserving the doctrine of justification by faith in its forensic setting, they have found in it an explanation of the method by which the soul is related to God, and made a partaker of the Divine and enduring life from which all the fruits of holiness spring.[1]

Campbell has correctly analyzed the Keswick movement that has misunderstood this doctrine. They have wrongly said to be "in Christ" was a mystical walk with Christ, which they described as the deeper Christian life. Donald Grey Barnhouse, while not exclusively Keswickian, has explained the experience of "in Christ":

> Then, still further, we find that the moment we believe in the Lord Jesus Christ as our personal Saviour from sin, not only does the Godhead come to dwell within us, but *we are said to be in God*. There are scores of references which speak of the believer as being *in* Christ. . . . Thank God, it is not necessary to live in accord with our condition! It is possible for us to know that condition altered, to realize day by day that our path shineth more and more to the perfect day, and to experience the reality of the good works which He has begun in us being perfected until the day when He shall come to complete that perfection. That life is ours, and that position is ours as children of God, heirs of God, and joint heirs with Christ. Sons? Yes, but to sum it all up in one word, we are "in Christ."[2]

There are reasons why the Keswickians say "in Christ" is experiential and mystical. When conversion is viewed as an experiential process, it is only natural to interpret the phrase "in Christ," which relates to conversion, as experiential. We realize that conversion is more than an intellectual reformation or a mental assent to the content of the gospel message. It begins more than a forensic religious exercise; conversion is the beginning of a new relationship with a person—Jesus Christ. A person's experience involves a total commitment of his total personality, not merely to a religious philosophy or dogma but to a person. As A. W. Tozer emphasizes:

To accept Christ is to form an attachment to the Person of our Lord Jesus altogether unique in human experience. The attachment is intellectual, volitional and emotional. The believer is intellectually convinced that Jesus is both Lord and Christ; he has set his will to follow Him at any cost and soon his heart is enjoying the exquisite sweetness of His fellowship.[3]

Perhaps because of their emphasis on this unique conversion experience and the theme of fellowship with Christ, the Pauline expression "in Christ" is a favorite Bible topic for study and preaching by certain deeper-life teachers. Many theologians also argue this was a fundamental theme in the theology of the Apostle Paul. In the thirteen epistles that bear his name, Paul uses this expression no fewer than 172 times. Edgar Young Mullins concludes:

The phrase "in Christ" is a favorite one in the writings of Paul. There is scarcely any phase of the Christian life which the apostle does not express by means of this or an equivalent expression. There is no condemnation to those who are "in Christ" (Rom. 8:1). Christians are alive unto God "in Christ Jesus," (Rom. 6:11). If any man is "in Christ," he is a new creature (2 Cor. 5:17). Paul declared that he had been crucified and that Christ lived in him (Gal. 2:20). We are baptized "into Christ" (Gal. 3:27). Christ dwells in the heart by faith (Eph. 3:17). We are created "in Christ Jesus unto good works" (Eph. 2:10).[4]

Albert Schweitzer further observes:

The concept of being-in-Christ dominates Paul's thought in a way that he not only sees in it the source of everything connected with redemption, but describes all the experience, feeling, thought and will of the baptized as taking place in Christ. Thus the phrase "in Christ Jesus" comes to be added to the most varied statements, almost as a kind of formula. The believer speaks the truth in Christ (Rom. ix. 1), knows and is convinced in Christ (Rom. xiv. 14), has a temper of mind in Christ (Phil. ii. 5), exhorts in Christ (Phil. ii. 1), speaks in Christ (2 Cor. ii. 17, xii. 19), gives out his Yes or his No in Christ (2 Cor. i. 19), salutes in the Lord (1 Cor. xvi. 19; Rom. xvi. 22), labours in the Lord (Rom. xvi. 3, 9, 12), labours abundantly in the Lord (1 Cor. xv. 58), presides in the Lord (1 Thess. v. 12), has freedom in Christ Jesus (Gal. ii. 4), rejoices in the Lord (Phil. iii. 1, iv. 4, 10), has hope in the Lord Jesus (Phil. ii. 19), has confidence in the Lord (Phil. ii. 24), is weak in Christ (2 Cor. xiii. 1), has power in the Lord (Phil. iv. 13), stands fast in the Lord (Phil. iv. 1), becomes rich in Christ Jesus (1 Cor. i. 5), glories in Christ Jesus (1 Cor. xv. 31; Rom. xv. 17; Phil. i. 26, iii. 3), is wise in Christ (1 Cor. iv. 10), is kept safe in Christ (Rom. xvi. 10), has love in Christ (1 Cor. xvi. 24; Rom. xvi. 8), receives a person in Christ Jesus (Rom. xvi. 2; Phil. ii. 29), is of one mind in Christ (Phil. iv. 2), has confidence in a person in the Lord (1 Cor. vii. 39), Paul's bonds become manifest in the Lord (Phil. i. 13).[5]

Therefore, we come to the place where we can ask what "in Christ" means. How does it apply to me?

Being "in Christ"

There are several interpretations of the phrase "in Christ." A person's theological suppositions will determine how he interprets this truth.

Mystery-Religion Influence. Some contemporary writers tend to interpret Paul in terms of the pagan mystery religions common to his time. They assume that to some extent the apostle borrowed concepts or at least the language of these cults to express his own view of Christianity. Kirrsopp Lake argues, "Christianity has not borrowed from the mystery-religions, because it was always, at least in Europe, a mystery religion itself." [6] D. Miall Edwards, on the other hand, seeks to limit the relationship between Pauline Christianity and the mystery religions to a coincidence of language:

Paul was after all a Jew (though a broad one), who always retained traces of his Pharisaic training, and who viewed idolatry with abhorrence; and the chief formative factor of his thinking was his own profound religious experience. It is inconceivable that such a man should so assimilate gentile modes of thought as to be completely colored by them. The characteristics which his teaching has in common with the pagan religions are simply a witness to the common religious wants of mankind, and not to his indebtedness to them.[7]

Sacramental Orientation. Some who argue for a relationship between Pauline Christianity and the Hellenistic mystery religions tend to interpret the expression "in Christ" sacramentally and view baptism and the Lord's Table as initiatory rites of Christianity. Albert Schweitzer, for instance argues:

We have seen how Pauline mysticism contrasts with Hellenistic; on the other hand it offers a striking analogy to the mysticism of the Hellenistic mystery-religions, and to primitive mysticism in general, in the fact that it is sacramental mysticism. . . . In primitive Christianity Baptism guaranteed the forgiveness of sins and allegiance to the coming Messiah, and the prospect of sharing the glory which is to dawn at His coming. In this significance Paul takes it over, but he explains its operation by his Christ-mysticism. On this basis he asserts that what takes place in Baptism is the beginning of the being-in-Christ and the process of dying and rising again which is associated therewith.[8]

The major problem with Schweitzer's interpretation of Paul is Paul himself. Paul's statement concerning baptism in 1 Corinthians 1:17 can hardly be the statement of one who viewed baptism as the initiatory rite into Christ. For Paul, baptism is not a means of grace effecting salvation but rather the symbolic testimony to the reception of the grace that brings salvation.

A Meaningless Idiomatic Expression. Another tendency among some writers is to deny any particular significance of the expression "in Christ." Accordingly, Michel Bouttier concludes his study of Pauline Christianity, noting that the phrase "in Christ" means nothing:

> We may have been able to analyze the different elements of *in Christo* which, when blended together, make up the whole; but in every passage where we meet the expression, its shade of meaning is so affected by the context as to enrich the latter. Strictly speaking, from an abstract point of view, it means nothing in itself; it always needs the appeal of particular circumstances to take shape and receive its extraordinary fullness.[9]

Similarly, others see the phrase "in Christ" as nothing more than a style of writing that has no implication of mysticism. Lucien Cerfaux questions any significance in the use of *en* over *dia* or *ek*:

> In the Pauline epistles, the preposition *en* is used about once in every two verses: in the epistle to the Romans alone it is used 170 times. It is also very frequently used with nouns, as *en dunamei*. The captivity epistles make use of these phrases, especially at the end of a sentence. They are not rare in the other epistles. We find them more or less everywhere in the New Testament and in the Septuagint, especially in the poetic parts. They often have a liturgical sound. It is clear that the expressions "in the Holy Spirit", "in Christ", and "in the Lord" become more frequent as the style becomes more rhetorical and they tend to become stylistic ornaments.[10]

The difficulty with Bouttier's and Cerfaux's position is evidenced in their failure to demonstrate the consistency of this use in Pauline literature. One can only conclude the apostle would 172 times make use of this "stylistic ornament" only if one assumes it has no other significance. The reasoning is circular. As Richard N. Longenecker notes:

> It is true that in many places the expression can be viewed as merely synonymous with the adjective and noun "Christian." . . . However, in most of the passages where it is

possible that Paul meant only Christian by the term, or where it is asserted that the instrumental, causal, source, or dynamic idea is uppermost in his thought, the local designation, if it were not for the revulsion of the interpreter to the seeming crudity of the idea, can just as easily be seen.[11]

The Republican View. A fourth view of this expression tends toward a republican or representative view of the union of Christ and the believer. Hence they deny a mystical union of Christ and believers. This view tends to limit this concept to the act of justification, assuming the role of Christ as only the federal head of the race. In describing the union of Christ and the believer in its nature, Alexander Archibald Hodge argues:

> It is a legal or federal union, so that all of our legal or covenant responsibilities rest upon Christ, and all of his legal or covenant mercies accrue to us. . . . This union is between the believer and the person of the God-man in his office as Mediator. Its immediate organ is the Holy Spirit, who dwells in us, and through him we are virtually united to and commune with the whole Godhead, since he is the Spirit of the Father as well as of the Son. — John xiv. 23: xvii. 21, 23.[12]

The difficulty with this view is not so much in what it states as in what it leaves unsaid. It is not to be disputed that justification is the believer's union with Christ, a conversion-related experience. The relationship is even closer, as it is "in Christ" that the believer is justified. The believer is clothed in the righteousness of Christ and is thereby justified not on the basis of his own merit but rather the merit of Christ. However, this is only one aspect of being in Christ. The believer is made a new creature "in Christ," which goes beyond the realm of justification (2 Corinthians 5:17).

Justification is an act whereby one's legal position in heaven is changed. Being declared justified is similar to the moment in which a government declares that an alien is a citizen. The moment the person is pronounced a citizen, nothing happens to him physically. His thought processes remain the same, as do his personality and pattern of speech. The only actual change is in his legal standing. While being in Christ involves the act of justification, it also involves far more than a mere change in one's legal standing before God.

A Metaphor for a Believer's Communion. A fifth view of the phrase "in Christ" interprets it as a metaphor of communion with Christ, either personally or corporately.

Historically the Roman Catholic Church has tended to emphasize this view from a corporate perspective, that is, to be "in Christ" is to be part of the "holy catholic church." More recently, however, non-Catholic writers have begun to argue along similar lines. According to Rudolph Bultmann, " 'in Christ,' far from being a formula for mystic union, is primarily an eschatological formula . . . to belong to the Christ Church is to be 'in Christ' or 'in the Lord.' "[13] Similarly John A. T. Robinson interprets this expression from the perspective of "the Church as literally now the resurrection 'body' of Christ."[14]

Again the failure of this view is not so much in what is stated but in what remains unstated. There can be no disputing that being "in Christ" is the basis for an intimate communion with Christ, both personally and corporately in the church, which is His body, but it cannot be limited to a mere metaphor of personal or corporate communion. As Augustus Hopkins Strong correctly notes:

> Lest we should regard the figures mentioned above as merely Oriental metaphors, the fact of the believer's union with Christ is asserted in the most direct and prosaic manner. . . . Thus the believer is said to be "in Christ," as the element or atmosphere which surrounds him with its perpetual presence and which constitutes his vital breath; in fact, this phrase "in Christ," always meaning "in union with Christ," is the very key to Paul's epistles, and to the whole New Testament. The fact that the believer is in Christ is symbolized in baptism: we are "baptized into Christ" (Gal. 3:27).[15]

Being in the Spirit of Christ. A sixth view of this phrase interprets it as, in the words of Adolph Deissmann, "a literal local dative of personal existence in the pneumatic Christ."[16] As one writer explains:

> Deissmann thought that St. Paul regarded Christ as a king of spiritual space in which the believer lives, as in an atmosphere, and maintained that "en Christo" had this mystical meaning every time it was mentioned. Though this cannot really be maintained, in the overwhelming number of cases it must mean what it says; it must be given a "locative" sense. To be "in Christ" is to possess an entirely different kind of life.[17]

Deissmann tended to use the analogy of air, which is in us at the same time we are in an atmosphere; and while the analogy is consistent with his view, he tended in doing so to deny the personality of Christ. More contemporary writers have corrected this error in following Deissmann's argument yet also insisting upon the personality of Christ. Richard N. Longenecker represents this modification as he notes:

> As the Old Testament can say that Abraham "trusted *in* Jahweh" (nine times out of eleven using the preposition *ba* rather than *la* with the hiphil form with its object as God), and as Jesus is reported to have spoken of His relationship to the Father as being "*in* the Father," all without diminishing the concept of the real personality of God, so Paul, with his high Christology, can speak of being "in Christ" without that concept of person "in" person softening or dissolving the fixed outlines of personality for either Christ or the Christian. To be forced to give a definite psychological analysis of this relationship would have left Paul speechless. But he was convinced that he had experienced just such an intimacy with Christ.[18]

In the Universal Church. Some dispensationalists have used the phrase to mean the believer is placed into the body of Christ which is the universal church. This action took place in the baptism of the Spirit (1 Corinthians 12:13). It produces a non-experiential position for the believer. As John F. Walvoord explains this position:

The expression "in Christ" in every one of its many instances in the New Testament refers only to the saints of this dispensation. As far as the expression "the dead in Christ" indicates, only those in Christ are raised. Of course, all the saints are in Christ in the sense that Christ is their substitute, but the question is whether they are in the body of Christ, baptized into His body, as the Scriptures picture. . . . There is no explicit teaching anywhere in the Bible that reveals that the Old Testament saints are resurrected at the time the church is resurrected. In other words, the two events are never brought together in any passage of Scripture. The best explanation of the expression "dead in Christ" is to refer it to the church alone.[19]

In the Person of Christ in the Heavenlies. This view is similar to the one immediately above, but notes that the believer is placed into the person of Christ in the heavenlies, not just a heavenly church entity. This is His body. Interpreting these ideas literally, the believer was placed "in Christ" historically on Golgotha and remains "in Christ." The believer was positionally placed in Christ on the day of Pentecost. He was actually placed in Christ at his conversion and symbolically placed in Christ when he is baptized in water.

The Pauline description of the believer "in Christ" is not too unlike the prenatal description of a child "in his mother." There is perhaps no more intimate relationship between two human beings than that of mother and child during that period. Yet at the same time both individuals have a distinct identity, so much so that some forms of medicine specialize in treating one party in this relationship without affecting the other. The baby is "in his mother," and at the same time the very lifeblood of the mother sustains the baby.

The position of the believer in Christ is only half the truth; Christ is in the believer. Jesus said, ". . . Ye in me, and I in you" (John 14:20). The first is nonexperiential; the believer is positionally "in Christ." The second is experiential and is based on the first, "Christ in me."

Just because we say to be "in Christ" is nonexperiential does not mean we do not have an experience related to it. You cannot be "in Christ" without having "Christ in you." So when you experience Christ in your life, the experience is based on your being "in Christ." Those who try to take the mystery or life out of this doctrine take the supernatural out of Christianity. According to Richard N. Longenecker:

> Endless debate will probably continue to gather around Paul's expression "in Christ," for it signifies that central aspect of the Christian life which is much better experienced than explained. Indeed, the more confident we are that we have reduced the expression to the cold prose of the psychologist's laboratory the more assured we can be that we have lost its central significance. The inexplicable must always remain in the truly personal relationship. Yet that relationship can be intellectually understood and expressed up to a point.[20]

This being "in Christ" is not merely some religious experience to be divorced from the rest of life and living. As noted above, Paul uses this expression in connection with virtually every aspect of Christian experience. Albert Schweitzer observes:

> Though the expression has thus almost the character of a formula, it is no mere formula for Paul. For him every manifestation of the life of the baptized man is conditioned by his being in Christ. Grafted into the corporeity of Christ, he loses his creative individual existence and his natural personality. Henceforth he is only a form of manifestation of the personality of Jesus Christ, which dominates that corporeity. Paul says this with trenchant clearness when he writes, in the Epistle to the Galatians, "I am crucified with Christ, so I live no longer as I myself; rather, it is Christ who lives in me" (Gal. ii. 19–20). The fact that the believer's whole being, down to his most ordinary everyday thoughts and actions, is thus brought within the sphere of the mystical experience has its effect of giving to this mysticism a breadth of permanence, a practicability, and a strength almost unexampled elsewhere in mysticism.[21]

Similarly, Watchman Nee argues the believer is placed "in Christ" as the believer accepts "Christ in him."

> But if God has dealt with us 'in Christ Jesus' then we have got to *be* in Him for this to become effective, and that now seems just as big a problem. How are we to 'get into' Christ? Here again God comes to our help. We have in fact no way of getting in, but what is more important, we need not try to get in, for we *are* in. What we could not do for ourselves, God has done for us. *He has put us into Christ.* Let me remind you of I Corinthians 1:30. I think that it is one of the best verses in the whole New Testament: 'Ye are in Christ.' How? 'Of him (That is, 'of God') are ye in Christ.' Praise God! It is not left to us either to devise a way of entry or to work it out. We need not plan how to get in. God has planned it; and He has not only planned it but He has also performed it. 'Of *him* are ye in Christ Jesus.' We are in; therefore we need not try to get in. It is a divine act, and it is accomplished.[22]

The experience of being placed in Christ occurs at conversion, whereas usually at some later point, the believer enters into or experiences the reality of this truth (some understand it at conversion). The key, according to Stuart Briscoe, is faith. Appealing to his Noah in the Ark illustration, he argues:

> The simple faith of Noah which motivated his step-in was evidenced as he stepped out. Noah heard the word "go forth," and "Noah went forth" (Genesis 8:18). To him, the one step of faith into the salvation of God was as logical as the series of steps of faith that were going to carry him to the extremities of the riches of a new land which God had made part of his salvation. Noah did not look out and long for the land. He did not have an all-night prayer meeting asking God to make the land his experience. Noah did not sit in his ark giving his testimony of how God saved him from the flood, and he did not plead with God to come and do a wonderful work in his heart that was going to bring the land to his own experience. He *looked* out, and he *stepped* out. If Noah had sat in his ark much longer, he would probably have suffered

from acute boredom and deep depression, e
was saved. But once he stepped out, he had
either bored or depressed. The man of God wh
depressed is the man who is still sitting in the   ,---
ing that his sins are forgiven, but hasn't reached the point of
stepping out and exploring the land. Remember boredom
and depression are aliens in the land of freshness and
newness.[23]

The holiness/Arminian view of "in Christ" is that it happens
in a sanctifying experience at some point in the Christian life.
The believer prays for sanctification and receives it in a second
work of grace. The Calvinist views sanctification as a continuous progress in Christian growth. The holiness/Arminian views
sanctification as a crisis experience, described as "placing all on
the altar, " "letting go and letting God," or "receiving" spiritual
truth, followed by a continued experience of continued growth.

Being "in Christ" is therefore a description of the believer not
only at conversion but also throughout his Christian experience. In identifying the believer's position "in Christ," Paul also
hints further at the intimacy that exists between the believer
and his Lord. As the child in his mother is an individual personality while very much a part of his mother, so the believer
retains his individual personality while being in Christ. This
concept involves a greater degree of intimacy than may be
implied in the togetherness statements or partnership statements of Paul. The truth of "in Christ" establishes a bridge
between the believer's association with Christ and living in
Christ.

— 7 —
UNION
AND
COMMUNION

The previous two chapters examined a believer's first contact with God, called union with Christ, and the second stage, communion with Christ. The believer who has experienced both union and communion understands the differences. Union and communion are different in motivation, results, and process.

Before I was saved, I had yearnings for God. I wanted to know Him as Saviour, because I knew I was lost. I wanted the peace I saw in Christians, because my life was empty. I prayed for long periods of time (at least at the time I thought they were long periods). I searched the Bible but didn't feel that God was speaking to me through it. I understood the natural meaning of its stories and words, but the Bible didn't have spiritual meaning to me.

Then I received Christ on July 25, 1950, in an experience that was real and satisfying. I talked to Christ and asked Him to come into my life. I know He heard me. The experience changed my life. The emptiness was gone. I no longer searched for God, because I had found Him. The Bible became a new book, and God spoke to me through it. My conversion is described by the phrase "union with God." The next phrase, "communion with God," describes continuing fellowship with God. These have also been called salvation (union with God) and sanctification (communion with God).

After I was saved, I had a constant desire to read the Bible and pray. Sometimes I enjoyed talking with friends. I had a paper route and enjoyed my work. I didn't want to quit these functions just to read the Bible and pray, but as I worked I meditated on Scripture and prayed to God. I was thirsty to know God and do His will. When I read the Bible, it was satisfying. This was communion. It was a new experience for me. Before I was saved, I thought about God and tried to talk to Him, especially when I had a problem. But I didn't sense God's presence, nor did I feel He answered my prayers.

Communion with God is like the tide; it comes and goes. At times I sense His presence more than at other times. When I feel that I have drifted from Him, I have a great thirst to get back in fellowship with Christ. During these times I search my life for sin, confess it, and attempt to draw close to God again in prayer and fellowship.

Some accuse those who walk in communion with God of being mystics. To a certain degree they are right. Such people are not emotional mystics but biblical mystics. Examine carefully W. R. Inge's classical definition of mysticism:

> Mysticism means communion with God, that is to say with a Being conceived as the supreme and ultimate reality. If what the mystics say of their experience is true, if they have really been in communion with the Holy Spirit of God, that is a fact of overwhelming importance, which must be taken into account when we attempt to understand God, the world, and ourselves.[1]

By this definition, one who enjoys any intimacy with God is a mystic. Certainly this would apply to every evangelical Christian who enters into the very presence of God through prayer or gets truth from God through personal Bible study. Yet we must be careful of claiming to be mystics. The literature of mysticism suggests communion with God is only one aspect of experience. Many mystics tend to go beyond deep communion with God to seeking to merge with Him. When Madame Guyon described union with God as "the ultimate stage of Christian experience,"[2] she meant the person became absorbed into God, losing his I-Thou relationship to God.

In the last chapter we saw that for the Christian union means nonexperiential joining of the believer to God. It happened when the experiential event of conversion took place. Union becomes the basis for communion. Henry Scougal explained his understanding of religion as a "divine life" within man:

> And so it may be called, not only in regard to its fountain and origin, having God for its author and being wrought in the souls of men by the power of His Holy Spirit, but also in regard of its nature, religion being a resemblance of the divine perfections, the image of the Almighty shining in the soul of man; nay, it is a real participation of his nature; it is a beam of the eternal light, a drop of that infinite ocean of goodness; and they who are endued with it may be said to have *God dwelling in their souls and Christ formed within them.*[3]

The difference between the deeper-life Christian and others is not so much found in their respective relationships with God as in their understanding of communion. The spokesman of the deeper life would argue that all believers are united with Christ (union), although relatively few experience the communion with Christ characteristic of the deeper life. According to Stuart Briscoe, "It is possible for a Christian to believe the doctrines of 'Union with Christ' or 'Position in Christ' and yet to remain remote, aloof, and untouched by the experience of the fullness of Christ which the Bible teaches is the experiential outcome of the doctrines."[4] A. W. Tozer agrees, "The new birth makes us partakers of the divine nature. There the work of undoing the dissimilarity between us and God. . . . From there it progresses by the sanctifying operation of the Holy Spirit till God is satisfied. That is the theology of it, but as I said, even the unregenerate soul may sometimes suffer from the feeling that God is far from him."[5]

The union of the believer with Christ is an act of God that though not accomplished by human effort is most often expressed in religious acts. Madame Guyon concludes, "This cannot be brought out merely by your own experience. Meditation will not bring divine union; neither will love, nor worship, nor your devotion, nor your sacrifice. Nor does it matter how much light the Lord gives you. Eventually it will take an *act of God* to make union a reality."[6]

According to Henry Scougal:

> The power of life of religion may be better expressed in ac-
> tions than in words, because actions are more lively things
> and do better represent the inward principle whence they
> proceed; and therefore we may take the best measure of those
> gracious endowments from the deportment of those in whom
> they reside, especially as they are perfectly exemplified in the
> holy life of our blessed Saviour, a main part of whose busi-
> ness in this world was to teach by his practice what he did
> require of others and to make his own conversation an exact
> resemblance of those unparalleled rules which he prescribed,
> so that if ever true goodness was visible to mortal eyes, it was
> then when his presence did beautify and illustrate this lower
> world.[7]

Historically, Catholic theologians have taken a sacramental view of this doctrine, defining union with Christ as a result or benefit of the sacraments. More contemporary writers, how-ever, have greatly modified this doctrine without abandoning the principle entirely. Expressing the more contemporary Cath-olic view of this doctrine, one writer notes:

> Now, though it is true that our life 'in Christ' is normally
> brought about by the Sacraments, the sacraments do not *in
> themselves* convey mystical experience. They are the 'outward
> and visible sign' of inward grace. Naturally, this does not
> mean that, at least in the case of the Eucharist, we may not
> 'taste and see', but only that the grace given in the sacraments
> is usually hidden from us, though it is not for that reason any
> less real and effective.[8]

An alternative view of attaining union with Christ identifies it closely with the liturgical practice of laying on of hands. Typical of the emphasis of many holiness evangelists, James

Gilchrist Lawson argues at length for the observance of the laying on of hands in connection with spiritual experience.[9]

Steps to Communion

But not all laying on of hands is associated with union; to some it is associated with communion and the spiritual experience. I traveled to the large churches in South America, preparing an article entitled "I Visited the Ten Largest Churches in the World" for *Christian Life* magazine. The Jotabache Church (Methodist Pentecostal) in San Diego, Chili, has the second largest membership in the world. Pastor John Maxwell of Skyline Wesleyan Church, San Diego, California, was with me. He was so impressed with the church that he asked the pastor of the church to pray over him. It was not during the invitation, but during a tour of the church. Maxwell went to the altar, and the pastor laid hands on him and prayed for Maxwell to have power in his ministry and personal life.

Maxwell came back to Skyline and every Sunday has about fifteen prayer partners meet him at 8:00 A.M., before he preaches. Maxwell kneels, and the men lay hands on him. They pray for power on the preaching for that day.

Union with Christ happens at conversion and is nonexperiential. It is accomplished by God apart from any involvement in any sacrament (ordinance) or liturgical exercise. It comes from conversion. Later a believer can act out his union with Christ and have intimate communion with Him. Communion is a postconversion experience that for many is even more meaningful than conversion. There are usually six acts in the experience of the believer associated with entering into communion with Christ. (Some may experience more or less than these steps.)

Knowledge. The first step in experiencing communion with Christ is knowledge. The Apostle Paul often used the "know ye not" formula when introducing some aspect of Christian experience (*see* Romans 6:3). For some, merely understanding aspects of the believer's togetherness with Christ—his position in Christ and full union with Christ—is the beginning of a deeper communion with Christ. One cannot fully appreciate truth he does not first at least partially understand intellectually.

Emotional mystics usually base their mysticism on their feelings. Some are depressed, hence they experience a passive God of dark colors and deep organ tones. Others are cheery, so they experience God in fast, racing tones of spring music. They experience God in light colors of yellow or misty green. The biblical mystic comes to God through the Scriptures. There is objectivity to his experience. Since feelings may or may not be a proper interpretation of communion, everyone needs a standard outside himself to determine the right approach to God. The Bible is the rule by which to judge all feelings. Feelings are not wrong but must be interpreted by the Word of God.

Repentance. Repentance of known sin is a second aspect of the entering into a deeper communion. It is known by other words: "turning from sin," "cleansing of sin," "purging," and so on. All those phrases mean the believer goes through the following actions:

1. He searches his heart for sin that blocks his fellowship with God.
2. He begs forgiveness for sin (1 John 1:9), making sure his intercession is sincere.
3. He asks God to forgive his sin by the blood of Jesus Christ (1 John 1:7).
4. He promises to learn lessons from the experience so it doesn't happen again.

Because they are happy at the time, and they *feel* cleansed, certain Christians think they are sinless. When they do sin and realize it, they either repeat the process or attempt to seek salvation again.

The Christian must not sin. Just because some Christians have taught an unattainable sinless perfection, we must not embrace sinful imperfection as a standard. We must realize we have a sinful nature and will sin, yet always attempt to gain victory over it. Sin has a hindering effect on the believer's relationship and experience with God. Henry Scougal advised a friend:

If we desire to have our souls molded to his holy frame, to become partakers of the divine nature and have Christ formed in our hearts, we must seriously resolve and carefully endeavor to avoid and abandon all vicious and sinful practices. There can be no treaty of peace till once we lay down these weapons of rebellion wherewith we fight against heaven; nor can we expect to have our distempers cured if we be daily feeding on poison. Every willful sin gives a mortal wound to the soul and puts it at a greater distance from God and goodness; and we can never hope to have our hearts purified from corrupt affections unless we cleanse our hands from vicious actions.[10]

Repentance is more than turning from known sin in our lives. It involves being aware of our lack of God consciousness or communion with Christ. We must recognize we do not always seek God in prayer, and we do not always try to walk by faith. A. W. Tozer advises:

Should the sense of remoteness persist in spite of prayer and what you believe is faith, look to your inner life for evidences of wrong attitudes, evil thoughts or dispositional flaws. These are unlike God and create a psychological gulf between you and him. Put away the evil from you, believe, and the sense of nearness will be restored. God was never away in the first place.[11]

Faith. Often, entering into communion with Christ is a matter of acting on the Word of God. Deeper-life speakers declare one should appropriate the deeper life by faith, just as one appropriates eternal life by faith at salvation. Stuart Briscoe explains:

The *initial act* of faith which allows Christ to enter and live within the heart, must be extended into a *continual attitude* of faith in His Person which allows Him to settle down and feel at home. It is amazing how many of God's people decide that once they have received Christ by faith, they no longer need to exercise faith. . . . Your faith must be a constant attitude of dependence upon Him: a continual appropriating of all the riches you have in Him, and a step-by-step expectation in Him to be Himself within you. This is faith, and this is your responsibility, but of course it is possible to accept the privilege and abuse the responsibility; to have Him *live* within you, and yet not *dwell* within you.[12]

Obviously, living by faith is an experience of the deeper-life (*see* chapter 3). Faith is more than a doctrinal statement of faith and saving faith; it is the basis of communion with Christ. A Christian can experience a faith greater than his own by living by the faith of Christ (Galatians 2:16, 20).

How does a believer enter the deeper-life faith? First, faith is acting on the Word of God, so he must obey the scriptural commands. Second, faith is applying the Word of God to his life so he knows what the Bible teaches about living in the power of "Christ's faith." Third, he must let Christ control him so the power of Christ's faith can flow through him.

The deeper life of faith is the result of the believer's intentional effort to have communion with God. A person does not accidentally stumble into spirituality, nor does it sneak up on him. The life of faith is an intentional walk with God. No one aimlessly meanders through the Bible to find communion with God.

Yielding. The idea of surrender or yielding to God is fundamental in virtually all deeper-life literature. Andrew Murray reflected this emphasis in calling a series of Keswick messages by the general title *Absolute Surrender.*[13] Phoebe Palmer, leader among revivalistic Methodists in the nineteenth century, urged her hearers to place all on the altar and allow the altar to sanctify.[14] A more contemporary writer urges:

Only God can steer the course of your life with divine discretion because *He* knows what *He* is doing. He is able to declare the end from the beginning to you. You have trusted Him to forgive and forget your past, and you expect Him to deliver you safely in heaven. Therefore, you *must* give Him the right to prove Himself to be as capable of organizing and directing in *time,* as you know and expect Him to be adequate for *eternity*. You have a throne room, which is His by right—is He at home sitting on His throne, ruling and reigning and signing the decrees? This is your responsibility to provide the King with a house fit for a King![15]

When a person yields his life to God, it is more than becoming passive. He does not become a vegetable. He takes control of his life by deciding where he will obey. When he yields to God, he decides not to yield it to his sinful nature or to the influences of ungodly friends. He decides not to yield it to unbiblical demands on his life. Yielding is an intentional act, done with the eyes open. It is *not* becoming a wimp. You know what should not control your life (sin, temptation, harmful influence, and so on); you know that God desires and is able to control your life; so you actively turn over the controls to Him.

Yielding your life to God is similar to yielding the wheel of your car to your son, who is learning to drive. Your son must know the rules of the road, how to handle the car, and have the privilege of driving. No one ignorantly yields a car to an adolescent, hoping he can drive. Correct yielding is based on knowledge and past experience.

Many things happen to your spiritual life when you yield your life to Christ. Yielding is a "neutral action" incorporated in various spiritual activities. These include, but are not limited to: being filled with the Spirit; understanding the Scriptures (illumination); praying effectively; living by faith; being led by the Spirit.

The action of yielding does not make you spiritual; the person to whom you yield makes you spiritual. Christ is the measure of your spirituality.

Obeying. The attitude of yielding must be continued through the act of obedience. Some oppose the idea of a deeper-life, charging that it is inherently antiaggressive in soul winning. In many cases Christians claiming to have the deeper life have been guilty of a passive approach to Christian experience and evangelism. But in all fairness, the great deeper-life men of the past were great soul winners. During his eighteen years as pastor of Moody Church, Chicago, Dr. H. A. Ironside saw public professions of faith in Christ on all but two Sundays. J. Hudson Taylor, founder of the China Inland Mission, wrote:

> The consecration of all to our Master, far from lessening our power to impart, increases both our power and our joy in ministration. The five loaves and two fishes of the disciples, first given up to and blessed by the Lord, were abundant supply for the needy multitudes, and grew, in the act of distribution, into a store of which twelve hampers full of fragments remained when all were fully satisfied. We have, then, in this beautiful section, as we have seen, a picture of unbroken communion leading to fellowship in service, to a being all for Jesus, ready for any experience that will fit for further service, surrendering all to Him, and willing to minister all for Him. There is no room for love of the world here, for union with Christ has filled the heart. There is nothing for the gratification of the world, for all has been sealed and is kept for the Master's use.[16]

Crucifying Self. A final aspect of maintaining intimacy in communion with Christ is crucifying self or taking up one's cross. In deeper-life literature this often takes the form of a call to holiness. Some believe this is a second experience after salvation, in which God eradicates the sin nature. Others believe this is a second work after salvation whereby God gives victory over sin so that a person can live without sin (but his sin nature is not eradicated). Still others believe they should continue the work of Calvary and constantly crucify the old nature called the self-life. These are given over to asceticism or legalism, trying to put the self-life into an iron cage to keep it from controlling their lives. Since all these are inadequate, what does the Bible teach about crucifying the old nature?

First, the Bible teaches that the old nature (old man, self, flesh, and so on) was crucified in the past act of Christ's death. Some misinterpretation of this doctrine comes from the King James Version of Romans 6:6, "Knowing this, that our old man is crucified with him, that the body of sin might be destroyed, that henceforth we should not serve sin." The phrase "is cru-

cified" implies two things: that a Christian should have his sin
nature *continually* crucified and that he can be the agent to
crucify his sinful nature (lust, temptations, and so on).

The problem is a believer cannot crucify his old nature. The
King James phrase in the present tense "is crucified" should be
translated "has been crucified." It is past action in the original
language. The old Adamic nature was *positionally* put to death
with Christ. As far as one's *standing* before God, a believer is
dead with Christ. This does not mean the old nature is no
longer active. Not at all. The old nature still has its urge to sin.
There still come lust and temptations from the old nature.

So what died? Just as a judge may hand down the death
sentence but it takes time to execute the criminal, so God has
judged the sin nature, but the eradication will not be carried out
until the death of the believer or the rapture. Eradication happens only at glorification.

Now the believer must act on what has happened. The sin
nature has been crucified; the believer cannot put his sinful
urges to death. He doesn't have the desire to crucify self, nor
does he have the power to do it. The answer is to act on the
power of Calvary to crucify self.

Jesus commands, "Whosoever doth not bear his cross, and
come after me, cannot be my disciple" (Luke 14:27), and, "If
any man will come after me, let him deny himself, and take up
his cross daily, and follow me" (Luke 9:23). He does not mean
we should physically nail ourselves to a cross or think that
self-denial is self-crucifixion. Rather we should: yield, not seek
sin, obey, and claim the power over sin that comes from the
accomplishments of the death and resurrection of Christ.

Some have mistakenly taught that in the act of self-crucifixion
a new relationship to God is formed. This idea of purging of self
is often defined in terms of bearing one's cross, the wilderness
period, or the trial of faith. Rather, to take up one's cross is to
apply the results of Calvary to one's life. Madame Guyon describes it as refinement:

> For two things to become one, the two must have similar
> natures. For instance, the impurity of dirt cannot be united

with the purity of gold. Fire has to be introduced to destroy the dross and leave the gold pure. This is why God sends a fire to the earth (it is called His Wisdom) to destroy all that is impure in you. Nothing can resist the power of that fire. It consumes *everything*. His Wisdom burns away all the impurities in a man for one purpose: *to leave him fit for divine union.*[17]

The deeper life offered by Christ is the life of Christ living in and through the believer. It begins with the concept of union with Christ. It is nonexperiential standing of the believer before God, not the merging of two personalities into one union. The Bible describes our union with Christ as a mystery no less understandable than the mystery of the Trinity. It happens at the conversion experience of every believer. To those believers who have to some degree understood and applied this doctrine to life, it has resulted in what they call "a deeper life." More correctly, union with Christ is the foundation of communion with Christ. When the believer attaches himself to Christ and depends on Christ in this earthly experience, he is walking in communion with Christ.

PART THREE

PRACTICAL APPLICATION OF EXPERIENCE

As a Christian seeks a deeper walk with God he will apply Christian truths to his life. What practical experiences are a part of this?

— 8 —
THE EXPERIENCE
OF THE
FULLNESS
OF THE SPIRIT

In the normal Christian experience, it should be anticipated that preconversion experiences, conversion-related experiences, and postconversion experiences with the Holy Spirit should exist. A survey of deeper-life literature, particularly that which records the testimony of deeper experiences with the Holy Spirit, will reveal a variety of terms describing these experiences with the Holy Spirit. To a large extent, the selection of these descriptive phrases is somewhat arbitrary and may be influenced to some degree by nonbiblical literature. A distinction should be made, however, between what might for lack of a better term be called part of the "normal" Christian experience and those more intense spiritual experiences more characteristic of revivalistic times. Further it seems that some of this confusion could be minimized if an attempt is made to apply biblical expressions only to those experiences that are similar to the biblical experiences originally described by the phrases.

Several biblical expressions are used to describe the relationship of the Holy Spirit to the believer. Some such as "baptism," "indwelling," and "sealing" appear to be closely related to one another and the conversion experience. In contrast, the idea of "the fullness of the Holy Spirit" in the New Testament is clearly a postconversion experience provided with biblical examples that demonstrate the possibility of multiple fillings of the Holy

Spirit not only after conversion but also after prior fillings. Understanding the biblical uses of these terms provides a reliable framework from which Christian experiences with the Holy Spirit can be analyzed and understood.

The Baptism of the Holy Spirit

After witnessing the descent of the Holy Spirit as a dove at the baptism of Jesus, John the Baptist spoke these words: ". . . He who sent me to baptize with water said to me, 'Upon whom you see the Spirit descending, and remaining on Him, this is He who baptizes with the Holy Spirit' " (John 1:33 NKJV).

Later Jesus promised His disciples, " . . . You shall be baptized with the Holy Spirit not many days from now" (Acts 1:5 NKJV). On the day of Pentecost, the disciples had a number of experiences involving the Holy Spirit, including the baptism of the Holy Spirit. Christians differ in their understanding of the facts recorded in Acts 2; some say it relates to conversion, while others see it as a second experience. A key to clearing up this confusion is to understand the difference between the terms "baptism" and "fullness."

The word *baptism* means "to immerse or totally surround something." The word *fullness*, on the other hand, refers to placing something into another and can carry with it the idea of control. On the day of Pentecost, the group in the Upper Room were both baptized and filled with the Holy Spirit. At conversion the person is baptized or placed into Jesus Christ. "For by one Spirit we were all baptized into one body . . ." (1 Corinthians 12:13 NKJV). Then there is the filling of the Spirit, which Paul commands for Christians: ". . . But be filled with the Spirit" (Ephesians 5:18 NKJV). This is a postconversion experience. The baptism of the Spirit is our new position in Jesus Christ, and the filling of the Spirit is His power working through us in Christian service.

On this basis I believe that the Bible quite clearly teaches that the baptism of the Holy Spirit is a nonexperience event occurring at conversion. That all the Christians at Corinth are said to have been baptized in the Spirit, yet many continued in pagan practices, is evidence in itself that this does not involve an eradication of the sin nature (1 Corinthians 12:13). This is apparently contrary to the claims of some teachers. The characteristics of the baptism of the Spirit are outlined in chart 12.

CHART 12

THE CHARACTERISTICS OF THE BAPTISM OF THE SPIRIT
1. Nonexperiential. 2. Once (nonrepeatable.) 3. All believers are placed in Jesus Christ. 4. New position in heaven. 5. Occurs at salvation.

One of the phenomena of the twentieth century has been the emergence and growth of Pentecostalism. From its humble beginnings in the first decade of this century, it has become a major influence in Christianity, not only in North America but around the world. Many of the world's largest and fastest-growing churches are affiliated with various Pentecostal denominations. One of the distinctives of this movement is its view of the baptism of the Holy Spirit. In an attempt to state the Pentecostal view of the Holy Spirit, Anthony A. Hoekema writes:

> Though it is difficult to sum up the views of a great many people from various Christian denominations in a single statement, the following is an attempt to reproduce what is commonly held by Neo-Pentecostals about this matter: the baptism in the Holy Spirit is an experience distinct from and usually subsequent to conversion in which a person receives the totality of the Spirit into his life and is thereby fully empowered for witness and service.[1]

Often the initial evidence of the Spirit baptism is identified by charismatic Christians by the practice of speaking in tongues. Article 8 of the *Statement of Fundamental Truths* of the Assemblies of God states in part, "The Baptism of believers in the Holy Ghost is witnessed by the initial physical sign of speaking with other tongues. . . ."[2]

CHART 13

PENTECOSTAL VIEW OF THE BAPTISM OF THE SPIRIT
1. Postconversion (second work of grace). 2. Power for holiness and service. 3. Comes by surrender and cleansing. 4. Evidenced by gift of tongues. 5. Experiential. 6. Available to every Christian, but must be sought.

The key to understanding the baptism of the Holy Spirit is the interpretation of 1 Corinthians 12:13, which I see as the central passage on this doctrine; it teaches that all Christians participate in this baptism. If the "one baptism" of Ephesians 4:5 is taken to mean the baptism of the Spirit, as it probably should be, this text constitutes added proof of the universality of this baptism among Christians. Romans 6 implies that this universal baptism of the Holy Spirit took place theologically in the historic death, burial, and resurrection of Christ and experientially at the moment of conversion. Historically, the baptism of the Holy Spirit occurred on the day of Pentecost (Acts 1:5; 2:1–4). When a Christian is baptized in water, he gives public testimony to having been baptized by the Spirit into the body of Christ.

CHART 14

WHEN DID THE BAPTISM OF THE HOLY SPIRIT OCCUR?	
THEOLOGICAL ANSWER	In the death, burial, and resurrection of Christ.
HISTORICAL ANSWER	On the day of Pentecost, the embryonic church was baptized with the Spirit.
EXPERIENTIAL ANSWER	At the moment of my conversion, I was baptized by the Spirit into the body of Christ.
TESTIMONIAL ANSWER	As I submitted to water baptism, I testified to my Spirit baptism.

The baptism of the Holy Spirit is unique to this dispensation. Until Pentecost, all references to the baptism of the Spirit were prophetic. This was one of the ministries of the Holy Spirit which began at Pentecost. Since it began at Pentecost, it is probable it will end at the rapture of the church. In Spirit baptism the Christian is baptized (placed positionally) into the body of Christ. The body of Christ is often used as a representation of the church in the Pauline epistles. Through the baptism of the Spirit, each individual is brought into a union with Christ. Thus there is a twofold identification in this baptism, with Christ and with His body, the church. When the church is removed at the rapture, this latter aspect of identification is apparently no longer possible. This is a second reason for limiting the baptism of the Holy Spirit to this dispensation.

On two occasions, references to the baptism with the Holy Spirit include the words "with fire" (Matthew 3:11; Luke 3:16). There are at least three interpretations of this expression. Some see this as little more than a reference to the tongues of fire that appeared on Pentecost. According to H. Leisegang, "Baptism with fire is nothing else than Baptism with the Spirit, which would, in Hellenistic circles of early Christianity, in reference to the Greek cult of Dionysus, to magic and mysteries, be thought of as bound up with an appearance of fire."[3]

Others consider this statement to be a reference to divine judgment. As Barret observes:

> Wellhausen and Bultmann are of the opinion that the original form of the saying was "He will baptize you with fire", and that this simple eschatological doom saying was corrupted to its present forms by the Christian experience of the Spirit. It seems even more plausible to conjecture that the earliest form of the logion was, "He will baptize you with *pneumati kai puri*", *pneumati* being taken to mean, not "spirit" but "wind". . . . Wind and fire are instruments of judgement.[4]

The third view sees the expression "fire" as a general statement concerning the mission and ministry of the apostles. Samuel Ragan explains:

This reference here is to the mission of the apostles and the proclamation of the Word. The Spirit is the Communicator of the Word. The creative Spirit and the creative Word work together. Pentecost is the immediate equipping of the disciples for their mission. Their words are to be words of fire, fire that destroys and consumes what is worthless, fire that purifies and makes ready for a new creation, a creation of brightness, genuineness, beauty, authenticity, effectiveness. When we relate or proclaim the Word, our self-expression has to be genuine and truly authentic.[5]

Since the creation, God made man to dwell with Him and enjoy fellowship with Him. In the Garden of Eden, God would come to walk and talk with Adam. After the fall, God spoke with various men to enjoy their fellowship. When men failed to live for God, even after the Flood, God established a unique relation with the heads of the patriarchal families. Later, on Mount Sinai, he gave Moses the plans for the tabernacle, which served as "the dwelling place of God's glory." When the tabernacle was replaced with a temple, the glory of the Lord moved into that place, where men could meet their God. During the life of Christ, God's desire to dwell with men was fulfilled when "the Word became flesh and dwelt among us. . . ." (John 1:14 NKJV). Today God dwells by His Holy Spirit in the bodies of those who have been redeemed.

"Or do you not know that your body is the temple of the Holy Spirit who is in you, whom you have from God, and you are not your own?" (1 Corinthians 6:19 NKJV). Our human bodies have become temples to house the Holy Spirit. A realization of this truth will assist us in our efforts to properly care for our physical bodies. It will also help to keep us spiritually pure and clean. Within the context of the apostle's question, he is discussing morality. Even if a man had no concern about engaging in immoral activity, the thought of involving "the temple of God" in such a practice should help prevent him from sinning. When we realize we are never alone but that the Holy Spirit is always with us, ever present inside, we will be more cautious in our efforts to live for God.

Catholic theologians believe the sacraments are a means of grace and that this is the means by which the Spirit of God enters the believer. Arguing this tenet, Edward Lien states:

> The Holy Communion might in a wide sense be called a means to the indwelling of the Blessed Trinity in the human soul. It is true that at the moment of baptism the Three Divine Persons take up their abode in the soul of the infant. But baptism involves in a certain way a desire of the Eucharist, since of its nature it tends toward it. In baptism there is a *votum improprie dictum* of the Blessed Sacrament.[6]

Actually, the Bible teaches the Spirit's indwelling occurs at conversion and is one of the proofs that one is a child of God. The Apostle Paul declared, ". . . Now if anyone does not have the Spirit of Christ, he is not His" (Romans 8:9 NKJV). The Holy Spirit within is the "earnest" of future blessing (2 Corinthians 1:22; 5:5; Ephesians 1:14). In the New Testament, even Christians living in sin are exhorted to righteousness on the basis of the indwelling Spirit (1 Corinthians 6:19).

Several passages have been interpreted by some to teach that not all Christians are indwelt by the Spirit or that the Spirit may withdraw this ministry. These passages describe conditions prior to Pentecost (1 Samuel 16:14; Psalms 51:11; Luke 11:13) or unique features of the transition into this present dispensation (Acts 5:32; 8:14–20; 19:1–6). The most difficult of the passages to explain is probably Acts 19:1–6. Here, twelve disciples of John engaged in an itinerant ministry are confronted by Paul concerning their relation with the Holy Spirit. Later they received the Holy Spirit and submitted to Christian baptism. The Anabaptists of the sixteenth century used this passage to justify their practice of baptizing believers who had been "baptized" prior to their conversion. Their assumption was that these disciples of John were not saved until they heard and responded to the preaching of the gospel by Paul. Regardless of how one might interpret the events of these verses, it would be unwise to use this passage against the many clear statements that all believers now have the Holy Spirit.[7]

The Bible also teaches that Christians are sealed by the Holy Spirit. ". . . You were sealed with the Holy Spirit of promise, who is the guarantee of our inheritance until the redemption of the purchased possession . . ." (Ephesians 1:13, 14 NKJV).

When a man and woman agree to marry, it is customary in our culture for the man to give the woman an engagement ring as a symbol of his commitment to her. Paul was drawing on a similar custom of the first century to explain this aspect of the ministry of the Holy Spirit in salvation. When we are born again, we immediately become heirs to all God has promised us. God gives us the Holy Spirit as a down payment of His commitment to someday give us all the other things He has promised. By way of application, it is important that we "do not grieve the Holy Spirit of God, by whom you were sealed for the day of redemption" (Ephesians 4:30 NKJV).

Concerning the seal as an emblem of the sealing of the Holy Spirit, F. E. Marsh states, "The Seal signifies the Holy Spirit. It is not some emotion or experience, but it is the presence of the Holy Spirit in the believer, witnessing to his full acceptance in Christ, telling us by the Word that as Christ is, so are we in this world (1 John iv. 17)."[8]

The Fullness of the Holy Spirit

The doctrine of the fullness of the Spirit is vital to the living experience of the normal Christian life. Unlike other ministries of the Spirit, the fullness of the Spirit is experiential and is the source of all spiritual experience in the life of the Christian. The importance of this doctrine has not gone unnoticed by the spiritual giants of the past. In a sermon entitled "The Outpouring of the Holy Spirit," Charles Haddon Spurgeon declared, "Let the preacher always confess before he preaches that he relies upon the Holy Spirit. Let him burn his manuscript and depend upon the Holy Spirit. If the Spirit does not come to help him, let him be still and let the people go home and pray that the Spirit will help him next Sunday."[9] Andrew Murray also sensed the importance of this doctrine when he wrote, "But one thing is needful. The Spirit did it all, on the day of Pentecost and afterwards. It was the Spirit who gave the boldness, the Spirit gave the wisdom, the Spirit gave the message, and the Spirit gave the converting power."

The characteristics of the filling or fullness of the Holy Spirit are shown in chart 15.

CHART 15

CHARACTERISTICS OF THE FILLING OF THE HOLY SPIRIT
1. Experiential.
2. For living and service.
3. Repeatable.
4. Yielding: "Not getting more of the Holy Spirit, but the Holy Spirit getting more of you."
5. Postconversion.
6. Not all believers take advantage of it.

When speaking of the fullness of the Spirit, not all writers use the same terms. John R. Rice designates it "the anointing of the Holy Spirit."[10] Stuart Briscoe describes the anointing as, "This is the meaning of the fullness of the Spirit. It is His overpowering. Men are filled with the Spirit when they are prepared to abandon themselves to His dominion and to rejoice in His control."[11] Similarily, C. Sumner Wemp also uses the term control to explain it, but calls it "the filling of the Spirit": "To be filled with the Holy Spirit means to be *controlled by* the Holy Spirit. This is it. The secret to the Christian life is being controlled by the Holy Spirit so that He can produce in and through the believer all that is His ministry today."[12]

Paul commanded the Ephesian Christians: "And do not be drunk with wine, in which is dissipation; but be filled with the Spirit" (Ephesians 5:18 NKJV). God has given men and women the opportunity to be continually filled with the Holy Spirit for effective service. Rather than allowing alcohol to control his mind, it is God's desire that His Holy Spirit control the Christian. As we establish our fellowship with God through confession of sins (1 John 1:9) and yield to Him (Romans 6:13) we can be filled with the Holy Spirit as commanded in Scriptures. In the light of Paul's command, no Christian can claim to be in the will of God who is not constantly being filled with the Holy Spirit.

The Scriptures speak of "the law of the Spirit of life" (Romans 8:2 NKJV). Among other things, this suggests certain eternal laws or principles govern the ministry of the Holy Spirit. When these laws are understood, particularly as they relate to the fullness of the Holy Spirit, any and every believer can experience this fullness. As F. B. Meyer observed, "The law of the Spirit of Life is for anybody and everybody who will obey. If a man is clean and pure in heart and lives near God, he can always count on the operation of the Spirit of God. . . . You can be filled with the light of the spirit of life if you will obey the law."[13]

The human responsibility concerning the fullness of the Holy Spirit includes both yieldedness and faith. As one yields his will to the Holy Spirit, he can by faith be filled with the Holy Spirit. Experiences associated with this fullness may vary with various personalities, but the eternal principles are unchanging. As Bill Bright observes:

> In like manner, and in different ways, sincere Christians are filled with the Spirit. It should be made clear at this point that to be "filled with the Spirit" does not mean that we receive more of the Holy Spirit, but that we give Him more of ourselves. As we yield our lives to the Holy Spirit and are filled with His presence, He has greater freedom to work in and through our lives, to control us in order to better exalt and glorify Christ.
>
> God is too great to be placed in a man-made mold. However, there are certain spiritual laws that are inviolate. Since the Holy Spirit already dwells within every Christian, it is no longer necessary to "wait in Jerusalem" as Jesus instructed the disciples to do, except to make personal preparation for His empowering. The Holy Spirit will fill us with His power the moment we are fully yielded. It is likewise possible for a man to be at a quiet retreat and become filled with the Holy Spirit. It is likewise possible for a man to be filled with the Holy Spirit while walking down a busy street in a great

city. . . . It is even possible for a man to be filled with the Holy Spirit and know something wonderful has happened, yet be completely ignorant at the time of what has actually taken place, provided he has a genuine desire to yield his will to the Lord Jesus Christ.[14]

While yielding to God is one aspect of being filled, faith is another. The two are so closely related that it is questionable if one can exist in experience without the other. Some Christian leaders speak of it as "spiritual breathing." In this analogy, yielding to Christ by confessing sin is likened to exhaling; appropriating the fullness of the Holy Spirit by faith is described as inhaling. Emphasizing the faith aspect of this act of being filled, C. Sumner Wemp writes:

Here, now, is the key to being controlled by the Holy Spirit. Ephesians 5:17 tells us emphatically to understand that to be filled with the Holy Spirit is *the will of God.* That means that if I ask for the Holy Spirit to fill me, to take control, He does! We *know* we have this petition (1 John 5:15, italics mine). How do we know? By feeling joy or a warm love oozing through us? No. We know by *faith* that God cannot lie, and so we live by faith. We walk by faith. We trust that at the moment we ask He gets behind the wheel and begins to take control. In the following days as He controls, we will see the fruit being produced. It will then be a fantastic experience to see the changes take place that He brings about. What's so amazing, and surprises even the believer, is that he finds himself loving people in a way so different from how he has in the past. He then is aware that God did it, and it was not the struggle of the flesh and his own efforts that brought it about.[15]

Receiving the fullness of the Holy Spirit involves two expressions of faith: asking and accepting. As W. H. Griffith Thomas observes:

Faith as revealed to us in Scripture is a two-fold nature; there is the faith that *asks* and the faith that *accepts;* the faith that

appeals and the faith that appropriates. This is probably the
reason why prayer and thanksgiving are so often associated
in the writings of Paul. They represent to us the aspects of
faith. Prayer is the faith that asks; thanksgiving is the faith
that takes.[16]

Some sincere Christians today seek spectacular signs to accompany the fullness of the Holy Spirit in their lives. I believe
the Bible does not teach these should be expected today. The
Holy Spirit's fullness within us is primarily to produce the fruit
of the Spirit (Galatians 5:22, 23). The evidence in the book of
Acts of the fullness of the Holy Spirit promised by Jesus was
power to witness (Acts 1:8). On some occasions (but not every
occasion) signs and wonders accompanied Christians' filling
with the Holy Spirit—the building shook (Acts 4:31) or they
spoke in tongues (Acts 10:44-46)—but always the gospel was
preached and people were saved. These occasional outward
occurrences were often tools God used at that time to accomplish the main objective of witnessing. These outward signs
were similar to the purpose miracles had in the early church;
they were an objective authority for the message of God. But
when God provided the full revelation of the Word of God as
the authoritative message, I believe the outward signs or authorities passed off the scene.

— 9 —
THE EXPERIENCE
OF REVIVAL

Revival is a misunderstood word. Some churches advertise a *Spring Revival*, but they mean "evangelistic meetings." Others plan a revival meeting that might include preaching, testimonies, singing, and even "tarrying at the altar," but they never experience revival. One pastor said, "I can't define revival, but I know it when I feel it!"

Is revival just a corporate feeling? Can revival be defined? Does it have an objective existence? Is revival from God or worked up by men?

The word *revival* comes from the Latin *revivere*, the prefix *re* means "again," and *vivere* means "to live." *Revival* means "a return of life," and spiritual revival means "a return of or stirring up of the spiritual life God originally gave."

Revival has a twofold application. First, it can mean an individual returns to the kind of life he began to experience at conversion. Second, it can mean a return to first-century Christianity or the experience of the believers on the day of Pentecost. The believers on the day of Pentecost were abundantly happy, shared their wealth with others, and had warm fellowship with one another. They spontaneously won others to Christ and sought time for prayer and Bible study.

Revival results in a good feeling, but more than feelings, the Bible says, ". . . the times of refreshing shall come from the presence of the Lord" (Acts 3:19). Revival cannot be worked up; it comes down sovereignly from God, when men meet the conditions of God.

I was saved in a genuine revival. Two young students from

Columbia (South Carolina) Bible College were pastoring the
Bonna Bella Presbyterian Church, outside Savannah, Georgia,
in the summer of 1950. Pastors Bill and Burt Harding were
gathering several people for prayer at 5:00 A.M. every morning,
and among others, they were praying for my salvation. The
church met in a new concrete-block building that was occupied
but unfinished.

People were being saved. The church community of Savannah was buzzing with news of stirrings in this little church of
less than one hundred attenders.

I was a seventeen-year-old who had just graduated from high
school. I attended a Youth for Christ rally and heard Burt Harding speak; next I went to a church banquet where Bill Harding
spoke. An excitement followed their ministry.

A revival meeting was held at the church in July. Mrs. Earnest Miller gave her testimony of how she, a Jehovah's Witness,
had been saved. Her husband was Jewish, and he was saved.
All six of their children received Christ. The neighborhood was
electrified.

Every night the altar was filled with people crying and seeking salvation. I had never seen anything like it in my life. It
seems everywhere I went people were talking about the Lord.
Everyone seemed interested in passing out gospel literature
and sharing Christ.

I even got swept up in the excitement. I went with a gospel
team to a local hospital and passed out tracts. There I confronted an elderly man, after giving him a gospel tract.

"Why do I want this piece of paper?" he asked.

"To go to heaven," I explained.

"Tell me how to get to heaven," the elderly patient asked.

"Believe in Christ, go to church, and do the best you can,"
was my sincere answer to him.

"That's not right," the crotchety old man rebuked me.

We argued about the plan of salvation. The man was
Lutheran and had a clear understanding of grace. I was de-
pending on works. He saw I was trying to work my way to
heaven. Finally he concluded, "I don't think you're going to
heaven."

The Lord used the elderly man to sting me with conviction. I never remember anyone ever telling me I was not right with God. During the next week I searched diligently for God. Each night people were going forward in the revival meeting to get saved. I refused to go forward thinking, *What will people say? They think I am a Christian.* Little did I know that a faithful group of people were interceding for me every morning. God was working. A bit of revival was being poured out on Savannah, Georgia. Out of that revival came the Evangelical Bible Institute (later called the Savannah Christian School). Also, over fifty young people surrendered for the ministry and went to Bible college. New churches were planted. Revitalization came to certain churches in the area—Presbyterian, Southern Baptist, Free Will Baptist, and Christian Missionary Alliance.

The spirit of revival had permeated the little Presbyterian church. When the week ended, the congregation voted overwhelmingly to continue another week. I read my Bible continuously but did not understand much. I went downtown and bought a religious book by Saint Thomas Aquinas; that did not help either. I constantly begged God—it seemed a hundred times a day—for forgiveness, but I felt nothing. I did not experience what others felt. I not only wanted to be forgiven, I wanted to feel it.

Thursday, July 25, 1950, was the turning point. That was the first night no one went forward to be saved. People seemed to sense a crisis because there were no results. It seemed as though revival would cease. Bill Harding came to the front of the little church and challenged the audience.

"I know someone is here who needs to come forward, but you are afraid to do it."

He must have looked into my heart, for he described me perfectly. I was afraid of what people thought about me. Bill Harding then challenged me, "I want you to go home, kneel by your bed, and pray these words. . . ."

Bill explained that we should not just ask for forgiveness, but meet a person. We were to ask Jesus Christ to come into our hearts.

I went home but refused to do what Bill had instructed. I prayed for a long time, asking God to be real to me. I prayed the Lord's Prayer sincerely. I asked God to forgive my sins. When I ran out of things to pray, I got in bed but could not go to sleep. Bill Harding's words kept going through my head . . . *meet a person*. Finally, I got on my knees and prayed, "Lord, I've never done it before. Jesus, come into my heart and save me."

Instantly, I experienced conversion and was born again. I had the feeling I had been searching for, but more important, I had inner assurance that I was saved. I cried for joy. I sang "Amazing Grace." I talked to God. I received assurance of my salvation, and to the day of this writing, I have never doubted my salvation.

When we examine the religious experiences of people, we cannot ignore the experience of the First and Second Great Awakenings in America. There were all-night prayer meetings, and working people skipped lunch to pray and fast. Saloons were shut down, and workers in the fields would fall to their knees, seeking salvation, because the power of God was so strong in an area. In the Welsh revival, the miners came to Christ, and the mules pulling out the coal could not respond to their drivers, because they had only been used to cursing and beatings.

The experience of revival can be nationwide at times, but on other occasions it is partial, touching one church or one denominational group of churches.

Two terms are used in revivalistic literature to describe the experience: "the outpouring of the Holy Spirit" and "the anointing of the Holy Spirit." While experiences of revival are described in revivalistic literature in many ways, the expression "outpouring of the Holy Spirit" usually refers to the general spirit of revival in an area or a church. At the same time, individuals such as soul winners or preachers are often described as being "anointed with the Holy Spirit."

Both phrases find their origin in the Scriptures and are constantly used in revivalistic literature to describe an intense experience with the Holy Spirit. However, the experience seems to be the same, whether it is the general experience (outpouring) or individually applied (anointing).

While many conservative Christians simply ignore these claims as expressions of fanaticism, those involved in revival know differently. Oswald J. Smith simply claims, "It is an undeniable fact that all down the centuries God has anointed men with the Holy Ghost."[1] He cites numerous examples from various ages to lend credibility to that claim. One of Smith's spiritual mentors declared concerning this experience with the Holy Spirit:

> Without the Holy Ghost you are unequal to the journey of life; you are unfit for the service of the Master; you are unwarranted in attempting to preach the gospel, or to win a soul for Christ, and you are unprepared for the future which He is immediately opening to you. Oh, let us wait at His feet; let us learn our weakness; let us realize our nothingness; let us get emptied for His filling, and then baptized with the Holy Ghost or filled anew with His utmost fullness; and we shall go forth not to our work, but to His, and find that "He is able to do exceedingly abundantly above all that we ask or think, according to the power that worketh in us. To whom be glory now and forever. Amen."[2]

The relationship between the outpouring and anointing of the Holy Spirit is such that the terms refer to different degrees of the same ministry of the Holy Spirit. When the Holy Spirit comes upon one, it is an anointing. When the Holy Spirit comes upon many, it constitutes an outpouring. Technically, the anointing is the same as the filling of the Spirit (Ephesians 5:18), also called "the infilling of the Spirit." When revivalists use the phrase "anointing" they describe the same experience theologians call "filling." Both refer to a postconversion experience with the Holy Spirit.

Not all biblical writers agree that the anointing and outpouring of the Holy Spirit are postconversion experiences. Commenting on the Greek term *chrisma*, W. E. Vine writes, "That believers have 'an anointing from the Holy One' indicates that this anointing renders them holy, separating them to God. The passage teaches that the gift of the Holy Spirit is the all-efficient means of enabling believers to possess a knowledge of the truth."[3]

Similarly, Watchman Nee at times seems to view the anointing of the Holy Spirit as a conversion-related experience. Using terms such as "the enduement with the Holy Spirit" and "baptism of the Holy Spirit" interchangeably, he writes:

> Because the Lord Jesus died on the Cross, I have received forgiveness of sins; because the Lord Jesus rose from the dead, I have received new life; because the Lord Jesus has been exalted to the right hand of the Father, I have received the outpoured Spirit. All is because of Him; nothing is because of me. Remission of sins is not based on merit, but on the Lord's crucifixion; regeneration is not based on human merit, but the Lord's resurrection; and the enduement of the Holy Spirit is not based on human merit, but on the Lord's exaltation. The Holy Spirit has not been poured out on you or me to prove how great we are, but to prove the greatness of the Son of God. . . . Some of you say, I agree with all of this, but I have no experience of it. Am I to sit down smugly and say I have everything, when I know perfectly well I have nothing? No, we must never rest content with objective facts alone. We need a subjective experience also; but that experience will only come as we rest upon divine facts. God's facts are the basis of our experience. . . . And enduement with the Holy Spirit becomes yours in exactly the same way, not by your doing anything yourself, but by your putting your faith in what the Lord has already done. If we lack experience, we must ask God for a revelation of this eternal fact, that the baptism of the Holy Spirit is the gift of the exalted Lord to His Church. Once we see that, effort will cease, and prayer will give place to praise.[4]

Some holiness writers argue that the practice of laying on hands in the New Testament was related to the anointing and outpouring of the Holy Spirit in power (*see* Acts 8:18). Even the few references to the anointing in the New Testament may be referring to a postconversion experience when the cultural backgrounds of the day are considered. Addressing this subject in an article on the "unction" of the Holy Spirit, Henry Barclay Swete notes:

> It has been customary to deny that the N.T. in these passages alludes to any post baptismal ceremony of unction. At Carthage in the early years of the third century a post baptismal unction preceded the laying on of hands. . . . Nevertheless, since anointing was with the Jews (cf. Ruth iii. 3, Ezek. xvi. 9) as well as with the Romans a normal accompaniment of a bath, it is not impossible that the anointing was followed almost from the first by the use of oil or unguent, which was to be regarded as symbolic of the descent of the anointing Spirit on Christ and His members. If so, a reference to this custom may be latent in 2 Cor. i. 21 and I Jo. i. 20, 27.[5]

That the anointing of the Holy Spirit is a postconversion experience is further suggested by the contrast of the nature and effects of the anointing and regeneration. Because the Holy Spirit is the agent of regeneration, it is to be expected that similarities are found between regeneration and other ministries of the same Spirit, but the differences serve to distinguish these various works. Writing more than a hundred years ago, Calvinist author C. R. Vaughan observed:

> Is then, this peculiar unction of the Spirit to be identified with regeneration, or, if not, in what does its power on the energies of spiritual discernment differ from that of regenerating grace? That the unction of the Spirit is not to be confounded with regeneration may be inferred from a number of circumstances. It is inferable from the fact of regeneration, with its effect on the spiritual vision, can occur *but once*, and its effect on the vision is to create the power to see where no such power existed before; but the oil of joy for mourning may be repeatedly applied, and its effect on the vision is simply to heal disorders which have impeded a vision already existing, but diseased and disordered.[6]

Under the Levitical law there were two occasions of a dual anointing, that is, the anointing of blood and the anointing of oil. This was practiced at the cleansing of a leper (Leviticus 14) and the consecration of a priest (Leviticus 8). Both have typical application to the Christian life, as the cleansed leper is a type of one cleansed from sin, and the New Testament identifies the believer as part of "a royal priesthood" (1 Peter 2:9). This dual anointing represents the twofold experience of the believer. He is anointed with blood, that is, in regeneration; and oil, that is, the anointing of the Holy Spirit.

Although the two are often confused, the anointing and fullness of the Holy Spirit should be distinguished. While the fullness of the Holy Spirit should be a regular part of Christian experience, the anointing tends to be more intense and specific. As Oswald J. Smith explains, "Thus we must distinguish between a normal Spirit-filled life, based on surrender and faith, as set forth under 'The Fullness of the Spirit,' and for which there need be no waiting, except for heart preparation, and repeated *anointings* of the Spirit which come as we tarry in prayer."[7]

The Nature of the Outpouring/Anointing

The phrase "outpouring of the Holy Spirit" is most commonly used in deeper-life literature to describe the conditions of revival. This becomes especially evident as one surveys both the writings of revivalists and the primary-source records and reports of actual revivals and awakenings. In his revision of his classic on revival, Arthur Wallis notes:

That sudden effusion of the Spirit that we call revival is one of the most powerful weapons God uses to further his kingdom plans. We should never view the outpouring of the Spirit as an end in itself, but always in the context of the on-going work of God's kingdom. It should not therefore be any surprise to find that the Bible not only encourages us to be hopeful about the ultimate success of the kingdom, but also about the prospect of coming revival.[8]

J. Edwin Orr similarly writes of revival in terms of the outpouring of the Holy Spirit. In the introduction to his trilogy on
the history of revival he notes:

> An Evangelical Awakening is a movement of the Holy Spirit
> bringing about a revival of New Testament Christianity in the
> Church of Christ and its related community. Such an awak-
> ening may change in a significant way an individual only; or
> it may affect a larger group of believers; or it may move a
> congregation, or the churches of a city or district, or the
> whole body of believers throughout a country or a continent;
> or indeed the larger body of believers throughout the world.
> The outpouring of the Spirit effects the reviving of the church,
> the awakening of the masses, and the movement of unin-
> structed peoples towards the Christian faith; the revived
> church, by many or by few, is moved to engage in evange-
> lism, in teaching, and in social action.[9]

This reference to God "pouring out His Spirit" is, in the context
of Pentecost, related to the prophecy of Joel. To understand the
biblical meaning of an outpouring of the Spirit, these two key
passages must be considered. The exact relationship between
Joel and Acts is not agreed upon among conservative theologians; nevertheless, all must agree that some relationship exists.

The outpouring of the Holy Spirit is one of several evidences
of the last days in the prophecy of Joel. Summarizing the
essential and relevant aspects of Joel's prophecy, Chester K.
Leham writes:

> Joel, one of the first writing prophets, saw in the last days the
> time when God would pour out His Spirit on all flesh. This
> would be marked by several characteristics. First, the manner
> of the Spirit's coming would be that of *a pouring out* of the
> Spirit. This metaphor becomes clear when we note that the
> psalmist *pours out* his soul and *pours out* his complaint. God
> *pours out* His wrath, His indignation, and His fury. God's
> pouring out His Spirit suggests the full gift of the Spirit.
> Second, God's Spirit would be poured out on all flesh. The *all
> flesh* stands in contrast with the few of Israel who had pos-

sessed the Spirit, such as kings, priests, prophets, and other devout individuals. The promise saw all of God's people experiencing the gift. Third, as Peter later observed, there was in Joel 2:32 the latent idea of the Spirit's coming upon all believers regardless of race. Fourth, the pouring out of the Spirit would manifest itself in prophecy, dreams, and visions. Fifth, the operation of the Spirit would lead men to call upon the name of the Lord for deliverance. Into their lives would flow all the blessing of Spirit possession.[10]

This was the passage to which Peter made reference on the day of Pentecost, in an attempt to explain the phenomena of Pentecost. The exact relation that exists between Joel's prophecy and Peter's experience is disputed among conservative Christians. Leham believes Pentecost was interpreted by Peter as the full and final fulfillment of the Joel prophecy. Explaining Pentecost as the full and final fulfillment of the Joel prophecy, Leham writes:

He testified that the things which happened on that day fulfilled Joel's prophecy. The last days had come. The pouring out of the Holy Spirit was proof of this. The gift of prophecy was no longer limited, as in the Old Testament times, to certain prophets, priests, or kings. Through the outpouring of the Spirit, prophecy was found among young men and women, as well as among the old. It reached beyond official servants to all God's people. . . . This coming of the Spirit was the fulfillment of God's promise to Christ and was the first work of the reigning Lord. The baptism with the Spirit is positive proof that Jesus is both Lord and Christ.[11]

The difficulty with Leham's view of Pentecost as the ultimate fulfillment of the Joel prophecy is twofold. First, not all the signs and conditions of the Joel prophecy were apparent on the day of Pentecost. For example, there is no record of blood, fire, pillars of smoke, a darkened sun, or a moon turning to blood on Pentecost (see Joel 2:30, 31). Further, there is no indication that a messianic kingdom that included the political liberation of

Jerusalem was at that time established in Jerusalem (see Joel 2:32). Another problem with Leham's view relates to the prospects of revival experience, that is, further outpourings of the Holy Spirit. If the Joel prophecy was fulfilled in the coming of the Holy Spirit on Pentecost, it could be argued that one should no more expect further outpourings of the Holy Spirit than one would expect further virgin births, a phenomenon attending the birth of Christ, which was also the fulfillment of prophecy.

While there are problems with seeing the events of Acts 2 as the fulfillment of a millennial prophecy, it cannot be denied that some relationship does exist. Perhaps it would be a better analogy to view Pentecost as a model of what is still to be anticipated on a much grander scale, that is, a foretaste of glory. This interprets Peter's affirmation, "But this is what was spoken by the prophet Joel" (Acts 2:16 NKJV) in the same sense as the Lord's claim, ". . . This is My body. . . . This cup is the new covenant in My blood . . ." (1 Corinthians 11:24, 25 NKJV). When Pentecost is understood in this sense, it becomes evident that the greatest outpouring of the Holy Spirit is not past but still future. Further, God's willingness to pour out His Spirit on Pentecost suggests the possibilities of yet further outpourings before the ultimate outpouring of the Spirit on the kingdom age. Most revivalist writers, therefore, tend to view Pentecost as a model or pattern by which further revivals may be recognized and evaluated. In this regard a charismatic holiness writer like Arthur Wallis and a Calvinistic Baptist writer like J. Edwin Orr are agreed. Wallis defines "Pentecost as a model outpouring of the Holy Spirit."[12] According to Orr:

> The major marks of an Evangelical Awakening are always some repetition of the Phenomena of the Acts of the Apostles, followed by the revitalizing of nominal Christians and by bringing outsiders into vital touch with the Divine Dynamic causing all such Awakenings—the Spirit of God. The surest evidence of the Divine origin of such quickening is its presentation of the evangelical message declared in the New Testament and its reenactment of the phenomena therein in the empowering of saints and the conversion of sinners.[13]

When the outpouring of the Holy Spirit is viewed from an individualistic perspective, it is called an anointing of the Holy Spirit. C. R. Vaughan emphasizes this relation'ship:

> The general grant of the Holy Spirit to renew the heart is spoken of as *an outpouring of the Spirit, and an anointing of the Spirit*. The expression is a figurative one, drawn from the practice of pouring oil on the head of one chosen to an office, or consecrated to a particular service. Oil was thus used as the official sign of setting apart to the office of king, priest, prophet, and captain of the host among the ancient Jews. It was thus figuratively transferred to the vocabulary of the gospel system in order to express different impressions made by the grant and the gifts of the Holy Spirit. The general significance of the unction of the Spirit was this general setting apart or consecration to the service of God.[14]

This experience should not be confused with the holiness idea of a once-and-for-all eradication of the sin nature. The outpouring/anointing is directed as a preparation for a specific task. In this sense the outpouring of the Spirit precedes and initiates times of revival and awakening. Individually, the anointing of the Spirit is a divine preparation for a specific act of service. The implication of this designation is that of repeated anointings. This is illustrated in type by David, who was three times anointed, once before three major periods of distinctive service. It is also an emphasis in deeper-life literature. Oswald Smith suggests, "The question is: What new anointing did I receive last week? Is my experience up-to-date? So many testify to something wonderful that occurred years ago, but their lives are so barren and dry that it is clear they long ago lost the freshness of what they received. We should be anointed again and again, a fresh anointing for each new service."[15]

The Evidences of the Outpouring/Anointing

To relate the outpouring of the Holy Spirit to a spirit of revival, common in deeper-life literature, is one thing; but specifically identifying the effect and evidence of such an outpouring/anointing individually is another matter. Few writers have chosen to address this aspect of the experience. F. B. Meyer alludes to these evidences when he suggests five tests of the fullness of the Holy Spirit:

> There are just *five tests* by which you may know that you have received this infilling. Let me give them to you.
> 1. Is the Lord Jesus Christ a living reality to you? (John 16:13, 14). How do you look at Jesus Christ?
> 2. Have you assurance that you are a child of God?
> 3. Have you victory over known sin? (Galatians 5:16–22)
> 4. Have you power in witness-bearing? (Acts 1:8)
> 5. Have you the spirit of Holy love? (Acts 2:45–47)[16]

Writing from a somewhat different perspective, Oswald Smith emphasizes four prominent evidences of the anointing of the Spirit, which in his opinion, surpass all others:

> There are four great results that follow the anointing, four evidences that can neither be disputed nor counterfeited. The first is victory over sin; the second, power in service; the third, the fruit of the Spirit; and the fourth, a burden for souls. Now I care not what else you may have received, even though visions and revelations have been yours—they fade into insignificance in the face of these tremendous results.[17]

A third opinion concerning evidences of the anointing of the Holy Spirit is that of C. R. Vaughan:

> The unction of the Spirit carries a dignity and a grace, a power and a comfort, or beauty and a universal blessedness, which can be gained from no other source, and can be matched in worth by no other value. It fills the mind with clear light, because it purges the visual energy with a "euphoria and rue" of nobler virtue than the gardens of earth ever grew. It fills the heart with holy and rejoicing affections toward God and man. It kindles hope until it rises like a column on which the sacred fires burn in imperishable brightness. It serves the will with heroic ardor. It fills the soul with intense desires,

and with staunch and unpresumptuous confidence of their fulfillment. It breathes out in prayers full of tenderness and pathetic solicitude; of faith and trustful love. It guides the conduct with a pure zeal into all the mazes of a full and loving obedience. It molds the whole character of the anointed man into a beautiful combination of serious pathos and exulting joy. It paints God on the soul.[18]

The Conditions of the Outpouring/Anointing

If the outpouring/anointing of the Holy Spirit is a legitimate postconversion experience with God that can have a positive influence on the ministry and character of the believer, then it is incumbent upon the believer to do what is necessary to get it. Again one encounters a difference of opinion in deeper-life literature. Some, like Watchman Nee, tend to emphasize a very passive role for the believer in this experience. Demonstrating this emphasis, Nee writes:

As with forgiveness, so equally with the coming upon us of the Holy Spirit, the whole question is one of faith. As soon as we see the Lord Jesus on the Cross, we know our sins are forgiven; as soon as we see the Lord Jesus on the Throne, we know the Holy Spirit has been poured out upon us. The basis upon which we receive the enduement of the Holy Spirit is not our praying and fasting and waiting, but the exaltation of Christ. Those who emphasize tarrying and hold "tarry meetings" only mislead us, for the gift is not for the "favoured few" but for all, because it is not given on the ground of what we are at all, but what Christ is. The Spirit has been poured out to prove *His* goodness and greatness, not ours. Christ has been crucified, therefore we have been forgiven; Christ has been glorified, therefore we have been endued with power from on high. It is all because of Him.[19]

Perhaps Nee's criticism of those holding an opposing view to his is somewhat unfair. Oswald Smith emphasized that the need to tarry is necessary, yet he did so emphasizing the anointing was available to all who would pay the price. While it is always difficult to accurately judge another man's motives, most would

agree Smith wrote without the intent to mislead. Addressing
the subject of receiving the anointing, he wrote:

> What is the secret of the Anointing of the Holy Spirit? Does
> God endue men in a sort of haphazard way? Has He favour-
> ites? Are some to be especially blessed irrespective of their
> qualifications and others passed over? Certainly not. God's
> difficulty is to find men who are willing to pay the price.
> There are so few who are ready to stand in the gap. Those
> who have been specially anointed of the Holy Ghost and
> whose work reads like a page out of the Acts of the Apostles,
> did not just happen to stumble on the blessing. They met
> God. And when we, too, after having counted the cost, are
> willing to pay the price, God will grant us the same endue-
> ment of power from on high. . . .
>
> And first of all I am persuaded that without an intense
> *desire and thirst* there will be no real blessing. "I will pour
> water upon him that is thirsty, and floods upon the dry
> ground" (Isa. 44:3). There must be a genuine thirst. The
> ground must realize that it is parched and dry. . . .
>
> Now the second great prerequisite is *earnest prayer*. So far as
> I have read the biographies of God's anointed men they have
> come from their knees with the power of God resting upon
> them and the fire of the Holy Spirit burning in their souls. I
> am perfectly confident that the man who does not spend
> hours alone with God will never know the anointing of the
> Holy Spirit. The world must be left outside until God alone
> fills the vision. . . .
>
> Then in the last place there will of course be an *expectant
> faith*. Everything we receive comes in response to faith. Now
> there are those who teach we are simply to "claim" from God,
> rise believing we have received, and pray no more. That may
> work sometimes for instantaneous faith is frequently given.
> But such can also be presumptuous faith which in reality is
> not faith at all. Receiving by faith means getting an answer.
> Taking by faith does not mean going without by faith. Real
> faith always brings a real experience. It is our privilege to
> tarry before the Lord until the deepest longings and desires of
> our heart are satisfied.[20]

The key to the reception of the blessing of God, particularly as it relates to the experience of revival, is the humbling of the believer. "For thus says the High and Lofty One Who inhabits eternity, whose name is Holy: 'I dwell in the high and holy place, with him who has a contrite and humble spirit, To revive the spirit of the humble, And to revive the heart of the contrite ones' " (Isaiah 57:15 NKJV). Ed Hindson notes this foundational aspect to the revival experience when he writes:

> Whenever Christ's people are truly humble before Him, whenever they deeply feel their own emptiness, whenever they are willing to be used as mere instruments in the hand of Almighty God, then you will find the outpouring of God's richest blessings. God is a jealous God. He will not share His glory with any man. Revival is not the result of some evangelist's clever statements, or invitation methods; it is not the result of pizza nights, "youth nights," and "junior nights." It is the result of God moving on the lives of those in need of His blessing. Revival has always come by the power of God, it will always come by the power of God, and it will come only by the power of God![21]

— 10 —

THE EXPERIENCE
OF SEEKING
AND SURRENDER

Obviously seeking God is *not* merely seeking an experience for experience' sake. To seek God is to hunger and thirst after knowledge, love, and fellowship. Those who seek after God: want to know God, want to know what God wants them to do in a specific situation, want to draw closer to God, or want power to do God's will. It is similar to a young man's seeking to be with the girl he loves, so he can know her, love her, and be loved in return.

There are many abuses surrounding the doctrine of seeking God. Some monks have prayed in the snow, thinking that physical denial or abuse would lead them to know God or be blessed by God. Some have spent years in solitude in a monastery cell or alone on a pole, as Simeon Stylites.

When I first went to Bible college, I did some foolish things in seeking God. In our dormitory the lights were turned out at 10:30, and we were to be in our beds. They also turned off the heat until the following morning. In my youthful sincerity, I felt I had to kneel by my bed to pray. But with only underwear on, it only took about five minutes of praying before my guilt gave way to common sense, and I would get under the covers and continue to pray. As I got warmer, my guilt would also crowd in to my prayers. I'd say something like this, *If you love Jesus, you would pray in the cold. . . . Any sacrifice for the Lord is worth it, even freezing.*

I would then get out onto my prayer rug beside my bed and again begin praying. Then I'd get cold and ultimately get back under the covers to pray. Some evenings I would get in and out of bed three or four times. This enthusiastic, but nonbiblical, practice continued for a couple of months. No event changed my practice, just a growing understanding of how to seek God.

While the deeper Christian life is described in various terms (*the abiding life, the victorious life,* and so on), it is ultimately a life characterized by seeking God and walking with Him. It is a life lived in relationship to God, and at the heart of this relationship is the believer's seeking God or surrender to God. Alexander MacLaren defined the essential nature of the Christian life: "The meaning of being a Christian is that in response for the gift of a whole Christ I give my whole self to Him."[1] Charles Hadden Spurgeon thought of the Christian life in terms of surrender to the will of God, and he questioned, "If a Christian can by possibility be saved while he conforms to this world, at any rate it must be so as by fire. Such a bare salvation is almost as much to be dreaded as desired."[2] In an evangelistic letter, Henry Scougal explained:

> Oh, the happiness of those souls that have broken the fetters of self-love, and disentangled their affection from every narrow and particular good; whose undertakings are enlightened by the Holy Spirit, and their wills enlarged to the extent of thine; who love thee above all things, and all mankind for thy sake! I am persuaded, O God! I am persuaded that I can never be happy, till my carnal and corrupt affections be mortified, and the pride and vanity of my spirit be subdued, and till I come seriously to despise the world and think nothing of myself.[3]

Although this idea of surrender of the will is fundamental to the nature of the Christian life, it is a concept that is verbalized much more easily than it is realized. Terms such as *revival*, *renewal*, and *rededication* exist in the Christian vocabulary to illustrate the difficulty with which this principle is applied. The constant struggle of the believer with self and personal ambition means there tend to be times when the will is not surrendered to God and thus must be revived, renewed, rededicated, recommitted, and so on. Andrew Murray explained his choice of a title for one of his books, noting:

In Scotland, I was in a company where we were talking about the condition of Christ's Church, and what the great need of the Church and believers is; and there was in our company a godly worker who has much to do in training workers, and I asked him what he would say was the great need of the Church, and the message that ought to be preached. He answered very quietly and simply and determinedly: *"Absolute surrender to God is the one thing."* The words struck me as never before. And that man began to tell how, in the workers with whom he had to deal, he finds that if they are sound on that point, even though they be backward, they are willing to be taught and helped, and they always improve; whereas, others who are not sound there very often go back and leave the work. The condition for obtaining God's full blessing is *absolute surrender* to Him.[4]

The Nature of Surrender

The terms *seeking* and *surrender* go hand in hand. When a Christian seeks God, it is a *process*; when he surrenders, it is the *product*. Seeking God is an action, described by a verb; the result is when the Christian has surrendered himself to God, hence it is a noun. A Christian does not automatically surrender, because he may not know what to surrender, how to surrender, or he may not have the ability to surrender. He just cannot give up his "sin" or "habit," or he cannot deny the flesh. So he prays, which is seeking God. The Christian seeks God's help to surrender, or he seeks a hidden sin or hidden Bible truth that will help him surrender. Seeking God usually comes from surrendering to Him. However, seeking and surrendering usually hopscotch. Seeking leads to surrender, which results in a deeper seeking that leads to a deeper level of surrender.

The biblical call to surrender is proclaimed throughout the pages of Scripture, but perhaps nowhere is it clearer than Romans 12:1, 2. Here the apostle concludes a largely theological treatise by calling upon the reader to make practical application by presenting himself "a living sacrifice." The sacrifice of his life is the same as surrendering to God.

I beseech you therefore, brethren, by the mercies of God, that you present your bodies a living sacrifice, holy, acceptable to God, which is your reasonable service. And do not be conformed to this world, but be transformed by the renewing of your mind, that you may prove what is that good and acceptable and perfect will of God.

Romans 12:1, 2 NKJV

The apostle used the term "beseech," *parakalo*, in his appeal to surrender, rather than another term, which might have had a greater degree of authority inherent in it. The term *beseech*, however, is an appeal to a sentiment already existing in the heart. It calls for an emotional response. In Romans 12:1 it occurs alongside "present," *parastesai*, which in contrast is a technical term referring to the presentation of a sacrificial animal to God (*compare* Luke 2:22). The term is here found in the aorist tense, suggesting the idea that the brethren should present themselves to God once and for all.

There are two aspects of surrendering to God. There is the initial surrender (once and for all). It is the surrender to the ownership of God. The second is a daily surrender for guidance. We may compare this to driving a car to a stop light. The once and for all surrender is the driver's attitude; he has made up his mind to obey all stop signs. Once and for all he will stop at all red lights. He has surrendered to the authority of the laws. The daily surrender is illustrated when he approaches a stop sign. He stops. He makes a daily submission to the authority of the stop sign because he made a once-and-for-all submission. The Christian once and for all surrenders to the authority of Christ. He will not lie. When the temptation to lie faces him, he doesn't debate the pragmatics of what a lie will do for him. He makes a daily submission to the authority of Christ. He tells the truth. Some have likened this to a big YES (once and for all surrender) and a little yes (daily surrender).

Oswald Chambers observed that a Christian's surrender is both external and internal.

Surrender is not the surrender of the external life, but of the will; when that is done, all is done. There are very few crises in life; the great crisis is the surrender of the will. God never crushes a man's will into surrender, He never beseeches him, He waits until the man yields up his will to Him. That battle never needs to be re-fought.[5]

Some commentators have stumbled over the apostle's use of the term "body" here, but there is no reason to believe he meant anything more than the presentation of the entire person. As James M. Stifler notes, " 'Bodies' is the comprehensive term for the whole man, body, soul, and spirit (I Thess. 5: 23). It is equivalent to 'yourselves,' but better suited than the latter word to Paul's sacrificial idea."[6] Alva J. McClain apparently agreed and taught:

> The body at the present time, is the instrument of the soul and the spirit, and God gets no service except it be manifested through the body: the hands, the feet, the mouth, the tongue. Therefore, he speaks of the body and that includes the soul and spirit, everything, the whole man. In fact the word *body* is a way of describing an organism in its entirety.[7]

The act of presenting oneself to God is foundational to the Keswick view of sanctification. This assumes a continual growth in grace after a postconversion crisis in which the will or self is definitely and completely surrendered or yielded to God. This is the means whereby the believer enters into the deeper Christian life. As Watchman Nee explains:

> Presenting myself to God implies a recognition that I am altogether His. This giving of myself is a definite thing, just as definite as reckoning. There must be a day in my life when I pass out of my own hands into His, and from that day forward I belong to Him and no longer to myself. That does not mean that I consecrate myself to be a preacher or a missionary. . . . Then to what are we to be consecrated? Not to Christian work, but *to the will of God, to be and to do whatever He requires*. . . . My giving of myself to the Lord must be an initial fundamental act. Then, day by day, I must go on giving to him, not finding fault with His use of me, but accepting

with praise even what the flesh finds hard. That way lies true enrichment. I am the Lord's, and now no longer reckon myself to be my own but acknowledge in everything His ownership and authority. That is the attitude God delights in, and to maintain it is true consecration. I do not consecrate myself to be a missionary or a preacher; I consecrate myself to God to do His will where I am, be it in school, office or kitchen or wherever He may, in His wisdom, send me. Whatever He ordains for me is sure to be the very best, for nothing but good can come to those who are wholly His.[8]

The surrender the apostle calls for here is none other than the surrender of the will. In many respects, the sacrifices of wealth or influence might be easier for some to offer than to surrender to the will of God. S. D. Gordon understood the severity of this call to surrender when he wrote:

The word will is one of the strongest in our language. A man's will is the imperial part of him. It is the autocrat upon the throne; the judge upon the bench of final appeal. Jesus is getting down to the root of matters here. He is appealing to the highest authority. No mere passing sentiment is this. Not attending a meeting and being swept along with the crowd by the hour's influence. But a *fixed purpose*, calmly, resolutely settled upon, rooted away down deep in the very vitals of the will to know Jesus absolutely, no matter what it may cost or where it may cut. I wonder how many of us would form such a purpose, to follow Jesus *blindly*, utterly regardless of what it might be found to mean as the days come and go?[9]

Total surrender or absolute surrender is total to the Christian, but relative to God. The Christian cannot experience an entire sanctification that makes him unable to sin, nor can he have no sin nature. Sin is so deceitful that some, who think they live without sin, are guilty of spiritual pride or hypocrisy. Since there is no perfect product (sinless living), there is no perfect process (absolute surrender).

The Christian dedicates his life as completely as possible, but it is not perfect. He may search out secret sin and yield it to God. Even in the act of complete surrender, he has some hidden sin that is unknown to him. His level of surrender moves him closer to God. He rejoices in his dedication and new depth of fellowship with God, but he is not sinlessly perfect, nor is his act of surrender perfect. Only after death or the rapture will he be sinless, a state also called glorification.

The image Paul used in calling for this surrender of will is that of a living sacrifice. His imagery naturally causes one to think in terms of the sacrificial system of Israel, particularly since this term is used in the context of a major discourse on Israel (Romans 9–11). Of the five principal sacrifices of the Levitical system, the whole burnt offering is most likely the context in which this challenge should be understood. As F. Godet observes:

> The practical part which we are now beginning corresponds to the second kind of sacrifice, which was the symbol of consecration after pardon had been received (the holocaust, in which the victim was entirely burned), and the communion reestablished between Jehovah and the believer (the peace offering, followed by a feast in the court of the temple). The sacrifice of expiation offered by God in the person of His Son should now find its response in the believer in the sacrifice of complete consecration and intimate communion.[10]

In the context of the whole burnt offering, several significant principles illustrate the nature of this surrender to God. First, it is a call to sacrifice that which is most prized. The whole burnt offering was to be "a male without blemish" (Leviticus 1:3, 10). While female animals were acceptable for some sacrifices, such was not the case in this offering. This principle is particularly evident when God called Abraham to offer a whole burnt offering, saying, " 'Take now your son, your only son Isaac, whom you love, and go to the land of Moriah, and offer him there as a burnt offering on one of the mountains of which I shall tell you' " (Genesis 22:2 NKJV).

Second, the "faith" nature of this sacrifice is seen in the practice of laying on of hands (Leviticus 1:4). The Hebrew word translated "put" here implies the idea of applying pressure, that is, leaning. This illustrates faith. To put one's hands on the lamb was an act of faith to identify with it. Third, this act was usually accompanied by the practice of confessing sin to God. Confession was part of the offerer's identification with the sacrifice. So also in surrendering to God there must be both a confession of sin and expression of faith in yielding.

Fourth, the unique feature of the whole burnt offering was that it was completely consumed on the altar. The blood (life) of the animal was literally splashed around the altar. The hide was removed, exposing any inner imperfections. Piece by piece the animal was taken to the altar and consumed by the fire, typical of the judgment of God. The actual act of sacrificing was in all probability an undesirable act, but the ultimate result was "a sweet aroma to the Lord" (Leviticus 1:9, 13, 17 NKJV). Similarly, Christians must surrender everything to God at the moment of giving themselves to God. Believers often testify of the struggle in surrendering to God, but the end result is a sacrifice that is sweetness to God and them.

The Intensity of Absolute Surrender

Because of their objection to the way certain Pentecostal and holiness groups emphasize "tarrying" and "seeking," some conservative Christians deny the biblical doctrine of seeking God both in faith and practice. Throughout the Scriptures, however, numerous commands, promises, and illustrations instruct a Christian to seek God. To neglect or ignore this doctrine is to neglect and ignore an important part of the revelation of God.

First, we must clearly identify the meaning of "seeking God." To seek God means more than searching after a hidden God, because God is in all places present to reveal Himself to those who have eyes of faith to behold Him. Neither can the phrase "seeking God" be passed off as a meaningless idiomatic expression. "Seeking God" is the sincere attempt to reestablish deep communion and fellowship with God through intense prayer, concentrated Bible study, and unswerving obedience to the revelation of God.

Conditions for Seeking God. Several Scriptures identify the need to prepare your heart to seek God (*see* 2 Chronicles 19:3). Chart 16 identifies several conditions of the heart named as prerequisite to seeking God in the Bible.

CHART 16

CONDITIONS FOR SEEKING GOD
Repentance (Jeremiah 26:19)
Brokenness (Jeremiah 50:4)
Separation (Ezra 6:21)
Humility (2 Chronicles 7:14; 33:12)
Desire (Psalms 119:10)
Faith (Romans 9:32)
Diligence (Hebrews 11:6)
Unity (Jeremiah 50:4)
Rejoicing (1 Chronicles 16:10)
Fear of the Lord (Hosea 3:5)
Meekness (Zephaniah 2:3)

Barriers to Seeking God. The Bible suggests many reasons why people do not seek God. Some do not know how, do not have an example of others seeking God, or have never heard about it. Beyond these reasons, there are the excuses given why people do not seek God (*see* chart 17).

CHART 17

BARRIERS TO SEEKING GOD
Sin (Acts 17:30; Psalms 119:155)
Pride (Psalms 10:4; Hosea 7:10)
Ignorance (Romans 3:11; Acts 17:30)
Security (Isaiah 31:1)
Faithlessness (Romans 9:32)
Failure to confess sin (Hosea 5:15)
Wrong motives (*see* Acts 8:18–24)

Seekers After God. Seeking after God is an experience of one who has already established a relationship with God by faith.

The idea of "seeking God for salvation" is totally contrary to the nature of salvation, that is, "the gift of God" (Ephesians 2:8). However, when the word *seeking* is used with salvation, it does not mean to "pray through" or to pray until you convince God to save you. The word "seeking" with salvation means to ask, to receive, or to believe. Paul observed the unsaved, noting, ". . . There is none who seeks after God" (Romans 3:11 NKJV). The Old Testament cites at least one illustration of pagans who tried to join the Jews in Jerusalem, presumably to seek God, but they were forbidden by Zerubbabel (Ezra 4:2, 3). This does not apply to salvation but to pagans who wanted to come to Jerusalem for commercial purposes.

CHART 18

SEEKERS AFTER GOD	
KINGS	1. David (2 Samuel 12:16) 2. Asa (2 Chronicles 14:7) 3. Jehosophat (2 Chronicles 17:4) 4. Uzziah (2 Chronicles 26:5) 5. Jehoahaz (2 Kings 13:4) 6. Hezekiah (2 Chronicles 31:21) 7. Josiah (2 Chronicles 34:3)
PROPHETS	1. Moses (Deuteronomy 3:23) 2. Man of God (1 Kings 13:6) 3. Daniel (Daniel 9:3)
APOSTLES	1. Paul (2 Corinthians 12:7, 8)
MY PEOPLE CALLED BY MY NAME	1. Israel (Exodus 33:7) 2. Residue (Acts 15:7)

Strategy for Seeking God. The Scriptures record no directions how to seek God, yet their repeated examples suggest various aspects of a biblical strategy before, during, and after the effort of seeking God. These principles are given in this section, yet seeking God is an emotional experience. There is no rational list of directions on how to kiss a girl, because a kiss is an expression of the heart and reflects a relationship. A kiss is similar to seeking God. To seek God, a person must first love God and want to please Him. Second, a person who loves another does not violate the rights of the one he loves. So in seeking God, we do not violate God's personhood, but we reverence Him and obey Him. We cannot seek God contrary to Scripture. A boy cannot express his love to a girl and embarrass her or constantly displease her. He must seek to please her; just so the one seeking God must obey the Scriptures to please God.

Chart 19 gives some Old Testament examples of how those who loved God and wanted to please Him sought Him and acted out their faith. Today, the same principles have general applications for us, though we should not seek to slavishly follow every point.

CHART 19

STRATEGY FOR SEEKING GOD	
PREPARATION	Commitment to seek God expressed by: 1. Covenant (2 Chronicles 15:12) 2. Expression of desire (Psalms 119:10) 3. Willingness to continue (1 Chronicles 16:10) 4. Vow (2 Chronicles 15:14)
PROCESS	1. Study of Scripture (Psalms 119:94) 2. Prayer (Exodus 32:11; Ezra 8:23) 3. Supplications (Daniel 9:3) 4. Fasting (2 Samuel 12:16) 5. Repentance (Jeremiah 26:19) 6. Obedience to Scripture (Ezra 7:10)
PRODUCT	1. Building of the temple (1 Chronicles 22:19) 2. Keeping the Passover (2 Chronicles 30:18, 19) 3. Teaching of the Law (Ezra 7:10)

The Implications of Seeking and Surrender

Ironically the result, surrendering to the will of God, comes from seeking God. Usually this results from a struggle with indwelling sin. The once-and-for-all surrender is followed by a daily transformation and renewing of one's mind (Romans 12:2). The practical strategy by which this is realized is found in four key verbs in Romans 6. Watchman Nee observed these four steps:

> As we study Chapters 6, 7, and 8 of Romans we shall discover that the conditions of living the normal Christian life are fourfold. They are (a) Knowing, (b) Reckoning, (c) Presenting ourselves to God, and (d) Walking in the Spirit, and they are set forth in that order. If we would live that life we shall have to take all four steps; not one or two or three, but all four. As we study each of them we shall trust the Lord by His Holy Spirit to illumine our understanding; and we shall seek His help now to take the first big step forward.[11]

Know. Three times Paul used the verb *know* to remind these Christians to recognize what they knew was true (Romans 6:3, 6, 9). He realized our actions usually result from sinful attitudes, and they can only be changed when they are built on an accurate intellectual basis. The key truth Paul wanted the Romans to know was their identification with Christ. "Or do you not know that as many of us as were baptized into Christ Jesus were baptized into His death?" (Romans 6:3 NKJV). When a Christian knows he was crucified with Christ, he should have victory over sin. "Knowing this, that our old man *has been* crucified with him" (*see* Romans 6:6). If we know the old man has received the death penalty on the cross, we do not have to allow Satan to tempt and condemn us. Knowledge of our cocrucifixion with Christ is the basis of our victory over sin.

At the heart of this passage Paul reminded the Christian he has been "united together" (Romans 6:5) with Christ in death. This phrase describes one of fifteen "togetherness" expressions that describe the believer's union with Christ (*see* chart 10). In each occurrence, when we know we are identified with Christ in the heavenlies, it becomes the basis for our daily victory.

Reckon. The second word Paul used is *reckon,* which carries the idea of "be counting on" or "relying upon." "Likewise you also, reckon yourselves to be dead indeed to sin, but alive to God in Christ Jesus our Lord" (Romans 6:11 NKJV). Part of the key to harmonizing our exalted standing in heaven with our state on earth is to rely upon what we know to be true and to act accordingly.

Present. The third important word is *present.* Based on what we know and how we have reckoned, we should surrender our lives on this earth to the designs of heaven. ". . . Present yourselves to God as being alive from the dead, and your members as instruments of righteousness to God" (Romans 6:13 NKJV). Yieldedness involves giving God the "right of way" to every aspect of our lives. It is impossible for a Christian desiring to serve God consistently to divide the sacred and secular in his life.

Obey. To obey Jesus Christ is to recognize His lordship in our lives. The one who is the Lord of our lives is the one we obey (Romans 6:16, 17). When a Christian refuses to do the will of God, he is denying the lordship of Christ in that area of his life.

The moment we are saved, we are risen with Christ into a new position and a new standing with God. But we still have human natures with sinful desires. Many times our walk with God will be inconsistent with our standing before God, yet as we apply these four verbs daily, those inconsistencies will decline in number. As we grow in our Christian walk, we begin to act more like Jesus.

— 11 —

THE EXPERIENCE
OF FAITH

A pastor in Florida took a step of faith and bought forty acres of ground to develop a complete Christian retirement city; he issued $4 million in church bonds. I wrote a lengthy story of the project in a Christian periodical. The venture failed, and everyone lost his money. A retired woman had put all her savings in the church bonds; all she had left was Social Security. Does everyone who says he is taking a step of faith have the same amount of faith? Can a person claim to be living by faith, yet be wrong?

A married student at a Christian college decided to live by faith; he refused to get a job. He often went to the altar to pray and seek God. Some money came in, but not enough to support a wife and two children. The family often went without food and did not have adequate clothes. He made several statements of faith in confidence that God would send him money. Most of the deadlines he set came and went without the miraculous supply of money he said would come. When he was almost out of fuel oil, he prayed into the night for God to intervene. He told me he was confident that God would supply heat for his family, right up to the moment he heard his furnace suck in air and stop. That crisis crushed him.

The next day he shared how God had failed him. I picked up the phone, called the pastor in the church who handled the benevolent fund, and the man had oil in his furnace within two hours. Also, several bags of groceries arrived on his kitchen table, from the church. It was not right for the family to suffer because this man misunderstood faith. His amount of faith was small, the object of his faith was wrong, and the expression of his faith was flawed. Later, he got a job and learned something more about faith. Living by faith is not just trusting God for groceries, although a few, such as George Mueller, have been able to do it. Living by faith means affirming the principles of Scripture. The man who works for wages can live by faith. Living by faith is not a mystical experience shrouded by the unknown; it is following the objective principles of the Word of God.

Chapter 2 examined six categories of faith. Each of these avenues of faith has a different purpose and result in life.

CHART 20

CATEGORIES OF FAITH
Doctrinal faith
Saving faith
Justifying faith
Indwelling faith
Living by faith
The gift of faith

Many Christians live by faith, but not all have the same amount of faith. On a scale of one to ten, it is possible for some Christians to have weak faith and only have the strength of a one or two in expressing their faith. Others have deep confidence in God and live at an eight or nine in faith.

Also there are many expressions of Christian experience, from Ex–1 to Ex–8. All these people can live by faith. They may understand their faith differently, and they may express it differently, but all faith has the same object, that is, the Lord Jesus Christ.

Because of the diversity of faith and its various expressions, there will be some failure or outward appearance of failure. But with the possibility of failure you also have the prospect of success. It is possible to walk by faith and move mountains by faith.

Indwelling Faith

As I have already implied above, the Scriptures use the word *faith* in several contexts, referring to its various aspects (*see* chart

20). Apparently the disciples did not know how to live by faith. Jesus commanded, "Have faith in God" (Mark 11:22). If someone asked you how to live by faith, what would you tell him? The King James translation obscures what Jesus might have meant. The original Greek reads *echete pistin theou* which is translated, "Have [the] faith of God." The secret of spiritual power was not their faith, but possessing the faith of God in them—indwelling faith.

One of the foundational verses in the Old Testament for faith is "the just shall live by his faith" (Habakkuk 2:4). Note this faith refers to His (God's) faith, not men's faith. God is faithful to enable His children to live for Him. This is one aspect of what has been called "the exchanged life" (*see* Isaiah 40:31).

Indwelling faith is someone else's faith at work for us. We cease all efforts to please God; we give up even our natural faith and let the faith of the Son of God work for us, as Paul noted, "knowing that a man is not justified by the works of the law but by faith in Jesus Christ . . ." (Galatians 2:16 NKJV). This means that the faith of Jesus Christ must be planted in our hearts—that is, indwelling faith. Later in the same chapter he repeats the same point but applies this power to sanctifying faith, ". . . I live by faith in the Son of God, who loved me and gave Himself for me" (Galatians 2:20 NKJV). The apostle is teaching that success in his Christian life was the result of the indwelling faith of Jesus Christ.

Therefore, faith does not spring from our hearts. Faith is not even natural faith helped along, dressed up for God, or given a new object—God Himself. Biblical faith is the indwelling of Christ's faith in our hearts; it is the experience of the deeper Christian life (*Ex–2*).

When Peter confessed that Jesus was " '. . . the Christ, the Son of the living God,' " Jesus responded, " '. . . Flesh and blood has not revealed this to you, but My Father who is in heaven' " (Matthew 16:16, 17 NKJV). Archibald Thomas Robertson interprets this as an assistance from the Father, aiding Peter's spiritual insight. "The Father had helped Peter get this spiritual insight into the Master's Person and Work."[1] Dispensational writer A. C. Gaebelein writes, "Flesh and blood could not produce such a revelation and such faith, it was the work of the Father."[2] On these words of Christ, Matthew Henry observes, "The revealing of Christ to us and in us is a distinguishing token of God's good will, and a firm foundation of true happiness; and blessed are they that are thus highly favoured."[3] Another expression in Scripture describing indwelling faith as a ministry of the Holy Spirit is the witness or testimony of the Spirit. According to Zacharius Ursinus:

> The most essential "evidence" or the "certainty of the Scriptures" is the testimony of the Holy Spirit. This testimony is unique, proper only to those reborn by the Spirit of Christ and known only to them. And it has such power that it not only attests and seals abundantly in our souls the truth of the prophetic and apostolic doctrine, but also effectually bends and moves our hearts to embrace and follow it.[4]

Apart from this illuminating ministry of the Holy Spirit, it would be impossible for man to know God. A. W. Tozer summarizes this truth:

> Man by reason cannot know God; he can only *know about God*. Through the light of reason certain important facts about God may be discovered. . . . Through the light of nature man's moral reason may be enlightened, but the deeper mysteries of God remain hidden to him until he has received illumination from above. . . . When the Spirit illuminates the heart, then a part of him sees which never saw before; part of him knows which never knew before, and that with a kind of knowing which the most acute thinker cannot imitate. He knows now in a deep and authoritative way, and what he knows needs no reasoned proof. His experience of knowing is above reason, immediate, perfectly convincing and inwardly satisfying.[5]

The importance of this "causing to see" ministry of the Holy Spirit is perhaps best understood in the historical context in which it was first clearly systematized. It is generally acknowledged that the witness of the Spirit was a doctrinal emphasis of all the Reformers generally, though Calvin is credited with the

systematizing of the doctrine of *testimonium* as part of his pro-
logomena. The conditions in Europe at that time were significant factors in both motivating the development and clarifying
the nature of this doctrine. Bernard Ramm suggests:

> In developing his doctrine of *testimonium* Calvin was faced
> with three alternative theories. (1) Christianity certainly was
> explained by Romanism as the gift of the infallible Church to
> the believing Catholic. (2) The enthusiasts, or fanatics, found
> their certainty of faith in an immediate revelation of the Holy
> Spirit, a revelation which was not bound to the contents of
> Scripture. (3) And some apologists were asserting that they
> could demonstrate the truthfulness of the Christian faith by
> purely rational evidence. Calvin was unhappy with all three
> theories, and developed his doctrine of the *testimonium* in
> opposition to each of them.[6]

The doctrine of *testimonium* is that the Holy Spirit witnesses to
the believer through the Word of God. The Christian can have
no knowledge of God apart from Scriptures.

Throughout his first general epistle, the Apostle John refers
to the special knowledge, *gnosis*, of a Christian, using the same
form of that term at least twenty-six times. Part of this emphasis
was no doubt due to the nature of this epistle as an apologetic
against gnosticism. Commenting on John's first usage of the
term in the epistle, Archibald Thomas Robertson states,
" 'Know that we have come to know and still know him,'
egnokamen the perfect active indicative of *ginosko*. The Gnostics
boasted of their superior knowledge of Christ, and John here
challenges their boast by an appeal to experimental knowledge
of Christ which is shown by keeping his (*autou*, Christ's)
commandments."[7]

Charles J. Rolls sees the significance of the expression beyond
a mere reference to gnosticism and suggests it refers to an
"intuitive knowledge" possessed by the Christian. Summarizing the nature and content of that knowledge, he writes:

> *CERTAIN KNOWLEDGE* (We know intuitively—by the in-
> stincts of our new nature).

Seven glorious facts of which none doubt.

1. Our *Prospect*. "We know" (what lies before us). "That, if He shall be manifested, we shall be like Him, for we shall see Him as He is." (Ch. 3, ver. 2).
2. Our *Position*. (Where we are). "That we have passed out of death into life, because we love the brethren." (Ch. 3, ver. 14).
3. Our *Prerogative*. "That He heareth us, whatsoever we ask." (Ch. 5, vers. 14, 15).
4. Our *Power in Prayer*. "That we have the petitions which we have asked of Him." (Ch. 5, ver. 15).
5. Our *Preservation*. "That whosoever is begotten of God sinneth not but He that was begotten of God keepeth him, and the evil one toucheth him not." (Ch. 5, ver. 18).
6. Our *Privilege*. "That we are of God . . . and the whole world lieth in the evil one." (Ch. 5, ver. 19).
7. Our *Portion*. "That the Son of God is come and hath given us an understanding that we know Him that is true." (Ch. 5, ver. 20).[8]

Faith Is More Than a Leap in the Dark

Faith is evident when it is expressed or confessed, ". . . I believed, and therefore have I spoken . . ." (2 Corinthians 4:13). Inward faith cannot be separated from our outward speech. The Lord does not give faith so that we might cherish it like a souvenir on a coffee table. Faith must be expressed in our outward experiences, and it grows as faith is properly acted upon.

I have interviewed many of the pastors who have built the largest churches in the world. I have studied their articles and sermons on faith. I consider them to be men of faith. When they have said publicly what they were going to do for God, their public statements were not egotistical bragging but rather an expression of their confidence in God. They have stepped out in faith in words and actions.

Faith takes many forms, but perhaps the greatest kind is evidenced by a confidence in God so deep that one not only knows he will get the thing for which he trusts, but he publicly tells others what he expects God to do. Faith expression in-

volves the total commitment of the person to God and to a task.
That person has confidence that God will do what He says in
His Word. The old farmer was wrong when he said, "Faith is
believing what ain't so." Faith is never a leap into the dark.
Rather, faith is a leap into the light. When we move by faith, we
know where we are stepping, because we are walking in the
light (by the principles) of the Word of God.

A faith expression must always agree with the principles of
the written Word. Since the Word of God gives confidence,
those who base their ministry upon the Bible will minister in
confidence.

Faith expression is not human faith directed toward God but
a supernatural ability of God whereby He plants in the human
heart the ability to trust Him for marvelous results. The Bible
teaches that faith expression increases the believer from weak
faith into strong faith. The faith of Abraham is described as
". . . not being weak . . ." (Romans 4:19 NKJV). He was ap-
proaching one hundred years of age, and both he and Sarah,
age ninety, were past the time of having children. Though
Abraham had failed in his faith on other occasions, in this
promise, Abraham did not stagger. The Bible says, "He . . .
was strengthened in faith . . ." (Romans 4:20 NKJV). It is possible
for a person to grow from "weak faith" to "strong faith." Evidently God gave Abraham occasions to trust Him. These experiences enabled Abraham to be led out of Ur and later into the
promised land, by faith.

A Christian can go from victory to victory, so our faith may
grow to the place where we see it accomplished. This is growing from faith expression to faith event. No man becomes the
heavyweight champion of the world unless he is continuously
victorious. He must go from victory to victory, until he gets the
ultimate prize.

Principles of Developing Greater Faith

We should not be discouraged if our faith is weak. Faith is not
set in concrete. It can grow. Many years ago I added the word
faith to the top of my prayer list and prayed fervently for God to
give me faith. I wanted to be a man of faith. My prayers were

not answered immediately. One cannot get faith by just praying for it. But my faith began to grow as I began to learn and apply the principles of growing and maturing faith. I had to act on what I was learning.

Paul wrote that we should go from initial faith, which saves us, to greater faith, by which we live. The apostle described this step as "... from faith to faith ..." (Romans 1:17). The experience of faith is simple, yet it appears difficult because living by faith flies in the face of those who want to be self-dependent.

How do we grow from weak faith to strong faith? We cannot strive for faith, nor can we work it up in the flesh. Getting faith is not like straining to pick up grocery bags. Even sincerity will not get more faith. We cannot stir up faith. Faith comes from without, and sometimes the less energy we expend, the more faith we have. It comes through yieldedness to God, who gives us faith. The following principles tell how we can encourage our faith to grow.

We Grow Faith Through the Word of God. As we make the Word of God the controlling principle of our lives, we begin to grow in faith. This growth does not come by simply acquiring biblical facts, but when the Word of God takes us to Jesus Christ, it takes us to faith (John 1:1, 14; 6:63; Revelation 19:13). The more the Word of God indwells and controls us, the more we are controlled by Jesus Christ. Then we have "the faith of Christ" (Galatians 2:16, 20). The more of His faith we get, the more we grow in our faith.

We Grow Faith Through Seeking. Today the practice of "seeking" the Lord is not emphasized. Maybe it is because we live in a day of "instant everything." We have fast food and instant replays. People think they can get immediate knowledge from television, seminars, or newspapers. As a result, we do not see many people seeking knowledge about God or seeking the Lord.

But it is biblical to search for God. "When You said, 'Seek My face,' My heart said to You, 'Your face, Lord, I will seek' " (Psalms 27:8 NKJV).

Our faith will grow as we seek God, because when the soul seeks God, it gets a clearer view of its own sinful desires. As a man seeks God, he identifies his selfish desires as separate from God's desires. Then he searches for a better relationship with his Saviour. He gets more than a theoretical understanding of God. He comes to know God on an experiential level. As he grows in faith, he asks, "Is my all on the altar?"

When we bring our sins to the cross, we are growing in faith. We Grow Faith Through the Blood. God constantly cleanses the Christian through the blood of Christ. "But if we walk in the light as He is in the light, . . . the blood of Jesus Christ His Son cleanses us from all sin" (1 John 1:7 NKJV).

Our position in heaven is perfect, but on earth we have sinful desires and sinful practices. When this happens, we must recognize sin each time it occurs and confess it for cleansing and restoration to fellowship with God. "If we confess our sins, He is faithful and just to forgive us our sins and to cleanse us from all unrighteousness" (1 John 1:9 NKJV).

Sometimes confession requires apologies and restitution. Not only must we deal with sin between us and God, we must deal with sin that hinders our fellowship with other Christians. Since confession of sin is a constant experience, so the Christian will constantly grow in his faith as he constantly relies upon the Lord.

We Grow Faith by Denying Self. It is difficult to tell who exercises faith and who deceives himself. When it comes to living by faith, some people actually experience communion with God day by day; they live by faith. Others deceive themselves, thinking they are living by faith, when they are simply feeding off the atmosphere of their church. As in self-hypnosis, their faith is perceptual, not real. These people usually give up when facing problems or failure.

Some have self-hypnotized faith. They have heard the expression "let go and let God." They think faith is a leap in the dark. Since they desire God, they leap for it. Out of desperation or a hope that lightning may strike, they live a charade. They claim to live by faith.

Faith is never blind—at least biblical faith is not blind. God doesn't bless ignorance. Since faith is grounded in the Bible and is directed by the Holy Spirit, a believer must live according to

Scripture, because faith will never go contrary to the nature of God or the principles by which God works. Blind faith may be contrary to the Word. There will be occasions when we will not understand, and it may seem we are exercising "blind faith." Paul described it, "For we walk by faith, not by sight" (2 Corinthians 5:7). But we should not call it "blind faith," because that is misleading. We look into the Bible to see biblical principles. That is biblical faith that is blinded to the world.

We Grow Faith by Surrendering. Those who live the deeper Christian life are constantly surrendered to the lordship of the Lord Jesus Christ. We do this initially when we are saved. But there are also subsequent times when we surrender to Christ— each time a crisis or problem arises.

When we were first saved, the act of surrender was called repentance. After we were saved, the act of surrender is called consecration, dedication, or yieldedness. In this act, the Christian abandons acts of sin and his commitment to future sins. In that act of surrender, he takes on the strength of the Lord Jesus Christ.

I'm not talking about sinless perfection or total eradication. The act of surrender means simply allowing the Lord to rule our lives. This act of yielding is in response to the Bible: "I beseech you therefore, brethren, by the mercies of God, that you present your bodies a living sacrifice, holy, acceptable to God, which is your reasonable service" (Romans 12:1 NKJV).

Here it should be noted that the deeper Christian life is not asceticism or denial of the physical. Faith is not a negative denial of self, but a positive identification with the Lord Jesus Christ. Therefore, a person may work hard for a better salary, possessions, and influence if his motives are surrendered to God. It is possible to live by faith and become a successful businessman. If faith means looking at the Lord Jesus Christ, then no matter what a Christian does—get wealth or give up wealth—he looks to the Lord Jesus Christ to guide his life.

Many years ago my little daughter was learning to swim. She ventured out of a quiet pool into the rapid current of a river. She screamed and fought the current. I could see sheer panic in her face but knew she was not in trouble. The water was shallow.

I jumped in and forced her to stand on the rock bottom. Many Christians respond like my daughter when faced with a threatening problem. They struggle to the point of exhaustion, when they need only to surrender and stand on the rock bottom.

Jesus described this action, "If anyone desires to come after Me, let him deny himself . . ." (Matthew 16:24 NKJV). When a man surrenders, he stops struggling for self-advancement or self-protection. However, surrender does not mean he quits working. He surrenders his ego and selfish pursuits. When faced with a problem, he has to work all the harder. But he works with different motives. He applies the principles of God's Word and commits the problem to the Lord. He no longer tries to solve the problem in his own way, for his own purpose. He surrenders to God's principles and allows the power of Christ to flow through him.

We Grow Faith Through Communion With Christ. If we want more faith, we must have constant communion with Jesus Christ. As we drive down the expressway, we can talk to Christ without closing our eyes. As we work in the kitchen, we can sense His presence without seeing Him with our physical eyes. The life of faith is the life of communion with the resurrected Jesus Christ.

We Grow Faith by Letting His Power Do It. The secret of the life of Paul was not his faith, but the faith of Jesus Christ. "I have been crucified with Christ; it is no longer I who live, but Christ lives in me; and the life which I now live in the flesh I live by faith in the Son of God, who loved me and gave Himself for me" (Galatians 2:20 NKJV). He had learned to live "by the faith of Jesus Christ" (literal translation). The secret of the deeper Christian life is living by the power of faith—Christ's faith.

Jesus said, ". . . I always do those things that please Him [the Father]" (John 8:29 NKJV), hence we please the Father through Christ. We can have the victory of Jesus Christ when we allow him to indwell our lives and live through us. Then we can learn the secret to overcoming the world. John said, ". . . And this is the victory that has overcome the world—our faith. Who is he who overcomes the world, but he who believes that Jesus is the Son of God?" (1 John 5:4, 5 NKJV.)

— APPENDIX —
DESCRIPTION OF
CHRISTIANS'
EXPERIENCES

I do not believe that all the experiences described here are valid biblical ones. Even though some use the same terms, they have different experiences. Others use different terms but have had similar experiences. Still others have had experiences that they claim are both valid and biblical, but their experiences are nonbiblical, and at times they deceive themselves and deceive others. Those who know better but deceive others by false claims are condemned by their own delusions. They are to be avoided. Those who are deceived by others are to be helped. Those who are self-deceived by their ignorance are to be pitied.

The following questionnaire is included to help you evaluate the biblical nature of the following testimonies. The chart is self-explanatory; fill it out with each testimony and draw your own conclusions.

1. I reject this person's experience.
2. I question the genuineness of the experience.
3. Average, I accept but do not understand this experience.
4. Above average, I understand the experience.
5. I have had this biblical experience.

EXPERIENCES OF CHRISTIANS	1	2	3	4	5
Booth					
Borden					
Brainerd					
Bramwell					
Bray					
Chapman					
Earle					
Evans					
Falwell					
Finney					
Fletcher					
Goforth					
Gordon					
Graham					
Ham					
Ironside					
Knapp					
Moody					
Palmer					
Roberts					
Rogers					
Smith					
Studd					
Taylor					
Torrey					
Wesley					

The Testimony of Catherine (Mrs. William) Booth

I struggled through the day until a little after six in the evening, when William joined me in prayer. We had a blessed season. While he was saying, "Lord, we open our hearts to receive Thee," that word was spoken to my soul: "Behold, I stand at the door and knock. If any man hear my voice, and open unto me, I will come in and sup with him." I felt sure He had been knocking, and oh, how I yearned to receive Him as a perfect Saviour! But oh, the inveterate habit of unbelief! How wonderful that God should have borne so long with me.

When we got up from our knees I lay on the sofa, exhausted with the effort and excitement of the day. William said, "Don't you lay all on the altar?" I replied, "I am sure I do!" Then he said, "And isn't the altar holy?" I replied in the language of the Holy Ghost, "The altar is most holy, and whatsoever toucheth it is holy." Then said he, "Are you not holy?" I replied with my heart full of emotion and with some faith, "Oh, I think I am." Immediately the word was given me to confirm my faith, "Now are ye clean through the word I have spoken unto you." And I took hold—true, with a trembling hand, and not unmolested by the tempter, but I held fast the beginning of my confidence, and it grew stronger, and from that moment I have dared to reckon myself dead indeed unto sin, but alive unto God through Jesus Christ, my Lord.[1]

The Testimony of William Whiting Borden

After this Dr. Torrey called for decisions. Fifty or sixty came forward and confessed Christ. Dr. Torrey told us to speak to those about us. I had an awful tussle, and almost didn't, for I thought the people around me were all Christians. However I wasn't sure, and so decided not to be the foolish man of "tomorrow" I spoke to a lady next to me, and others, but they were all saved. However, I felt much better, and know it will be easier to do next time.

In the After Meeting, Miss Davis sang the song, "I surrender all" and an invitation was given to those who had never publicly done so, whether Christians or not, to do so then. I stood up with several others, and we sang the chorus:

> I surrender all, I surrender all;
> All to Thee, my blessed Saviour,
> I surrender all.

Dr. Torrey then gave us a little talk on, The Way of Life. He also spoke on, How to keep on with the Christian Life when it is begun:

1. Look always to Jesus.
2. Keep confessing Jesus everywhere.
3. Keep studying God's Word, Matt. 4.4.
4. Keep praying every day, 1 Thes. 5.17.
5. Go to work.

The first four I am doing and the fifth I will do.

Well, when I got home that night I felt there was a difference. You know the expression, "for heaven's sake", that I have used so much. I knew it was wrong and yet I couldn't stop it. Before last Sunday I had been praying about it, but not very earnestly I am afraid, for though I managed to keep it from my lips, it got started several times. That night I prayed not only that my life might be controlled but my thoughts also, and I meant it. I expected a direct answer and got it the next day, and I have kept in that matter ever since. I don't think I ever had any real definite experience like that before, and it has strengthened my faith. And now I am praying more earnestly about things for which we have been praying some time. . . . [2]

The Testimony of David Brainerd

In the morning, I felt my soul *hungering and thirsting* after *righteousness*. In the forenoon, while I was looking on the sacramental elements, and thinking that Jesus Christ would soon be "Set forth crucified before me," my soul was filled with light and love, so that I was almost in an ecstasy; my body was so weak I could hardly stand. I felt at the same time an exceeding tenderness, and most fervent love towards all mankind; so that my soul, and all the powers of it seemed, as it were, to melt into softness and sweetness. This love and joy cast out fear, and my soul longed for perfect grace and glory.[3]

I felt exceeding dead to the world and all its enjoyments: I was ready to give up life, and all its comforts, as soon as called to it; and yet then had as much comfort of life as almost ever I had. Life itself appeared but an empty bubble; the riches, honors, and enjoyments of it extremely tasteless. I longed to be entirely *crucified* to all things here below. My soul was sweetly resigned to God's disposal of me; and I saw there had nothing happened to me but what was best for me. . . . It was my meat and drink to be holy, to live to the Lord, and die to the Lord. And I then enjoyed such a heaven, as far exceeded the most sublime conceptions of an unregenerate soul; and even unspeakably beyond what I myself could conceive at another time.[4]

The Testimony of Willam Bramwell

When in the house of a friend at Liverpool, whither I had gone to settle some temporal affairs, previously to my going out to travel, while I was sitting, as it might be, on this chair [pointing to his chair], with my mind engaged in various meditations concerning my present affairs and future prospects, my heart now and then lifted up to God, but not particularly about this blessing, *heaven came down to earth*; it came to my soul. The Lord, for whom I had waited, came suddenly to the temple of my heart; and I had an immediate evidence that this was the blessing I had for some time been seeking. My soul was then all wonder, love and praise.[5]

The Testimony of Billy Bray

I remember being at Hick's Mill Chapel one Sunday morning at class-meeting when a stranger led the class. The leader asked one of our members whether he could say that the Lord had cleansed him from all sin, and he could not. "That," I said in my mind, "is sanctification; I will have that blessing by the help of the Lord;" and I went on my knees at once, and cried to the Lord to sanctify me wholly, body, spirit, soul. And the Lord said to me, "Thou art clean through the word I have spoken unto thee." And I said, "Lord, I believe it." When the leader came to me I told him, "Four months ago I was a great sinner against God. Since that time I have been justified freely by His grace, and while I have been here this morning, the Lord has sanctified me wholly." When I had done telling what the Lord had done for me, the leader said, "If you can believe it, it is so." Then I said, "I can believe it." When I had told him so, what joy filled my heart I cannot find words to tell. After the meeting was over, I had to go over a railroad, and all around me seemed so full of glory that it dazzled my sight: I had a "joy unspeakable and full of glory."[6]

The Testimony of J. Wilbur Chapman

One incident connected with my own Christian experience can never be effaced from my memory. I was seated in my country home reading the accounts of the Northfield conferences, before I had even thought of attending the same, when one sentence in an address delivered by Mr. Meyer arrested my attention. It was concerning the life of surrender, and the sentence was as follows: "If you are not willing to give up everything to God, then can you say, *I am willing to*

be made willing?" It was like a star in the midnight darkness of my life
and led to a definite surrender of myself in October 1892. But after that
there were still some discouragements and times of depression, and
standing one morning very early in front of Mr. Moody's house with
the Rev. F. B. Meyer, I said to him, "Mr. Meyer, what is my difficulty?" I told him of my definite surrender and pointed out to him my
times of weakness and discouragement, and in a way which is peculiar
to himself he made answer, "My brother, your difficulty is doubtless
the same as the one I met. Have you ever tried to breathe out six times
without breathing in once?" Thoughtlessly I tried to do it and then
learned that one never breathes out until he breathes in, that his
breathing out is in proportion to his breathing in; that he makes his
effort to breathe in and none to breathe out. Taking my hand in his,
my distinguished friend said, "it is just so in one's Christian life, we
must be constantly breathing in of God, or we shall fail," and he
turned to make his way to Mr. Moody's house for breakfast while I
hastened up to my room in Weston Hall thanking God that I had had
a message better to me than any sermon I had ever heard.[7]

The Testimony of A. B. Earle

About ten years ago, I began to feel an inexpressible hungering and
longing for the fulness of Christ's love. I had often had seasons of
great joy and peace in Christ, and in His service. I had seen many
precious souls brought into the fold of Christ. I fully believe I then
belonged to Christ, that my name was in His family record.

I loved the work of the ministry, but had long felt an inward unrest,
a void in my soul that was not filled. Seasons of great joy would be
followed by seasons of darkness and doubt. If I had peace, I feared it
would not continue; and it did not.

In this state I was exposed to severe temptations and attacks of the
enemy. I made strong and repeated resolutions that I would be faithful, but could not keep them. Then I sought and found forgiveness
again, and was happy, and said, "Oh, that I could always enjoy such
peace!" But it was soon disturbed by some word, or act, or heart-
wandering.

Thus I lived on for many years. . . .

I frequently met Christians who claimed sinless perfection: many of
them were, indeed, a better type of Christian than ordinary profes-
sors; but they did not seem perfect to me. The rest in Jesus, for which
I longed, was still unfound.

At last I felt that the question for me to settle was this,—Can an imperfect Christian sweetly and constantly rest in a perfect Saviour, without condemnation?

This I revolved in my mind for a long time. I read, as far as I could, the experiences of those who seemed to live nearest to Christ. I searched the Scriptures for light, and asked such as I believed had power with God to pray with and for me, that I might be led aright on this great question. At length I became satisfied that Christ had made provision for me and all His children to abide in the fulness of His love without one moment's interruption.

Having settled this, I said: "I need this; I long for it; I cannot truly represent religion without it, and Christ is dishonored by me everyday I live without it."

I therefore deliberately resolved, by the help of my Redeemer, to obtain it at any sacrifice; little realizing how unlike Christ I then was, or how much would be needed, to bring me there.

I first procured a blank book, which I called my "Consecration Book," and slowly and solemnly, on my knees, wrote in it the following dedication:

Andover, February 10, 1859.
This day I make a new consecration of my all to Christ.

Jesus, I now forever give myself to Thee; my soul to be washed in Thy blood and saved in heaven at last; my whole body to be used for Thy glory; my mouth to speak for Thee at all times; my eyes to weep over lost sinners, or to be used for any purpose to Thy glory; my feet to carry me where Thou shalt wish me to go; my heart to be burdened for souls, or used for Thee anywhere; my intellect to be employed at all times for Thy cause and glory. I give to Thee my wife, my children, my property, all I have, and all that ever shall be mine. I will obey Thee in every known duty.

A. B. E.

I then asked for grace to enable me to carry out that vow, and that I might take nothing from the altar. I supposed, with this consecration, entire as far as knowledge went, I should soon receive all that my longing heart could contain; but in this I was sadly mistaken.

I then came nearer to Christ. But as clearer light began to shine into my heart, I saw more of its vileness. . . .

I felt like a patient who, though in the hands of a skilful physician, groans and writhes under the severe treatment which has been found necessary in order to save his life. But my constant prayer was, "Be

thorough with me, Jesus,—be thorough." Many a discouraging day
followed this consecration and these heart-searchings. I grew weak
and small and unworthy in my own estimation.

At times my joy and peace were almost unbounded. Sometimes I
felt that I grasped the prize so earnestly sought, but was shown
hidden sin in my heart which greatly humbled and distressed me. . . .

One sin that troubled me most, and was the hardest to overcome,
was a strong will,—a desire, and almost a determination to have my
own way;—and thus—even in regard to little things, or any little
injury or supposed wrong—to speak without reflection, and sometimes severely, even to those I knew were my friends; to say, "I will do
this," and "I will do that."

This I clearly saw must be overcome, if I would become a consistent
and useful Christian. As I could not do it myself, I gave it over to Jesus:
He could give me grace to overcome even this. But I found I gave
nothing into the hands of Jesus, except by a sinful faith. My faith was
very deficient and weak: to believe the promises fully was not easy. I
believed the theory of religion; but to have my heart grasp the reality,
without wavering, was more difficult. Yet I found my faith growing
stronger, until at last I came to believe just what God had said in His
Word. I found first the blade of faith, then the ear, and then the full
corn in the ear. No rest could be obtained until I could believe just
what God had said, and trust Him fully.

I felt that I must have in my heart something that I did not then
possess. Before I could be filled with the fullness of Christ's love I must
be emptied of self. Oh, the longing of my heart for what I then
believed, and now believe, to be sweet and constant rest in Jesus! I
believed I should receive, and thought it was near.

I soon found it easier to resist temptation. I began to trust Christ and
His promise more fully.

With this mingling of faith, desire, and expectation, I commenced a
meeting on Cape Cod. After re-dedicating myself, in company with
others, anew to God, I was in my room alone, pleading for the fulness
of Christ's love, when all at once a sweet, heavenly peace filled all the
vacuum in my soul, leaving no longing, no unrest, no dissatisfied
feeling in my bosom. I felt, I knew, that I was accepted fully in Jesus.
A calm, simple, childlike trust took possession of my whole being. . . .

Then, for the first time in my life, I had the rest which is more than
peace. I had felt peace before, but feared I should not retain it; now I
had peace without fear, which really became rest. . . .

This change occurred about five o'clock, on the evening of the second day of November, 1863; and although I never felt so weak and small, yet Jesus has been my all since then. There has not been one hour of conscious doubt or darkness since that time. A heaven of peace and rest fills my soul. Day and night the Saviour seems by me.

My success in leading souls to Jesus has been much greater than before. . . .

Temptation is presented, but the power of it is broken. I seem to have a present Saviour in every time of need; so that for several years I have done the trusting and Jesus the keeping. . . . [8]

The Testimony of Christmas Evans

I was weary of a cold heart towards Christ and His sacrifice, and the work of His Spirit—of a cold heart in the pulpit, in secret prayer, and in study. Fifteen years previously, I had felt my heart burning within, as if going to Emmaus with Jesus.

On a day ever to be remembered by me, as I was climbing up towards Cader Idris, I considered it to be incumbent upon me to pray, however hard I felt in my heart, and however worldly the frame of my spirit was. Having begun in the name of Jesus, I soon felt, as it were, the fetters loosening, and the old hardness of heart softening, and, as I thought, mountains of frost and snow dissolving and melting within me.

This engendered confidence in my soul in the promise of the Holy Ghost. I felt my whole mind relieved from some great bondage; tears flowed copiously, and I was constrained to cry out for the gracious visits of God, by restoring to my soul the joys of His salvation; and that He would visit the churches of the saints, and nearly all the ministers in the principality by their names.

This struggle lasted for three hours: it rose again and again, like one wave after another, or a high flowing tide, driven by a strong wind, until my nature became faint by weeping and crying. Thus I resigned myself to Christ, body and soul, gifts and labours—all my life—every day, and every hour that remained for me; and all my cares I committed to Christ.

From this time I was made to expect the goodness of God to churches, and to myself. In the first religious meetings after this, I felt as if I had been removed from the cold and sterile regions of spiritual frost, into the verdant fields of Divine promises. The former striving with God in prayer, and the longing anxiety for the conversion of

sinners, which I experienced at Leyn, were now restored. I had a hold
of the promises of God.

The result was, when I returned home, the first thing that arrested
my attention was that the Spirit was working also in the brethren in
Anglesea, inducing in them a spirit of prayer, especially in two of the
deacons, who were particularly importunate that God would visit us
in mercy, and render the Word of His grace effectual amongst us for
the conversion of sinners.[9]

The Testimony of Jerry Falwell

When Falwell entered Baptist College, he was a typical first-year
student, searching for answers to questions. Through the years at
Baptist Bible College, Falwell was not aware of what he was going to
do. He had never preached. During his first year an event changed his
life. He asked for a Sunday school class at the High Street Baptist
Church and was given a little area with a curtain around it, a class
book and one eleven-year-old boy. Young Falwell taught this boy for
three or four weeks; finally the embarrassed boy brought a friend.
Falwell got discouraged and went to the superintendent with the
intention of giving up the class. He told young Falwell, "I didn't want
to give you the class when you asked because my better judgement
told me you were not serious and dedicated." Then the superintendent criticized the immature preacher, "I don't think you will make it
in the ministry, but I went against my judgement and gave you the
class." The middle-aged man finished, "I was right in my first judgement; you're worthless, so give me the book." Falwell's eyes spit fire.
The young student replied, "I won't give you the book. I'd like to
consider the class and pray about it." Falwell went back and asked the
dean of students for a key to the empty room on the third floor. Each
afternoon for a week, Falwell went and prayed from 1:30 to 5:00 P.M.
There was no mattress on the bed and Falwell stretched his body over
the springs. God broke his heart over his failure with the small Sunday
school class. "I realized if I wasn't going to be faithful in little things,
God would never bless me in big things." Falwell prayed for that boy,
his family, the other boy, his family. Next Jerry prayed for himself and
his own needs, praying that God would lead him to the right place.
God blessed the class and new kids came. Falwell prayed for them and
their friends. On Saturday he cut a swath across every playground and
empty lot, seeking eleven-year-old boys. He would gather the class
members, then go looking for their buddies and friends, for anyone
who was eleven years old. When Falwell left school in May of

that year, he had fifty-six eleven-year-old boys in that class. All had been saved and many of their mothers, dads, and friends also. Falwell realized for the first time, that if he would pray and work there was unlimited potential in the service of Christ.[10]

The Testimony of Charles Grandison Finney

As I turned and was about to take a seat by the fire, I received a mighty baptism of the Holy Ghost. Without any expectation of it, without ever having the thought in my mind that there was any such thing for me, without any recollection that I had ever heard the thing mentioned by any person in the world, the Holy Spirit descended upon me in a manner that seemed to go through me, body and soul. I could feel the impression, like a wave of electricity going through and through me. Indeed it seemed to come in waves and waves of liquid love; for I could not express it in any other way. It seemed like the very breath of God. I can recollect distinctly that it seemed to fan me, like immense wings.

No words can express the wonderful love that was shed abroad in my heart. I wept aloud with joy and love; and I do not know but I should say, I literally bellowed out the unutterable gushings of my heart. These waves came over me, and over me, and over me, one after the other, until I recollect I cried out, "I shall die if these waves continue to pass over me." I said, "Lord, I cannot bear any more"; yet I had no fear of death. . . .

When I awoke in the morning . . . instantly the baptism that I had received the night before returned upon me in the same manner. I arose upon my knees in bed and wept aloud with joy, and remained for some time too much overwhelmed with the baptism of the Spirit to do anything but pour out my soul to God.[11]

The Testimony of John Fletcher

My dear brethren and sisters, God is here! I feel Him in this place; but I would hide my face in the dust, because I have been ashamed to declare what He has done for *me*. For many years, I have grieved His Spirit; I am deeply humbled; and He has again restored my soul. Last Wednesday evening, He spoke to me by these words. *"Reckon yourselves to be dead indeed unto sin, and alive unto God through Jesus Christ our Lord."* I obeyed the voice of God; I now obey it; and tell you all, to the praise of His love—*I am freed from sin.* Yes, I rejoice to declare it, and to be a witness to the glory of His grace, that *I am dead unto sin, and alive unto God, through Jesus Christ*, who is my Lord and King! I received this blessing four or five times before; but I lost it, by not observing the order of God; who has told us, *With the heart man believeth unto righteousness and with the mouth confession is made unto salvation.* But the enemy offered his bait, under various colors, to keep me from a public declaration of what God had wrought.

When I first received this grace, Satan bid me to wait awhile, till I saw more of the *fruits;* I resolved to do so; but I soon began to doubt the witness, which, before, I had felt in my heart; and in a little time, I was sensible I had lost both. A second time, after receiving this salvation, I was kept from being a witness for my Lord, by the suggestion, "Thou art a public character—the eyes of all are upon thee—and if, as before, by *any* means thou lose the blessing, it will be a dishonor to the doctrine of *heart-holiness.*" I held my peace, and again forfeited the gift of God. At another time, I was prevailed upon to hide it by reasoning, "How few, even of the children of *God*, will receive this testimony; many of them supposing that every transgression of the Adamic law is sin; and, therefore, if I profess to be *free* from sin, *all* these will give my profession the lie; because I am not free in *their* sense; I am not free from ignorance, mistakes, and various infirmities; I will, therefore, enjoy what God has wrought in me; but I will not say, *"I am perfect in love."* Alas! I soon found again, He that hideth his *Lord's talent, and improveth it not, from that unprofitable servant shall be taken away even that he hath.*

Now, my brethren, you see my folly. I have confessed it in your presence; and *now* I resolve before you all to confess my Master. I will confess Him to all the world. And I declare unto you, in the presence of God, the Holy Trinity, I am now *dead indeed unto sin.* I do not say, *I am crucified with Christ,* because some of our well-meaning brethren say, by *this* can only be meant *gradual* dying; but I profess unto you, *I am dead unto sin, and alive unto God;* and, remember, all *this is through Jesus Christ our Lord.*[12]

The Testimony of Rosalind (Mrs. Jonathan) Goforth

I do not remember the time when I did not have in some degree a love for the Lord Jesus Christ as my Saviour. When not quite twelve years of age, at a revival meeting, I publicly accepted and confessed Christ as my Lord and Master.

From that time there grew up in my heart a deep yearning to know Christ in a more real way, for He seemed so unreal, so far away and visionary. One night when still quite young I remember going out under the trees in my parents' garden and, looking up into the starlit heavens, I longed with intense longing to feel Christ near me. As I knelt down there on the grass, alone with God, Job's cry became mine, "Oh, that I knew where I might find him!" Could I have borne it had I known then that almost forty years would pass before that yearning would be satisfied?

With the longing to know Christ, literally to "find" Him, came a passionate desire to *serve* Him. But, oh, what a terrible nature I had! Passionate, proud, self-willed, indeed just full was I of those things that I knew were unlike Christ.

The following years of halfhearted conflict with sinful self must be passed over till about the fifth year of our missionary work in China. I grieve to say that the new life in a foreign land with its trying climate, provoking servants, and altogether irritating conditions, seemed to have developed rather than subdued my natural disposition.

One day (I can never forget it), as I sat inside the house by a paper window at dusk, two Chinese Christian women sat down on the other side. They began talking about me, and (wrongly, no doubt) I listened. One said, "Yes, she is a hard worker, a zealous preacher, and—yes, she dearly loves us; but, oh, what a temper she has! *If she would only live more as she preaches!*"

Then followed a full and true delineation of my life and character. So true indeed was it, as to crush out all sense of annoyance and leave me humbled to the dust. I saw then how useless, how worse than useless, was it for me to come to China to preach Christ and not *live* Christ. But how could I live Christ? I knew some (including my dear husband) who had a peace and a power—yes, and something I could not define—that I had not; and often I longed to know the secret.

Was it possible, with such a nature as mine, ever to become patient and gentle?

Was it possible that I could ever really stop worrying?

Could I, in a word, ever hope to be able to live Christ as well as preach Him?

I knew I loved Christ; and again and again I had proved my willingness to give up all for His sake. But I knew, too, that one hot flash of temper with the Chinese, or with the children before the Chinese, would largely undo weeks, perhaps months of self-sacrificing service.

The years that followed led often through the furnace. The Lord knew that nothing but fire could destroy the dross and subdue my stubborn will. Those years may be summed up in one line: "Fighting [not finding], following, keeping, *struggling*." Yes, and failing! Sometimes in the depths of despair over these failures; then going on determined to do *my* best—and what a poor best it was!

In the year 1905, and later, as I witnessed the wonderful way the Lord was leading my husband, and saw the Holy Spirit's power in his life and message, I came to seek very definitely for the fullness of the Holy Spirit. It was a time of deep heart-searching. The heinousness of sin was revealed as never before. Many, many things had to be set right toward man and God. I learned then what "paying the price" meant. Those were times of wonderful mountaintop experiences, and I came to honor the Holy Spirit and seek His power for the overcoming of sin in a new way. But Christ still remained, as before, distant, afar off, and I longed increasingly to know—to find Him. Although I had much more power over besetting sins, yet there were times of great darkness and defeat.

It was during one of these latter times that we were forced to return to Canada, in June, 1916. My husband's health prevented him from public speaking, and it seemed that this duty for us both was to fall on me. But I dreaded facing the home church without some spiritual uplift—a fresh vision for myself. The Lord saw this heart-hunger, and in His own glorious way He fulfilled literally the promise, "He satisfieth the longing soul, and *filleth* the hungry soul with goodness" (Ps. 107:9).

A spiritual conference was to be held the latter part of June at Niagara-on-the-Lake, Ontario, and to this I was led. One day I went to the meeting rather against my inclination, for it was so lovely under the trees by the beautiful lake. The speaker was a stranger to me, but from almost the first his message gripped me—Victory Over Sin! Why, this was what I had fought for, had hungered for, all my life! Was it possible?

The speaker went on to describe very simply an ordinary Christian life experience—sometimes on the mountaintop, with visions of God; then again would come the sagging, the dimming of vision, coldness, discouragement, and perhaps definite disobedience, and a time of downgrade experience. Then perhaps a sorrow, or even some special mercy, would bring the wanderer back to his Lord.

The speaker asked for all those who felt this to be a picture of their experience to raise the hand. I was sitting in the front seat, and shame only kept me from raising my hand at once. But I did so want to get all God had for me, and I determined to be true; and after a struggle I raised my hand. Wondering if others were like myself, I ventured to glance back and saw many hands were raised, though the audience was composed almost entirely of Christian workers, ministers, and missionaries.

The leader then went on to say *that* life which he had described was *not* the life God planned or wished for His children. He described the higher life of peace, rest in the Lord, of power and freedom from struggle, worry, care. As I listened I could scarcely believe it could be true, yet my whole soul was moved so that it was with the greatest difficulty I could control my emotion. I saw then, though dimly, that I was nearing the goal for which I had been aiming all my life.

Early the next morning, soon after daybreak, on my knees I went over carefully all the passages on the victorious life that were given in a little leaflet. What a comfort and strength it was to see how clear God's Word was that victory, not defeat, was His will for His children, and to see what wonderful provision He had made! Later, during the days that followed, clearer light came. I did what I was asked to do—I quietly but definitely accepted Christ as my Saviour from the *power* of sin as I had so long before accepted Him as my Saviour from the *penalty* of sin. And on this I rested.

I left Niagara, realizing, however, there was still something I did not have. I felt much as the blind man must have felt when he said, "I see men as trees, walking." I had begun to see light, but dimly.

The day after reaching home I picked up a little booklet, *The Life That Wins*, which I had not read before, and going to my son's bedside I told him it was the personal testimony of one whom God had used to bring great blessing into my life. I then read it aloud till I came to the words, "At last I realized that Jesus Christ was actually and literally within me." I stopped amazed. The sun seemed suddenly to come from under a cloud and flood my whole soul with light. How blind I had been! I saw at last the secret of victory—it was simply Jesus Christ Himself—His own life lived out in the believer. But the thought of victory was for the moment lost sight of in the inexpressible joy of realizing *Christ's indwelling presence!* Like a tired, worn-out wanderer finding home at last I just *rested* in Him. Rested in His love—in Himself. And, oh, the peace and joy that came flooding my life! A restfulness and quietness of spirit I never thought could be mine took possession of me so naturally. Literally a new life began for me, or rather *in* me. It was just "the Life that is Christ."

The first step I took in this new life was to stand on God's own Word, and not merely on man's teaching or even on a personal experience. And as I studied especially the truth of God's indwelling, victory over sin, and God's bountiful provision, the Word was fairly illumined with new light.

The years that have passed have been years of blessed fellowship with Christ and of joy in His service. A friend asked me not long ago if I could give in a sentence the after-result in my life of what I said had come to me in 1916, and I replied, "Yes, it can be all summed up in one word, *resting*."[13]

The Testimony of George C. Needham Concerning A. J. Gordon

Dr. Gordon, unlike some Christians, believed there was something always beyond. This he ever sought to attain. Some years ago, during the first Northfield convention, he was desirous to secure what he yet needed as a saint and servant of Christ. Toward the close of those memorable ten days, spent more in prayer than in preaching, my beloved friend joined me in a mid-night hour of great heart-searching and in-filling of the Spirit. He read with peculiar tenderness of our Lord's intercessory prayer of John xvii. The union of the believer with Christ and the Father, as taught by our Lord in that chapter, called out fervent exclamations, while with deep pathos he continued reading. During united prayer which followed, the holy man poured his soul with a freedom and unction indescribable. I never heard him boast of any spiritual attainment reached during that midnight hour. Soul experiences were to him very sacred, and not to be rehearsed on every ordinary occasion. But I have no doubt that he received then a divine touch which further ennobled his personal life and made his ministry of ever-increasing spirituality and of ever-widening breadth of sympathy.[14]

The Testimony of William Franklin (Billy) Graham

In my own life there have been times when I have also had the sense of being filled with the Spirit, knowing that some special strength was added for some task I was being called upon to perform.

We sailed for England in 1954 for a crusade that was to last for three months. While on the ship, I experienced a definite sense of oppression. Satan seemed to have assembled a formidable array of his artillery against me. Not only was I oppressed, I was overtaken by a sense of depression, accompanied by a frightening feeling of inadequacy for the task that lay ahead. Almost night and day I prayed. I knew in a new way what Paul was telling us when he spoke about "praying without ceasing." Then one day in a prayer meeting with my wife and colleagues, a break came. As I wept before the Lord, I was filled with deep assurance that power belonged to God and he was faithful. I had been baptized by the Spirit into the body of Christ when I was saved, but I believe God gave me a special anointing on the way to England. From that moment on I was confident that God the Holy Spirit was in control for the task that lay ahead.

That proved true.

Experiences of this kind had happened to me before, and they have happened to me many times since. Sometimes no tears are shed. Sometimes as I have lain awake at night the quiet assurance has come that I was being filled with the Spirit for the task that lay ahead.

However, there have been many more occasions when I would have to say as the apostle Paul did in 1 Corinthians 2:3: "I was with you in weakness and in fear and in much trembling." Frequently various members of my team have assured me that when I have had the least liberty in preaching or the greatest feeling of failure, God's power has been most evident.[15]

The Testimony of Mordecai F. Ham

Two sisters were living in a log hut near the church. Both were just young girls and were dying with tuberculosis. At the start of the meeting I was asked to pray for them, which I did, but with no apparent result. I was to visit them on a certain day, and the night before, after I had finished the service and retired to my room in the home where I was residing, I had an overwhelming experience of the Lord's presence. I felt so powerfully overcome by the nearness of the Holy Spirit that I had to ask the Lord to draw back, lest He kill me. It was so glorious that I couldn't stand more than a small portion of it.[16]

The Testimony of Henry Allen (Harry) Ironside

Being saved myself, the first great desire that sprang up in my heart was an intense longing to lead others to the One who had made my peace with God.

At the time of which I write, the Salvation Army was in the zenith of its energy as an organization devoted to going out after the lost. . . . Naturally therefore, when the knowledge of salvation was mine, I went at the first opportunity, the night after my conversion, to an "Army" street-meeting, and there spoke for the first time, in the open air, of the grace of God so newly revealed to my soul. . . .

As nearly as I can now recollect, I was in the enjoyment of the knowledge of God's salvation about a month when, in some dispute with my brother, who was younger than I, my temper suddenly escaped control, and in an angry passion I struck and felled him to the ground. Horror immediately filled my soul. I needed not his sarcastic taunt, "Well, you are a nice Christian! You'd better go down to the Army and tell what a saint you've become!" to send me to my room in anguish of heart to confess my sin to God in shame and bitter sorrow, as afterwards frankly to my brother, who generously forgave me.

From this time on mine was an "up-and-down experience," to use a term often heard in "testimony meetings." I longed for perfect victory over the lusts and desires of the flesh. Yet I seemed to have more trouble with evil thoughts and unholy propensities than I had ever known before. For a long time I kept these conflicts hidden, and known only to God and to myself. But after some eight or ten months, I became interested in what were called "holiness meetings," held weekly in the "Army" hall, and also in a mission I sometimes attended. At these gatherings an experience was spoken of which I felt was just what I needed. It was designated by various terms: "The Second Blessing"; "Sanctification"; "Perfect Love"; "Higher Life"; "Cleansing from Inbred Sin"; and by other expressions.

Substantially, the teaching was this: When converted, God graciously forgives all sins committed up to the time when one repents. But the believer is then placed in a lifelong probation, during which he may at any time forfeit his justification and peace with God if he falls into sin from which he does not at once repent. In order, therefore, to maintain himself in a saved condition, he needs a further work of grace called sanctification. This work has to do with sin the root, as justification had to do with sins the fruit.

The steps leading up to this second blessing are, firstly, conviction as to the need of holiness (just as in the beginning there was conviction of the need of salvation); secondly, a full surrender to God, or the laying of every hope, prospect and possession on the altar of consecration; thirdly, to claim in faith the incoming of the Holy Spirit as a refining fire to burn out all inbred sin, thus destroying *in toto* every lust and passion, leaving the soul perfect in love and as pure as unfallen Adam. This wonderful blessing received, great watchfulness is required lest, as the serpent beguiled Eve, he deceive the sanctified soul, and thus introduce again the same kind of an evil principle which called for such drastic action before. . . .

Eagerly I began to seek this precious boon of holiness-in-the-flesh. Earnestly I prayed for this Adamic sinlessness. I asked God to reveal to me every unholy thing, that I might truly surrender all to Him. I gave up friends, pursuits, pleasures—everything I could think of that might hinder the incoming of the Holy Ghost and the consequent blessing. I was a veritable "book-worm," an intense love for literature possessing me from childhood; but in my ignorant desire I put away all books of pleasurable or instructive character, and promised God to read only the Bible and holiness writings if He would only give me "the blessing." I did not, however, obtain what I sought, though I prayed zealously for weeks.

At last, one Saturday night (I was now away from home, living with a friend a member of the "Army"), I determined to go out into the country and wait on God, not returning till I had received the blessing of perfect love. I took a train at eleven o'clock, and went to a lonely station twelve miles from Los Angeles. There I alighted, and, leaving the highway, descended into an empty *arroyo*, or water-course. Falling on my knees beneath a sycamore tree, I prayed in an agony for hours, beseeching God to show me anything that hindered my reception of the blessing. Various matters of too private and sacred a nature to be here related came to my mind. I struggled against conviction, but finally ended by crying, "Lord, I give up *all*—everything, every person, every enjoyment, that would hinder my living alone for Thee. Now give me, I pray Thee, the blessing!"

As I look back, I believe I was fully surrendered to the will of God at that moment, so far as I understood it. But my brain and nerves were unstrung by the long midnight vigil and the intense anxiety of previous months, and I fell almost fainting to the ground. Then a holy ecstasy seemed to thrill all my being. This I thought was the coming into my heart of the Comforter. I cried out in confidence, "Lord, I believe Thou dost come in. Thou dost cleanse and purify me from all sin. I claim it now. The work is done. I am sanctified by Thy blood. Thou dost make me holy. I believe; I believe!" I was unspeakably happy. I felt that all my struggles were ended.

With a heart filled with praise, I rose from the ground and began to sing aloud. Consulting my watch, I saw it was about half-past three in the morning. I felt I must hasten to town so as to be in time for the seven o'clock prayer-meeting, there to testify to my experience. Fatigued as I was by being up all night, yet so light was my heart I scarcely noticed the long miles back, but hastened to the city, arriving just as the meeting was beginning, buoyed up by my new-found experience. All were rejoiced as I told what great things I believed God had done for me. Every meeting that day added to my gladness. I was literally intoxicated with joyous emotions. . . .

For some weeks after the eventful experience before described, I lived in a dreamily-happy state, rejoicing in my fancied sinlessness. One great idea had possession of my mind; and whether at work or in my leisure hours, I thought of little else than the wonderful event which had taken place. But gradually I began to "come back to earth," as it were. I was now employed in a photographic studio, where I associated with people of various tastes and habits, some of whom ridiculed, some tolerated, and others sympathized with, my radical views on things religious. Night after night I attended the meetings, speaking on the street and indoors, and I soon noticed (and doubtless others did too) that a change came over my "testimonies." Before, I had always held up Christ, and pointed the lost to Him. Now, almost imperceptibly, my own experience became my theme, and I held up *myself* as a striking example of consecration and holiness! This was the prevailing characteristic of the brief addresses made by most of the "advanced" Christians in our company. The youngest in grace magnified Christ. The "sanctified" magnified themselves. . . .

As time went on, I began to be again conscious of inward desires toward evil—of thoughts that were unholy. I was nonplused. Going to a leading teacher for help, he said, "These are but temptations. Temptation is not sin. You only sin if you yield to the evil suggestion." This gave me peace for a time. I found it was the general way of excusing such evident moving of a fallen nature, which was supposed to have been eliminated. But gradually I sank to a lower and lower plane, permitting things I would once have shunned; and I even observed that all about me did the same. The first ecstatic experiences seldom lasted long. The ecstasy departed, and the "sanctified" were in very little different from their brethren who were supposed to be "only justified." We did not commit overt acts of evil: therefore we were sinless. Lust was not sin unless yielded to; so it was easy to go on testifying that all was right. . . .

When but sixteen years of age I became a cadet; that is, a student preparing for officership in the Salvation Army. During my probation in the Oakland Training Garrison I had more trouble than at any other time. The rigorous discipline and enforced intimate association with young men of so various tastes and tendencies, as also degrees of spiritual experience, was very hard on one of my supersensitive temperament. I saw very little holiness there, and I fear I exhibited much less. In fact, for the last two out of my five months' terms I was all at sea, and dared not profess sanctification at all, owing to my low state. I was tormented with the thought I had backslidden, and might be lost eternally after all my former happy experiences of the Lord's goodness. Twice I slipped out of the building when all were in bed, and made my way to a lonely spot where I spent the night in prayer, beseeching God not to take His Holy Spirit from me, but to again cleanse me fully from all inbred sin. Each time I "claimed it by faith," and was brighter for a few weeks; but I inevitably again fell into doubt and gloom, and was conscious of sinning both in thought and in word, and sometimes in unholy actions, which brought terrible remorse.

Finally, I was commissioned as Lieutenant. Again I spent the night in prayer, feeling that I must not go out to teach and lead others unless myself pure and holy. Buoyed up with the thought of being free from the restraint I had been subjected to so long, it was comparatively easy this time to believe that the work of full inward cleansing was indeed consummated, and that I was now, if never before, actually rid of all carnality. . . .

As lieutenant for a year, and then as captain, I thoroughly enjoyed my work, gladly enduring hardship and privation that I fear I would shrink from now; generally confident that I was living out the doctrine of perfect love to God and man, and thereby making my own final salvation more secure. And yet, as I now look back, what grave failures I can detect—what an unsubdued will—what lightness and frivolity—what lack of subjection to the word of God—what self-satisfaction and complacency! Alas, "man at his best estate is altogether vanity."

I was between eighteen and nineteen years of age when I began to entertain serious doubts as to my actually having attained so high a standard of Christian living as I had professed, and as the Army and other Holiness movements advocated as the only real Christianity. . . .

Nearly eighteen months of an almost constant struggle followed. In vain I searched my heart to see if I had made a full surrender, and tried to give up every known thing that seemed in any sense evil or doubtful. Sometimes, for a month at a time, or even longer, I could persuade myself that at last I had indeed again received the blessing. But invariably a few weeks would bring before me once more that which *proved* that it was in my particular case all a delusion. . . .

At last I became so troubled I could not go on with my work. I concluded to resign from the Salvation Army, and did so, but was persuaded by the colonel to wait six months ere the resignation took effect. At his suggestion I gave up corps work and went out on a special tour—where I did not need to touch the holiness question. But I preached to others many times when I was tormented by the thought that I might myself be finally lost, because, "without holiness no man shall see the Lord"; and, try as I would, I could not be sure I possessed it. I talked with any who seemed to me to really have the blessing I craved; but there were very few who, upon an intimate acquaintanceship, seemed genuine. . . .

Finally, I could bear it no longer, so asked to be relieved from all active service, and at my own request was sent to the Beulah Home of Rest, near Oakland.

It was certainly time; for five years' active work, with only two brief furloughs, had left me almost a nervous wreck, worn out in body and most acutely distressed in mind.

The language of my troubled soul, after all those years of preaching to others, was, "Oh that I knew where I might find Him!" Finding Him not, I saw only the blackness of despair before me; but yet I knew too well His love and care to be completely cast down.

At last I found myself becoming cold and cynical. Doubts as to everything assailed me like a legion of demons, and I became almost afraid to let my mind dwell on these things. For refuge I turned to secular literature, and sent for my books, which some years before I had foresworn on condition that God would give me the "second blessing." How little I realized the Jacob-spirit in all this! God seemed to have failed; so I took up my books once more, and tried to find solace in the beauties of essays and poetry, or the problems of history and science. I did not dare to confess to myself that I was literally an agnostic; yet for a month at least I could only answer, "I do not know" to every question based on divine revelation. . . .

Deliverance came at last in a most unexpected way. A lassie-lieutenant, a woman some ten years my senior in age, was brought to the Home from Rock Springs, Wyo., supposedly dying of consumption. From the first my heart went out to her in deep sympathy. To me she was a martyr, laying down her life for a needy world. I was much in her company, observed her closely, and finally came to the conclusion that she was the only wholly sanctified person in that place.

Imagine my surprise when, a few weeks after her arrival, she, with a companion, came to me one evening and begged me to read to her; remarking, "I hear you are always occupied with the things of the Lord, and I need your help." *I* the one to help her! I was dumbfounded, knowing so well the plague of my own heart, and being so fully assured as to her perfection in holiness. At the very moment they entered my room I was reading Byron's "Childe Harold." And I was supposed to be entirely devoted to the things of God! It struck me as weird and fantastic, rather than as a solemn farce—all this comparing ourselves with ourselves, only to be deluded every time.

I hastily thrust the book to one side, and wondered what to choose to read aloud. In God's providence a pamphlet caught my attention which my mother had given me some years before, but which I had dreaded to read lest it might upset me; so afraid had I been of anything that did not bear the Army or Holiness stamp. Moved by a sudden impulse, I drew it forth and said, "I'll read this. It is not in accordance with our teaching; but it may be interesting any way." I read page after page, paying little attention, only hoping to soothe and quiet this dying woman. In it the lost condition of all men by nature was emphasized. Redemption in Christ through His death was explained. Then there was much as to the believer's two natures, and his eternal security, which to me seemed both ridiculous and absurd. The latter part was occupied with prophecy. Upon that we did not enter. I was startled after going over the first half of the book when Lieut. J—— exclaimed, "O Captain, do you think that can possibly be true? If I could only believe that, I could die in peace!"

Astonished beyond measure, I asked, "What! do you mean to say you could not die in peace as you are? You are justified and sanctified; you have an experience I have sought in vain for years; and are you troubled about dying?" "I am miserable," she replied, "and you mustn't say I am sanctified. I cannot get it. I have struggled for years, and I have not reached it yet. This is why I wanted to speak with you, for I felt so sure you had it and could help me!"

We looked at each other in amazement; and as the pathos and yet ludicrousness of it all burst upon us, I laughed deliriously, while she wept hysterically. Then I remember exclaiming, "Whatever is the matter with us all? No one on earth denies himself more for Christ's sake than we. We suffer, and starve, and wear ourselves out in the endeavor to do the will of God; yet after all we have no *lasting* peace. We are happy at times; we enjoy our meetings; but we are never certain as to what the end will be."

"Do you think," she asked, "that is because we depend upon our own efforts too much? Can it be that we trust Christ to save us, but we think we have to keep saved by our own faithfulness—?"

"But," I broke in, "to think anything else would open the door to all kinds of sin!"

And so we talked till, wearied out, she arose to go, but asked if she and others might return the next evening to read and talk of these things we had gone over—a permission which was readily granted. For both Lieut. J—— and myself that evening's reading and exchange of confidences proved the beginning of our deliverance. We had frankly owned to one another, and to the third party present, that we were *not* sanctified. We now began to search the Scriptures earnestly for light and help. I threw all secular books to one side, determined to let nothing hinder the careful, prayerful study of the word of God. Little by little, the light began to dawn. We saw that we had been looking within for holiness, instead of without. We realized that the same grace that had saved us at first alone could carry us on. Dimly we apprehended that *all* for us must be in Christ, or we were without a ray of hope.

Many questions perplexed and troubled us. Much that we had believed we soon saw to be utterly opposed to the word of God. Much more we could not understand, so completely warped had our minds become through the training of years. In my perplexity I sought out a teacher of the Word who, I understood, was in fellowship with the writer of the pamphlet I have referred to above. I heard him with profit on two occasions, but still was in measure bewildered, though I began to feel solid ground beneath my feet once more. The great truth was getting a grip of me that holiness, perfect love, sanctification, and every other blessing, were mine *in Christ* from the moment I had believed, and mine forevermore, because all was pure grace. I had been looking at the wrong man—all was in another Man, and in that Man for me! But it took weeks to see this. . . .

Miss J—— saw it ere I did. The light came when she realized that she was eternally linked up with Christ as Head, and had eternal life in Him as the Vine, in her as the branch. Her joy knew no bounds, and she actually improved in health from that hour, and lived for six years after; finally going to be with the Lord, worn out in seeking to lead others to Christ. Many will be disappointed to know that she maintained her connection with the Army to the last. She had a mistaken (I believe) notion that she should remain where she was, and declare the truth she had learned. But ere she died she repented of this. Her last words to a brother (A. B. S.) and me, who were with her very near the end, were: "I have everything in Christ—of that I am sure. But I wish I had been more faithful as to the truth I learned about the

Body—the Church. I was misled by zeal which I thought was of God, and *it is too late to be faithful now!"*

Four days after the truth burst upon her soul in that Home of Rest, I too had every doubt and fear removed, and found my all in Christ. To go on where I was, I could not. Within a week I was outside of the only human system I had ever been in as a Christian, and for many years since I have known no head but Christ, no body but the one Church which He purchased with His own blood. They have been happy years; and as I look back over all the way the Lord has led me, I can but praise Him for the matchless grace that caused Him to set me free from introspection, and gave me to see that perfect holiness and perfect love were to be found, not in me, but in Christ Jesus alone.[17]

The Testimony of Jacob Knapp

At length I was advised by Dr. Nathaniel Kendrick to take an appointment from the Board of the Baptist Convention of the State of New York, as an evangelist in Jefferson and Oswego Counties. I thought favorably of this suggestion, imagining that such an appointment would increase my influence and tend to silence my opposers. I therefore went to the meeting of the Convention, about a hundred and forty miles distant. I had not mingled with the brethren long before I found that some, whom I had counted as friends, were disposed to treat me with coolness. Though endorsed by such a man as Dr. Kendrick, whose weight of personal influence was everywhere recognized, yet my application was instantly met by a decided opposition. One must tell what he had heard, another explain his views of the gospel method, until, after a lengthy debate, in which some cried one thing and some another, it was resolved to refer the question of my appointment to a committee. This committee made an adverse report, and my application was rejected. . . .

For a short time the effect of my rejection by the Board of the Convention was very disheartening. I had hoped to secure, by an appointment, a greater influence among the churches, the more positive countenance of some of the ministers who had hitherto been sitting on the fence, hesitating as to which side to get down on, and also to silence the active opposition of those who had avowed their hostility to my course; but it was not long before I found that my difficulties in these directions were on the increase. The non-committed became outspoken against me, and those heretofore opposed became violent and abusive. My soul was in deep trouble and I knew not which way to turn.

But in distress I cast my burdens on the Lord. I sought to know the will of God. I cried unto the Lord; and, blessed be His name, very soon He made known His ways, and lifted upon me the light of His countenance. After spending one whole day in fasting and prayer, and continuing my fast until midnight, the place where I was staying was filled with the manifested glory of God. His presence appeared to me, not exactly in visible form, but as real to my recognition as though He had come in person, and a voice seemed to say to me, "Hast thou ever lacked a field in which to labor?" I answered, "Not a day." "Have I not sustained thee, and blessed thy labors?" I answered, "Yea, Lord." "Then learn that henceforth thou art not dependent on thy brethren, but on me. Have no concern but to go on in thy work. My grace shall be sufficient for thee."

From that night I felt willing to sacrifice the good opinion of my brethren, as I had previously sacrificed the favor of the world, and swing off from all dependencies but God. Up to this time I had concerned myself too much about the opinions of other and older brethren, distrusting my youth and inexperience. But the Lord taught me that He was my only and infallible guide. I joyously acquiesced in His will, and from that day to this have rested in His divine manifestation. . . .

In the manifestation of God's presence to me, He cast no reflections on those of my ministerial brethren who differed from me, but, in the most tender manner, bade me to leave them to pursue their own way, and cleave only to Him. Thus was I cured of all yearning for denominational promotion, led to make an unreserved consecration of all my powers to one end,—the conversion of men to Christ; and made willing to labor on, through evil and good report, leaving my vindication until the day of judgement.[18]

The Testimony of Dwight Lyman Moody

The blessing came upon me suddenly like a flash of lightning. For months I had been hungering and thirsting for power in service. I had come to that point where I think I would have died if I had not got it. I remember I was walking the streets of New York. I had no more heart in the business I was about than if I had not been in the world at all. Well, one day—oh, what a day! I cannot describe it, I seldom refer to it; it is almost too sacred an experience to name—right there on the streets the power of God seemed to come upon me so wonderfully I had to ask God to stay His hand. I was filled with a sense of God's goodness, and I felt as though I could take the whole world to my heart. I took the old sermons I had preached before without any power, it was the same old truth, but there was new power. Many were impressed and converted. This happened years after I was converted myself. I would not now be placed back where I was before that blessed experience if you should give me all the world—it would be as the small dust in the balance.[19]

I can myself go back almost twelve years and remember two holy women who used to come to my meetings. It was delightful to see them there, for when I began to preach, I could tell by the expression of their faces they were praying for me. At the close of the Sabbath evening services they would say to me, "We have been praying for you." I said, "Why don't you pray for the people?" They answered, "You need power." "I need power," I said to myself; "why I thought I had power." I had a large Sabbath school and the largest congregation in Chicago. There were some conversions at the time, and I was in a sense satisfied. But right along these two godly women kept praying for me, and their earnest talk about "the anointing for special service" set me thinking. I asked them to come and talk with me, and we got down on our knees. They poured out their hearts, that I might receive the anointing of the Holy Ghost. And there came a great hunger into my soul. I knew not what it was. I began to cry as I never did before. The hunger increased. I really felt that I did not want to live any longer if I could not have this power for service. I kept on crying all the time that God would fill me with His Spirit. Well, one day, in the city of New York—O, what a day! I cannot describe it; I seldom refer to it; it is almost too sacred an experience to me. Paul had an experience of which he never spoke for fourteen years. I can only say, God revealed Himself to me, and I had such an experience of His love that I had to ask Him to stay His hand.

I went to preaching again. The sermons were not different; I did not present any new truths, and yet hundreds were converted. I would not be placed back where I was before that blessed experience if you would give me all Glasgow. It is a sad day when the convert goes into the church, and that is the last you hear of him. If, however, you want this power for some selfish end, as for example, to gratify your ambition, you will not get it. "No flesh," says God, "shall glory in my presence." May he empty us of self and fill us with His presence.[20]

The Testimony of Phoebe Palmer

Over and over agian, previous to the time mentioned, had she endeavored to give herself away in covenant to God. But she had never, till this hour, deliberately resolved on counting the cost, with the solemn intention to "reckon herself dead *indeed* unto sin, but alive unto God through Jesus Christ our Lord" (Rom. 6:11); to account herself permanently the Lord's, and in truth no more at *her own* disposal; but *irrevocably the Lord's property*, for time and eternity. Now, in the name of the Lord Jehovah, after having deliberately "counted the cost," she resolved to enter into the bonds of an everlasting covenant, with the fixed purpose to *count all things but loss* for the excellency of the knowledge of Jesus, that she might know Him and the power of His resurrection, by being made conformable to His death, and raised to an entire newness of life. . . . On doing this, a hallowed sense of consecration took possession of her soul.[21]

The Testimony of Evan Roberts

For thirteen years I had prayed for the Spirit; and this is the way I was led to pray. William Davies, the deacon, said one night in the society: "Remember to be faithful. What if the Spirit descended and you were absent? Remember Thomas! What a loss he had!"

I said to myself: "I will have the Spirit"; and through every kind of weather and in spite of all difficulties, I went to the meetings. Many times, on seeing other boys with the boats on the tide, I was tempted to turn back and join them. But, no. I said to myself: "Remember your resolve," and on I went. I went faithfully to the meetings for prayer throughout the ten or eleven years I prayed for a Revival. It was the Spirit that moved me thus to think.

[At a certain morning meeting which Evan Roberts attended, the evangelist in one of his petitions besought that the Lord would "bend us." The spirit seemed to say to Roberts: "That's what you need, to be bent." And thus he describes his experience:] I felt a living force coming into my bosom. This grew and grew, and I was almost bursting. My bosom was boiling. What boiled in me was that verse: "God commending His love." I fell on my knees with my arms over the seat in front of me; the tears and perspiration flowed freely. I thought blood was gushing forth." [Certain friends approached to wipe his face. Meanwhile he was crying out, "O Lord, bend me! Bend me!" Then the glory broke.]

After I was bent, a wave of peace came over me, and the audience sang, "I hear Thy welcome voice." And as they sang I thought about the bending at the Judgment Day, and I was filled with compassion for those that would have to bend on that day, and I wept.

Henceforth, the salvation of souls became the burden of my heart.

From that time I was on fire with a desire to go through all Wales, and if it were possible, I was willing to pay God for the privilege of going.[22]

The Testimony of Adrian Rogers

I'm not sure exactly how the "germ-thought" that God might want me to preach got into my heart. But I found it there. "Lord, do You really want me to preach?" I would ask Him. As a high-school football player, I was not afraid of much that moved on the gridiron, but the thought of being a public speaker was disturbing. More candidly, it scared me to death.

Yet, this little seed of a thought would not go away. For weeks I would pray like this: "Lord, I think You want me to preach." Then for days I would pray, "Lord, if You don't want me to preach, You had better let me know." Finally it was, "Lord, You are calling me, and I know it."

I made a public commitment, and it was settled. From that point on I did not look back. I was thrilled—and still am—that God would call me to serve Him. My high school sweetheart, who is now my wife, was also thrilled. In her heart, she sensed God calling her into His full-time service as well.

As a would-be preacher, I knew I needed God's might and power in my life. I also knew I was totally inadequate. I had not heard much about the power of God available to the Christian, but I knew I needed something.

Our home was near the field where we practiced football. I went alone to that field one night to seek the Lord. It was a beautiful South Florida summer night. I walked and prayed, "Lord Jesus, I want You to use me." Then I knelt down and repeated, "Lord Jesus, I want You to use me." Then, wanting to humble myself before Him, I stretched out prostrate, face down on the grass and said, "Lord Jesus, I am Yours. Please use me." That still did not seem low enough. So I made a hole in the dirt and placed my nose into it. "Lord Jesus, I am as low as I know how to get. Please use me."

(I did not know it then, but I learned later the English word "humble" comes from a Latin root humus meaning "ground" or "earth.")

Again, something happened in my life that night. I didn't have ecstasies or a vision of any kind, but there was a transformation. At that time, I knew very little theology. But I would be less than honest to deny that God graciously released His power into my young heart and life. There was a great joy present and a desire to share Christ with everyone.

Shortly after that time, I entered college and was asked to serve as pastor of a small country church. I was nineteen years of age and utterly untrained. I am sure my preaching was greatly lacking in form and content, but God graciously and visibly worked. I was often surprised at His power. There were commitments for repentance and tears of joy from the start in that little congregation. People were brought to Christ in unusual numbers for such a small church and town. There was no mistaking the mighty hand of God.[23]

The Testimony of Oswald J. Smith

It was in Tampa, Florida, February 10th, 1927. I had delivered a message on The Highest Form of Christian Service; viz., Intercessory Prayer. At the close I called for a season of prayer, and knelt where I was, beside the pulpit on the platform in the Alliance Tabernacle.

Now I am handicapped for words. How am I going to describe it? What can I say? Nothing was farther from my mind. Not for a moment had I expected anything unusual that morning. But as the people prayed, I was conscious of an unusual Presence. God seemed to hover over the meeting. Presently the blessing began to fall. I was melted, broken, awed, my heart filled with unutterable love; and as my soul rose to meet Him, the tears began to come. I could do nothing but weep and praise my precious Lord.

It seemed as though my whole body was bathed in the Holy Ghost, until I was lost in wonder, love and praise. I felt as though I wanted to love everybody. The world and all its troubles faded from my sight. My trials appeared, oh, so insignificant, as God, God Himself filled my whole vision. Oh, it was glorious!

The people saw it. I was conscious of their wonder as they looked up and breathed a "Praise the Lord!" "Hallelujah!" etc. Presently I began to pray, but only exclamations of praise and adoration poured from my lips. I saw no one save Jesus only. As I prayed the audience joined in, some in tones subdued and low, others in ejaculations of thanksgiving. All seemed conscious of God's presence and power. Tears still flowed from my eyes.

After a while I quietly slipped out, and hurried to my room in John Minder's home. There I saw my mail for which I had been eagerly waiting, lying on the table. But it remained untouched. Back and forth I walked, my face uplifted, my heart thrilled, praising and blessing God. Oh, how near the Saviour was!

As I continued to praise God, the door suddenly opened and a young man came in. I did not give him time to tell me what he wanted, but with quivering voice and yearning heart, I pleaded with him for Christ, and a minute later got him on his knees and poured out my heart in prayer on his behalf. It had been so easy to speak to him just then.

After a while I stopped long enough to glance at my mail. Then, feeling that I could not bear to meet people at the dinner table, I left the house, and wandered I know not where. Every now and again as I walked along the street praising God, the tears would start to my eyes until they became so red that I wondered what the people would think was the matter with me. Time after time I was choked with unutterable outbursts of worship and love that seemed to almost overwhelm me. I sang, deep down in my soul, my own chorus:

Alone, dear Lord, ah yes, alone with Thee!
My aching heart at rest, my spirit free;
My sorrow gone, my burdens all forgotten,
When far away I soar alone with Thee.

I seemed shut in with God. For a while as I walked I would think of something else, but in a moment my thoughts would fly back to God, and again the tears gushed forth as my heart was melted, humbled and broken in His presence.

At last I wended my way back to my room with a sweet, settled peace in my heart and a light that never shone on land or sea in my soul. The glow passed, but the Anointing remained. I did not speak in tongues and I never have, but I had a foretaste of what shall be hereafter. Oh, how I love and adore Him! Jesus, my Lord, my God![24]

The Testimony of Charles T. Studd

Having spent three months in reading my Bible and praying to God for guidance, I came back much better, but still not knowing what I was to do. I decided to read for the Bar until He should show me. I found, however, when I got back to town, that it was absolutely impossible for me conscientiously to go into any business or profession. It seemed so thoroughly inconsistent. God had given me far more than was sufficient to keep my body and soul together, and, I thought, how could I spend the best years of my life in working for myself and the honours and pleasures of this world, while thousands and thousands of souls are perishing every day without having heard of Christ?

About this time I met with a tract written by an atheist. It read as follows: "Did I firmly believe, as millions say they do, that the knowledge and practice of religion in this life influences destiny in another, religion would mean to me everything. I would cast away earthly enjoyments as dross, earthly cares as follies, and earthly thoughts and feelings as vanity. Religion would be my first waking thought, and my last image before sleep sank me into unconsciousness. I should labour in its cause alone. I would take thought for the morrow of Eternity alone. I would esteem one soul gained for heaven worth a life of suffering. Earthly consequences should never stay my hand, nor seal my lips. Earth, its joys and its griefs, would occupy no moment of my thoughts. I would strive to look upon Eternity alone, and on the Immortal Souls around me, soon to be everlastingly happy or everlastingly miserable. I would go forth to the world and preach to it in season and out of season, and my text would be, WHAT SHALL IT PROFIT A MAN IF HE GAIN THE WHOLE WORLD AND LOSE HIS SOUL?" I at once saw that this was the truly consistent Christian life. When I looked back upon my own life I saw how inconsistent it had been. I therefore determined that from that time forth my life should be consistent, and I set myself to know what was God's will for me. But this time I determined not to consult with flesh and blood, but just wait until God should show me.

About three days afterwards a great friend of mine came back to town, and asked me to go to a Bible meeting with him. I went, and after we had read the Bible for some time, and spoken about it among ourselves, he said, "Have you heard of the extraordinary blessing Mrs. W. has received?" "No." "Well, you know she has been an earnest Christian worker nearly her whole life, and she has had a good deal of sorrow and trouble, which has naturally influenced and weighed upon her. But lately somehow God has given her such a blessing that it does not affect her at all now. Nothing, in fact, seems to trouble her. She lives a life of perfect peace. Her life is like one of heaven upon earth." We began at once looking into the Bible to see if God had promised such a blessing as this, and it was not long before we found that God had promised it to believers, a peace which passeth all understanding, and a joy that is unspeakable. We then began to examine ourselves earnestly, and we found that we had not got this. But we wanted the best thing that God could give us, so we knelt down and asked Him to give us this blessing. Then we separated.

I was very much in earnest about it, so when I went up to my own room I again asked God to give me this peace and joy. That very day I met with the book, *The Christian's Secret of a Happy Life*. In it was stated that this blessing is exactly what God gives to everyone who is ready and willing to receive it. I found that the reason why I had not received it was just this, that I had not made room for it, and I found, as I sat there alone thinking, that I had been keeping back from God what belonged to Him. I found that I had been bought with the price of the precious blood of the Lord Jesus, and that I had kept back myself from Him, and had not wholly yielded.

As soon as I found this out, I went down on my knees and gave myself up to God in the words of Frances Ridley Havergal's Consecration Hymn:

> "Take my life and let it be,
> Consecrated, Lord, to Thee."

I found the next step was to have simple, childlike faith, to believe that what I had committed to God, He was also willing to take and keep. I knew I had committed my soul to His keeping and He was able to keep that; how much more then was He able to keep me and what belonged to me in this world? I realized that my life was to be one of simple, childlike faith, and that my part was to trust, not to do. I was to trust in Him and He would work in me to do His good pleasure. From that time my life has been different, and He has given me that peace that passeth understanding and that joy which is unspeakable.

It was not very long before God led me to go to China. I had never thought of going out of the country before. I had felt that England was big enough for me. But now my mind seemed constantly to run in the direction of the Lord's work abroad. I went one day with my friend Mr. Stanley Smith to Mr. McCarthy's farewell, and I shall never forget the earnest and solemn way in which he told us of the need of earnest workers to preach the Gospel. I thought, however, that I would not decide at once, because people would say I was led by impulse. I therefore resolved that after the meeting I would go and ask God. I prayed to God to guide me by His Word. I felt that there was the love of my mother; but I read that passage, "He that loveth father or mother more than me is not worthy of me," after which I knew it was God's will, and I decided to go.[25]

The Testimony of J. Hudson Taylor

As to work—mine was never so plentiful, so responsible or so difficult, but the weight and strain are all *gone*. The last month or more has been, perhaps, the happiest of my life, and I long to tell you a little

of what the Lord has done for my soul. I do not know how far I may
be able to make myself intelligible about it, for there is nothing new or
strange or wonderful—and yet, all is new! . . .

Perhaps I may make myself more clear if I go back a little. Well,
dearie, my mind has been greatly exercised for six or eight months
past, feeling the need personally and for our Mission of more holiness,
life, power in our souls. But personal need stood first and was the
greatest. I felt the ingratitude, the danger, the sin of not living nearer
to God. I prayed, agonized, fasted, strove, made resolutions, read the
Word more diligently, sought more time for meditation—but all without avail. Every day, almost every hour, the consciousness of sin
oppressed me.

I knew that if only I could abide in Christ all would be well, but I
could not. I would begin the day with prayer, determined not to take
my eye off Him for a moment, but pressure of duties, sometimes very
trying, and constant interruptions apt to be so wearing, caused me to
forget Him. Then one's nerves get so fretted in this climate that temptations to irritability, hard thoughts and sometimes unkind words are
all the more difficult to control. Each day brought its register of sin and
failure, of lack of power. To will was indeed "present with me," but
how to perform I found not.

Then came the question, is there no rescue? Must it be thus to the
end—constant conflict, and too often defeat? How could I preach with
sincerity that, to those who receive Jesus, "to them gave he power to
become the sons of God" (i.e., Godlike) when it was not so in my own
experience? Instead of growing stronger, I seemed to be getting weaker
and to have less power against sin; and no wonder, for faith and even
hope were getting low. I hated myself, I hated my sin, yet gained no
strength against it. I felt I was a child of God. His Spirit in my heart
would cry, in spite of all, "Abba, Father." But to rise to my privileges
as a child, I was utterly powerless. . . .

All the time I felt assured that there was in Christ all I needed, but
the practical question was—how to get it out. He was rich truly, but I
was poor; He was strong, but I weak. I knew full well that there was
in the root, the stem, abundant fatness, but how to get it into my puny
little branch was the question. As gradually light dawned, I saw that
faith was the only requisite—was the hand to lay hold on His fulness
and make it mine. But I had not this faith.

I strove for faith, but it would not come; I tried to exercise it, but in
vain. Seeing more and more the wondrous supply of grace laid up in
Jesus, the fulness of our precious Saviour, my guilt and helplessness

seemed to increase. Sins committed appeared but as trifles compared with the sin of unbelief which was their cause, which could not or would not take God at His word, but rather made Him a liar! Unbelief was I felt the damning sin of the world; yet I indulged in it. I prayed for faith, but it came not. What was I to do?

When my agony of soul was at its height, a sentence in a letter from dear McCarthy was used to remove the scales from my eyes, and the Spirit of God revealed to me the truth of our *oneness with Jesus* as I had never known it before. McCarthy, who had been much exercised by the same sense of failure but saw the light before I did, wrote (I quote from memory):

"But how to get faith strengthened? Not by striving after faith, but by resting on the Faithful One."

As I read, I saw it all! "If we believe not, he abideth faithful." I looked to Jesus and saw (and when I saw, oh, how joy flowed!) that He had said, "I will never leave thee."

"Ah, *there* is rest!" I thought. "I have striven in vain to rest in Him. I'll strive no more." For has not *He* promised to abide with *me*—never to leave me, never to fail me?" And, dearie, *He never will*.

Nor was this all He showed me, nor one half. As I thought of the Vine and the branches, what light the blessed Spirit poured direct into my soul! How great seemed my mistake in wishing to get the sap, the fulness *out* of Him! I saw not only that Jesus will never leave me, but that I am a member of His body, of His flesh and of His bones. The vine is not the root merely, but all—root, stem, branches, twigs, leaves, flowers, fruit. And Jesus is not that alone—He is soil and sunshine, air and showers, and ten thousand times more than we have ever dreamed, wished for or needed. Oh, the joy of seeing this truth! I do pray that the eyes of your understanding too may be enlightened, that you may know and enjoy the riches freely given us in Christ. . . .

And since Christ has thus dwelt in my heart by faith, how happy I have been! I wish I could tell you about it, instead of writing. I am no better than before. In a sense, I do not wish to be, nor am I striving to be. But I am dead and buried with Christ—ay, and risen too! And now Christ lives in me, and "the life that I now live in the flesh, I live by the faith of the Son of God, who loved me and gave himself for me."[26]

The Testimony of R. A. Torrey

I recall the exact spot where I was kneeling in prayer in my study. . . . It was a very quiet moment, one of the most quiet moments

I ever knew. . . . Then God simply said to me, not in any audible voice, but in my heart, "It's yours. Now go and preach." . . . He had already said it to me in His Word in 1 John 5:14, 15; but I did not then know my Bible as well as I know it now, and God had pity on my ignorance and said it directly to my soul. . . . I went and preached, and I have been a new minister from that day to this. . . . Some time after this experience (I do not recall just how long after), while sitting in my room one day . . . suddenly . . . I found myself shouting (I was not brought up to shout and I am not of a shouting temperament, but I shouted like the loudest shouting Methodist), "glory to God, glory to God, glory to God," and I could not stop. . . . But that was not when I was baptized with the Holy Spirit. I was baptized with the Holy Spirit when I took Him by simple faith in the naked Word of God.[27]

The Testimony of John Wesley

About three in the morning as we were continuing instant in prayer, the power of God came mightily upon us, insomuch that many cried out for exceeding joy, and many fell to the ground. As soon as we recovered a little from the awe and amazement at the presence of His Majesty, we broke out with one voice, "We praise Thee, O God, we acknowledge Thee to be the Lord."[28]

— SOURCE NOTES —

Chapter 1

1. R. H. Strachan, *The Authority of Christian Experience: A Study in the Basis of Religious Authority* (London: Student Christian Movement, 1929), 208.
2. William Barclay, *William Barclay: A Spiritual Autobiography* (Grand Rapids, Mich.: William B. Eerdmans Publishing Co., 1977), 56, 57.
3. Augustine, *The Confessions of Augustine in Modern English*, trans. Sherwood E. Wirt (Grand Rapids, Mich.: Zondervan Publishing House, 1977), 4.
4. Lady Julian of Norwich, *Revelations of Divine Love* (London: Methuen, 1911), 12.
5. Norman P. Grubb, "Foreword," Ernest and Marie Williams, *A Closer Walk: Fifty-two Meditations* (London: Christian Literature Crusade, 1959), xi.
6. Perry Miller, *The New England Mind in the Seventeenth Century* (Cambridge, Mass.: Harvard University Press, 1953), 3.
7. Donald Grey Barnhouse, *Life by the Son: Practical Lessons in Experimental Holiness* (Philadelphia: Revelation Publications American Bible Conference Association, 1939), 33.
8. Watchman Nee, *The Normal Christian Life* (Fort Washington, Penn.: Christian Literature Crusade, 1973), 9.
9. Oswald J. Smith, *The Enduement of Power* (London: Marshall, Morgan & Scott, 1974), 55.
10. A. W. Tozer, *The Divine Conquest* (Harrisburg, Penn.: Christian Publications, 1950) 121, 122.
11. John R. Rice, *The Power of Pentecost or the Fullness of the Spirit* (Murfreesboro, Tenn.: Sword of the Lord Publishers, 1976), 277, 278.
12. Alan Redpath, "The Price of Christian Service," *The People and the King*, ed. David Porter (Kent, England: STL Books, 1980), 154.
13. D. W. Lambert, *Oswald Chambers: An Unbribed Soul* (London: Marshall, Morgan & Scott, 1972), 62.
14. Oswald Chambers, *My Utmost for His Highest* (New York: Dodd, Mead & Co., 1935), 101.

15. W. Stewart, "Prayer as Connected With Revivals of Religion," *Canadian Baptist Register 1861*, 29.
16. Charles Grandison Finney, *Revivals of Religion* (Old Tappan, N.J.: Fleming H. Revell Co., n.d.), 14.
17. Norman P. Grubb, "Introduction," Roy and Revel Hession, *The Calvary Road* (Fort Washington, Penn.: Christian Literature Crusade, 1977), 7.
18. Pat Robertson, *The Secret Kingdom* (Nashville, Tenn.: Thomas Nelson Publishers, 1982), 50.
19. R. A. Torrey, *How to Bring Men to Christ* (Chicago: Fleming H. Revell Co., 1893), 104, 111, 112.
20. Andrew Murray, *Absolute Surrender* (London: Marshall, Morgan & Scott, n.d.), 35.
21. Bud Robinson, *The Moth-eaten Garment* (Kansas City, Mo.: Beacon Hill Press, 1961), 38, 39.
22. David Wilkerson with John and Elizabeth Sherrill, *The Cross and the Switchblade* (Westwood, N.J.: Fleming H. Revell Co., 1967), see chapters 20, 21.
23. Helen E. Bingham, *An Irish Saint: The Life Story of Ann Preston Known Also as "Holy Ann"* (Toronto: Evangelical Publishers, 1927), 80, 81.
24. Kenneth Scott Latourette, *A History of Christianity* (New York: Harper & Row, 1953), 432.

Chapter 2

1. Arthur T. Pierson, *George Müller of Bristol and His Witness to a Prayer-Hearing God* (New York: Loizeaux Brothers/Bible Truth Depot, 1944), 303.
2. James I. Packer, "Faith," *Baker's Dictionary of Theology*, ed. Everett F. Harrison (Grand Rapids, Mich.: Baker Book House, 1960), 209.
3. Augustus Hopkins Strong, *Systematic Theology* (Old Tappan, N.J.: Fleming H. Revell Co., 1907), 838.
4. D. Martyn Lloyd–Jones, *Romans: An Exposition of Chapter 5: Assurance* (Grand Rapids, Mich.: Zondervan Publishing House, 1975), 7.
5. George Mueller, *Autobiography of George Mueller* (London: J. Nisbet & Co., 1905), 173.
6. Russ Johnston with Maureen Rank, *God Can Make It Happen* (Wheaton, Ill.: Victor Books, 1977), 7.
7. Donald Gee, *Concerning Spiritual Gifts* (Springfield, Mo.: Gospel Publishing House, 1972), 42.
8. Albert Barnes, *Barnes Notes on the New Testament: James, Peter, John and Jude* (Grand Rapids, Mich.: Baker Book House, 1974), 302.

9. Willoughby C. Allen, *The International Critical Commentary: A Critical and Exegetical Commentary on the Gospel According to Matthew* (Edinburgh: T & T Clark, 1972), 9.

10. John Gill, *An Exposition of the New Testament* (London: Matthews & Leigh, 1976), 559.

11. John Charles Ellicott, *A New Testament Commentary for English Readers* (London: Cassell & Co., 1897), 38.

12. Henry Alford, *The Greek New Testament* (Chicago: Moody Press, 1968), 1:83, 84.

13. R. C. H. Lenski, *The Interpretation of St. Matthew's Gospel* (Minneapolis, Minn.: Augsburg Publishing House, 1961), 539.

14. Heinrich August Wilhelm Meyer, *Commentary on the New Testament* (New York: Funk & Wagnalls Pub., 1887), 314.

15. Ibid., 523.

16. Lenski, *St. Matthew's Gospel*, 117.

Chapter 3

1. Dan Basham, *A Handbook on Holy Spirit Baptism* (Monroeville, Penn.: Whitaker Books), cited by Erling Jorstad, *The Holy Spirit in Today's Church: A Handbook of the New Pentecostalism* (New York: Abingdon Press, 1973), 78, 79.

2. Sir Robert Anderson, *Spirit Manifestations and the Gift of Tongues* (New York: Loizeaux Brothers/Bible Truth Depot, n.d.), 3.

3. George W. Dollar, *The New Testament and New Pentecostalism* (Maple Grove, Minn.: Nystrom Publishing Co., 1978), 2, 3. *See also* John Thomas Nichol, *Pentecostalism* (New York: Harper, 1966), 7; Jorstad, *Holy Spirit*, 12.

4. Mortan T. Kelsey, *Tongue Speaking: An Experiment in Spiritual Experience* (Garden City, N.Y.: Doubleday & Co., 1968). Kelsey devotes chapter 3, "A Peculiar History," to a survey of church history, claiming statements of the existence of these phenomena in the experience of these groups and several other individuals, including Martin Luther, Dante, and Francis Bacon.

5. Dollar, *New Testament*, 7–11; Jorstad, *Holy Spirit*, 16–18. Dollar also includes the ministry of David J. du Plessis in ecumenical and academic circles as significant in giving credibility to the movement.

6. *The Statement of Fundamental Truths of the Assemblies of God*, Article 8.

7. Joseph Smith, *Statement of Faith*, Article 7.

8. George W. Peters, *Indonesia Revival: Focus on Timor* (Grand Rapids, Mich.: Zondervan Publishing House, 1975), 80–83.

9. Ibid., 72.
10. Anderson, *Spirit Manifestations*, 11, 12.
11. S. I. McMillen, *None of These Diseases* (New York: Pyramid Books, 1968), 58.
12. Peters, *Indonesia Revival*, 74.
13. Carl G. Jung, *Modern Man in Search of a Soul* (New York: Harcourt, Brace & Co., 1933), 261.
14. Joseph G. Moore, "Religious Syncretism in Jamaica," *Practical Anthropology* (1965) 12:64.
15. M. J. Field, *Search for Security: An Ethno Psychiatric Study of Rural Ghana* (Evanston, Ill.: Northwestern University Press, 1960), 59.
16. George W. Peters, *Indonesia Revival*, 58–63.
17. Douglas Porter, "The Children of God," *Evangelical Baptist* (March, 1975), 9.
18. Peters, *Indonesia Revival*, 57, 58.
19. Kathryn Kuhlman, *I Believe in Miracles* (Englewood Cliffs, N.J.: Prentice-Hall, 1968).
20. Charles Grandison Finney, *Revivals of Religion* (Old Tappan, N.J.: Fleming H. Revell Co., n.d.), 4.
21. Augustus Hopkins Strong, *Systematic Theology* (Old Tappan, N.J.: Fleming H. Revell Co., 1907), 118.
22. Henry C. Theissen, *Lectures in Systematic Theology* (Grand Rapids, Mich.: William B. Eerdman Publishing Co., 1949), 35.
23. Peters, *Indonesia Revival*.
24. C. S. Lewis, *Miracles: A Preliminary Study* (New York: Macmillan Co., n.d.), 9.
25. W. E. Vine, *Vine's Expository Dictionary of Old and New Testament Words*, ed. F. F. Bruce, vol. 4 (Old Tappan, N.J.: Fleming H. Revell Co., 1981), 29, 30.
26. Peters, *Indonesia Revival*, 79, 80.

Chapter 4

1. Augustus Hopkins Strong, *Systematic Theology* (Old Tappan, N.J.: Fleming H. Revell Co., 1907), 32.
2. Roland H. Bainton, *The Reformation of the Sixteenth Century* (Boston: Beacon Press, 1952), 124, 125.
3. Earle E. Cairns, *Christianity Through the Centuries* (Grand Rapids, Mich.: Zondervan Publishing House, 1979), 271, 272.
4. Kenneth Scott Latourette, *A History of Christianity* (New York: Harper & Row, 1953), 542.
5. A. W. Tozer, *The Divine Conquest* (Harrisburg, Penn.: Christian Publications, 1950), 11, 12.

6. William Ralph Enge, *Christian Mysticism* (London: Methuen, 1899), 5.
7. Cairns, *Christianity* 108, 109.
8. Strong, *Systematic Theology*, 31.
9. Bainton, 124.
10. A. J. Gordon, *Ministry of the Spirit* (Grand Rapids, Mich.: Zondervan Publishing House, 1949), 116.
11. Andrew Murray, *Absolute Surrender* (London: Marshall, Morgan & Scott, n.d.), 64, 69.
12. Madame Jeanne Guyon, *Experiencing the Depths of Jesus Christ*, ed. Gene Edwards (Goleta, Calif.: Christian Books, 1981), x, xi.
13. Henry Scougal, *The Life of God in the Soul of Man* (Philadelphia: Westminster Press, 1948), 30.
14. Bainton, *Reformation*, 212.
15. Cited by Oswald J. Smith, *The Enduement of Power* (London: Marshall, Morgan & Scott, 1974), 59.
16. R. A. Torrey, *The Holy Spirit, Who He Is and What He Does* (New York: Fleming H. Revell Co., 1927), 198, 199.
17. Cited by W. R. Moody, *The Life of Dwight L. Moody*, 2nd. ed. (Kilmarnock: John Ritchie, n.d.), 135.
18. Smith, *Enduement*, 66.
19. Charles Grandison Finney, *Memoirs of Charles G. Finney* (New York: Fleming H. Revell, 1876), 20.
20. Cited by Oswald J. Smith, *The Revival We Need* (London: Marshall, Morgan & Scott, 1950), 42, 43.
21. Ibid., 43.
22. Ibid., 43, 44.
23. A. M. Hills, *Holiness and Power* (Cincinnati: Revivalist Office, n.d.), 336.
24. These terms are those used by James H. McConkey, *The Threefold Secret of the Holy Spirit* (Chicago: Moody Press, 1897).
25. Not all writers would agree with the conclusion that mystics are essentially ascetic. In an attempt to make a distinction, *The Catholic Encyclopedia* (New York: Applebon, 1907), vol. 1, 768 argues, "asceticism is ethical; mysticism, largely intellectual." Similarly, this distinction is emphasized by evangelical author Kenneth Ronald Davis, *Anabaptism and Asceticism* (Kitchener, Ontario: Herald Press, 1974), 38, when he defines asceticism: " . . . Three factors emerge as essential ingredients for a balanced understanding of Christian asceticism: (1) negatively, the resistance to and struggle against the evil impulses of the "fallen" flesh, with separation from this— worldly society and its temptations as a corollary; (2) positively, the development of virtues that lead towards spiritual perfection;

and (3) an otherworldly conditioned ethical and moral thrust (heroic ethics) which distinguishes it from mysticism."
26. Dr. Curtis Hutson, editor of *The Sword of the Lord*, has sold and advocated the book by James Gilcrest Lawson, *Deeper Experiences of Famous Christians* (Anderson, Ind.: Warner Press, 1978) in his meetings and conferences. However, Hutson's theology is different from the holiness implications of the experiences of the Roman Catholic mystics in the book, including the extremes of Savonarola, which he uses as an example.

Chapter 5

1. Augustus Hopkins Strong, *Systematic Theology* (Old Tappan, N.J.: Fleming H. Revell Co., 1907), 795.
2. C. H. M., *Miscellaneous Writings*, vol. 3, "The Christian: His Position and Work" (New York: Loizeaux Brothers/Bible Truth Depot, n.d.), 2.
3. There are, of course, significant exceptions to this general rule, including Major Ian Thomas's exposition of the resurrection life, *The Saving Life of Christ* (Grand Rapids, Mich.: Zondervan Publishing House, 1961), and H. A. Ironside's commentary on Ephesians, emphasizing the theme of the believer's position "in the heavenlies." Still, L. E. Maxwell's *Born Crucified* (Chicago: Moody Press, 1945), is more typical in content of the theme of both preaching and publications dealing with the believer's togetherness with Christ.
4. Archibald Alexander Hodge, *Outlines of Theology* (London: Thomas Nelson & Sons, 1883), 484.
5. E. M. Bounds, *Power Through Prayer* (Grand Rapids, Mich.: Baker Book House, 1973), 18, 19.
6. A. W. Tozer, *The Root of the Righteous* (Harrisburg, Penn.: Christian Publications, 1955), 66.
7. Watchman Nee, *The Normal Christian Life* (Fort Washington, Penn.: Christian Literature Crusade, 1973), 35.
8. "Fellowship With Christ," *The Present Testimony 9*, no. 15, 353.
9. John Murray, *The Epistle to the Romans: The English Text With Introduction, Exposition and Notes* (Grand Rapids, Mich.: William B. Eerdmans Publishing Co., 1977), 213.
10. Strong, *Systematic Theology*, 797, 798.
11. Archibald Thomas Robertson, *Word Pictures in the New Testament*, vol. 2 (New York: Richard R. Smith, 1930), 70.
12. Albert Barnes, *Notes on the New Testament Explanatory and Practical:*

James, Peter, John, and Jude (Grand Rapids, Mich.: Baker Book
House, 1949), 220.
13. "Fellowship With Christ," 17.
14. Earl D. Radmacher, *The Nature of the Church* (Portland, Ore.: Western Baptist Press, 1972), 268, 269.
15. Cited by Strong, *Systematic Theology*, 808.
16. J. Robert Nelson, *The Realm of Redemption* (London: Epworth Press, 1953), 93–95.
17. J. B. Lightfoot, *St. Paul's Epistles to the Colossians and to Philemon* (Grand Rapids, Mich.: Zondervan Publishing House, n.d.), 157.
18. Cited by Strong, *Systematic Theology*, 808.
19. A note on Ephesians 5:30, 31 in *The Scofield Reference Bible* (1917) specifically identifies Eve, Rebecca, Asenath and Zipporah as "bride types."
20. M. L. H., *Song of Songs* (New York: Our Hope, n.d.); Andrew Miller, *Meditations on The Song of Solomon* (London: G. Monish, 1877); J. Hudson Taylor, *Union and Communion* (Minneapolis, Minn.: Bethany Fellowship, n.d.).
21. Lehman Strauss, *Devotional Studies in Galatians and Ephesians* (New York: Loizeaux Brothers, 1958), 210.
22. H. C. G. Moule, *The Epistle of Paul the Apostle to the Ephesians With Introduction and Notes* (Cambridge: Cambridge University Press, 1910), 143.
23. Cited by Strong, *Systematic Theology*, 808.
24. A. R. George, *Communion With God in the New Testament*, 133.
25. Hodge, *Outlines of Theology*, 484, 485.
26. Russell Benjamin Miller, "Communion (Fellowship)," *The International Standard Bible Encyclopedia*, ed. James Orr (Grand Rapids, Mich.: William B. Eerdmans Publishing Co., 1974), 689.
27. A. W. Tozer, *That Incredible Christian* (Harrisburg, Penn.: Christian Publications, 1964), 33, 34.
28. Taylor, *Union and Communion*, 25.
29. Tozer, *Incredible Christian*, 67.
30. Miller, *Meditations*, v.
31. Robert E. Coleman, *The Mind of the Master* (Old Tappan, N.J.: Fleming H. Revell Co., 1977), 67, 68.
32. Taylor, *Union and Communion*, 94.

Chapter 6

1. James M. Campbell, *Paul the Mystic: A Study in Apostolic Experience* (London: Andrew Melrose, 1907), 66, 67.

2. Donald Grey Barnhouse, *Life By the Son: Practical Lessons in Experimental Holiness* (Philadelphia: Revelation Publication, 1939), 47, 48, 59.
3. A. W. Tozer, *That Incredible Christian* (Harrisburg, Pa.: Christian Publications, 1964), 18.
4. Edgar Young Mullins, *The Christian Religion in Its Doctrinal Expression* (New York: Roger Williams Press, 1917), 10.
5. Albert Schweitzer, *The Mysticism of Paul the Apostle*, trans. William Montgomery (New York: Henry Holt & Co., 1931), 124, 125.
6. Kirrsopp Lake, *The Earlier Epistles of St. Paul* (London: Christophers, 1934), 215.
7. D. Miall Edwards, "Mystery," *The International Standard Bible Encyclopedia*, ed. James Orr (Grand Rapids, Mich.: William B. Eerdmans Publishing Co., 1974), 2106.
8. Schweitzer, *Mysticism*, 18, 19.
9. Michel Bouttier, *Christianity According to Paul*, trans. Frank Clarke (Naperville, Ill.: Alec R. Allenson, 1966), 118.
10. Lucien Cerfaux, *The Christian in the Theology of St. Paul*, trans. Lillian Soiron (New York: Herder & Herder, 1967), 358.
11. Richard N. Longenecker, *Paul: Apostle of Liberty* (Grand Rapids, Mich.: Baker Book House, 1980), 167, 168.
12. Archibald Alexander Hodge, *Outlines of Theology* (London: Thomas Nelson & Sons, 1883), 484.
13. Rudolf Bultmann, *The Theology of the New Testament*, vol. 1 (New York: Macmillan, 1951), 311.
14. John A. T. Robinson, *The Body* (London: SCM Press, 1957), 51.
15. Augustus Hopkins Strong, *Systematic Theology* (Old Tappan, N.J.: Fleming H. Revell Co., 1907), 797.
16. Adolph Deissmann, *Die Neutestamentliche Formel "in Christo Jesu"* (Marburg: Elwert, 1892), cited by Longenecker, *Paul*, 164 ff.
17. Sister Sylvia Mary, *Pauline and Johannine Mysticism* (London: Barton, Longman & Todd, 1964), 22.
18. Longenecker, *Paul*, 170.
19. John F. Walvoord, *The Thessalonian Epistles* (Grand Rapids, Mich.: Zondervan Publishing House, 1973), 72, 73.
20. Longenecker, *Paul*, 167.
21. Schweitzer, *Mysticism*, 125.
22. Watchman Nee, *The Normal Christian Life* (Fort Washington, Penn.: Christian Literature Crusade, 1973), 29, 30.
23. Stuart Briscoe, *The Fullness of Christ* (Grand Rapids, Mich.: Zondervan Publishing House, 1965), 59, 60.

Chapter 7

1. W. R. Inge, *Mysticism in Religion* (London: Hutchinsons' Universal Library), 8.

2. Madame Guyon, *Short and Very Easy Method of Prayer*, 125.
3. Henry Scougal, *The Life of God in the Soul of Man* (Philadelphia: Westminster Press, 1948), 33, 34.
4. Stuart Briscoe, *The Fullness of Christ* (Grand Rapids, Mich.: Zondervan Publishing House, 1965), 63.
5. A. W. Tozer, *Born After Midnight* (Ferndale, Mich.: Christian Pub., n.d.), 122.
6. Guyon, *Method of Prayer*, 125.
7. Scougal, *Life of God*, 40.
8. Sister Sylvia Mary, *Pauline and Johannine Mysticism* (London: Darton, Longman & Todd, 1964), 105.
9. James Gilchrist Lawson, *Deeper Experiences of Famous Christians* (Anderson, Ind.: Warner Press, 1978), 42–57.
10. Scougal, *Life of God*, 69.
11. Tozer, *Born*, 122.
12. Briscoe, *Fullness*, 82, 83.
13. Andrew Murray, *Absolute Surrender* (London: Marshall, Morgan & Scott, n.d.).
14. Cited by Lawson, *Deeper Experiences*, 268.
15. Briscoe, *Fullness*, 96.
16. J. Hudson Taylor, *Union and Communion* (Minneapolis, Minn.: Bethany Fellowship, n.d.), 55.
17. Guyon, *Method of Prayer*, 127.

Chapter 8

1. Anthony A. Hoekema, *Holy Spirit Baptism* (Grand Rapids, Mich.: William B. Eerdmans Publishing Co., 1972), 10.
2. *The Statement of Fundamental Truths of the Assemblies of God*, Article 8.
3. H. Leisegang, "Pneuma Hagion," *Studies in Early Christianity*, ed. S. J. Case (New York: Century, 1928), 76.
4. Barret, *The Holy Spirit and Gospel Tradition* (New York: Macmillan, 1947), 127.
5. Samuel Ragan, *Breath of Fire: The Holy Spirit: The Heart of the Christian Gospel* (London: Geoffrey Chapman, 1979), 13.
6. Edward Lien, *The Holy Ghost and His Work in Souls* (New York: Sheed & Ward, 1937), 136.
7. The King James Version of verse 2 is unfortunate. "Have ye received the Holy Ghost since ye believed?" should be more literally translated, "Did you receive the Holy Spirit, having believed?" or "Did you receive the Holy Spirit when you believed?"

8. F. E. Marsh, *Emblems of the Holy Spirit* (London: Pickering & Inglis, 1923), 28.
9. Charles Haddon Spurgeon, *Twelve Sermons on the Holy Spirit*, (Grand Rapids, Mich.: Baker Book House, 1973), 51.
10. John R. Rice, *The Power of Pentecost or Fullness of the Spirit* (Murfreesboro, Tenn.: Sword of the Lord Publishers, 1976), 792.
11. Stuart Briscoe, *Living Dangerously: A Challenge to Daring and Dynamic Commitment* (Grand Rapids, Mich.: Zondervan Publishing House, 1974), 118.
12. C. Sumner Wemp, *How on Earth Can I Be Spiritual?* (New York: Thomas Nelson Publishers, 1978), 49.
13. F. B. Meyer, *Back to Bethel: Separation From Sin and Fellowship With God* (Chicago: The Bible Institute Colportage Association, 1901), 93.
14. Bill Bright, *The Christian and the Holy Spirit* (Arrowhead Springs, Calif.: Campus Crusade for Christ, 1968), 16.
15. Wemp, *How on Earth?*, 56, 57.
16. W. H. Griffith Thomas, *The Christian Life and How to Live It* (Chicago: Moody Press, 1919), 97.

Chapter 9

1. Oswald J. Smith, *The Enduement of Power* (London: Marshall, Morgan & Scott, 1974), 55.
2. A. B. Simpson, *The Holy Spirit or Power From on High, Part 2, The New Testament* (Harrisburg, Penn.: Christian Publications, n.d.), 76.
3. W. E. Vine, *An Expository Dictionary of New Testament Words*, vol. 1 (Old Tappan, N.J.: Fleming H. Revell Co., n.d.), 59.
4. Watchman Nee, *The Normal Christian Life* (Fort Washington, Penn.: Christian Literature Crusade, 1973), 84, 86.
5. Henry Barclay Swete, *The Holy Spirit in the New Testament: A Study of Primitive Christian Teaching* (London: Macmillan and Co., 1910), 385, 386.
6. C. R. Vaughan, *The Gifts of the Holy Spirit to Unbelievers and Believers* (Edinburgh: Banner of Truth Trust, 1984), 278.
7. Oswald J. Smith, *Enduement*, 64.
8. Arthur Wallis, *Rain From Heaven: Revival in Scripture and History* (London: Hodder & Stoughton, 1979), 119.
9. J. Edwin Orr, *The Flaming Tongue: Evangelical Awakenings, 1900–* (Chicago: Moody Press, 1973), vii; *The Fervent Prayer: The World-*

wide Impact of the Great Awakening of 1858 (Chicago: Moody Press, 1974), vii; *The Eager Feet: Evangelical Awakenings, 1790–1830* (Chicago: Moody Press, 1974), vii.
10. Chester K. Leham, *The Holy Spirit and the Holy Life* (Scottdale, Penn.: Herald Press, 1959), 65.
11. Ibid., 70.
12. Wallis, *Rain From Heaven*, 52.
13. Orr, *Flaming Tongue; Fervent Prayer; Eager Feet*, vii.
14. Vaughan, *Gifts*, 276, 277.
15. Smith, *Enduement*, 59, 60.
16. F. B. Meyer, *Back to Bethel: Separation From Sin and Fellowship With God* (Chicago: The Bible Institute Colportage Association, 1901), 97–101.
17. Smith, *Enduement*, 71.
18. Vaughan, *Gifts*, 290.
19. Watchman Nee, *Normal Christian Life*, 87.
20. Smith, *Enduement*, 61–64.
21. Edward E. Hindson, *Glory in the Church: The Coming Revival* (New York: Thomas Nelson Publishers, 1975), 63.

Chapter 10

1. Alexander MacLaren, cited by Mrs. Howard Taylor, *Bordan of Yale '09: "The Life that Counts"* (Toronto: China Inland Mission, 1957), 71.
2. Charles Haddon Spurgeon, *Morning and Evening: Daily Readings* (Grand Rapids, Mich.: Zondervan Publishing House, 1976), 577.
3. Henry Scougal, *The Life of God in the Soul of Man* (Philadelphia: Westminster Press, 1948), 62.
4. Andrew Murray, *Absolute Surrender* (London: Marshall, Morgan & Scott, n.d.), 54, 55.
5. Oswald Chambers, *My Utmost for His Highest* (New York: Dodd, Mead & Co., 1935), 297.
6. James M. Stifler, *The Epistle to the Romans: A Commentary Logical and Historical* (Chicago: Moody Press, 1977), 204.
7. Herman A. Hoyte, *Romans: The Gospel of God's Grace: The Lectures of Alva J. McClain* (Chicago: Moody Press, 1980), 207.
8. Watchman Nee, *The Normal Christian Life* (Fort Washington, Penn.: Christian Literature Crusade, 1973), 69, 70, 72.
9. S. D. Gordon, *Quiet Talks on Power* (New York: Fleming H. Revell Co., n.d.), 128, 129.

10. F. Godet, *Commentary on St. Paul's Epistles to the Romans*, trans. A. Cusin (Edinburgh: T. & T. Clark, 1890), 228, 229.
11. Nee, *Normal Christian Life*, 33.

Chapter 11

1. Archibald Thomas Robertson, *Word Pictures in the New Testament*, vol. 1 (New York: Harper & Brothers 1930), 131.
2. A. C. Gaebelein, *The Gospel of Matthew: An Exposition*, vol. 2 (New York: Our Hope, 1910), 47.
3. Matthew Henry, *Matthew Henry's Commentary on the Whole Bible*, vol. 5 (Old Tappan, N.J.: Fleming H. Revell Co., n.d.), 230.
4. Cited by Heinrich Heppe, *Reformed Dogmatics, Set Out and Illustrated from the Sources*, trans. G. T. Thomson (London: George Allen & Unwin, 1950), 24.
5. A. W. Tozer, *The Divine Conquest* (Old Tappan, N.J.: Fleming H. Revell Co., 1950), 77–78.
6. Bernard Ramm, *The Witness of the Spirit* (Grand Rapids, Mich.: William B. Eerdmans Publishing Co., 1959), 12.
7. Robertson, *Word Pictures*, vol. 6, 210.
8. Charles J. Rolls, *A Synoptical Study of the Books of the Bible: The First Epistle of John* (Strathfield, Australia: Sydney Bible Training Institute, 1937), 69, 70.

Appendix

1. From a letter by Catherine Booth to her parents, cited by James Gilchrist Lawson, *Deeper Experiences of Famous Christians* (Anderson, Ind.: Warner Press, 1978), 255, 256.
2. From a letter to his mother concerning the closing meeting of R. A. Torrey in London, England, July 2, 1905, cited by Mrs. Howard Taylor, *Borden of Yale '09: "The Life That Counts"* (Toronto: China Inland Mission, 1957), 81, 82.
3. From his journal entry of October 19, 1740, cited by Lawson, *Deeper Experiences*, 264, 265.
4. From his journal entry of March 10, 1743, cited by Lawson, *Deeper Experiences*, 265.
5. Cited by Oswald J. Smith, *The Enduement of Power* (London: Marshall, Morgan & Scott, 1933), 59.

6. From F. W. Bourne, *The King's Son, A Memoir of Billy Bray*, cited by Lawson, *Deeper Experiences*, 187, 188.
7. J. Wilbur Chapman, *The Life and Work of Dwight L. Moody* (New Haven, Conn.: Butler & Alger, 1900), 199, 200.
8. From A. B. Earle, *The Rest of Faith* (1871), cited by Lawson, *Deeper Experiences*, 216–220.
9. Cited by Oswald J. Smith, *The Revival We Need* (London: Marshall, Morgan & Scott, 1933), 43–45.
10. Elmer L. Towns, *Church Aflame* (Nashville, Tenn.: Impact Books, 1971), 27, 28.
11. Charles G. Finney, *Memoirs of Rev. Charles G. Finney* (New York: Fleming H. Revell Co., 1876), 20–23.
12. From a letter by Hester Ann Rogers, describing a meeting with John Fletcher, held in 1781; cited by Lawson, *Deeper Experiences*, 142, 143.
13. Rosalind Goforth, *How I Know God Answers Prayer: The Personal Testimony of One Lifetime* (Lincoln, Neb.: Back to the Bible Publishers, n.d.), 118–124.
14. Cited by Chapman, *Dwight L. Moody*, 198, 199.
15. Billy Graham, "The Holy Spirit," *Christian Herald* (Oct. 1978), 16, 18.
16. Cited by Edward E. Ham, *Fifty Years on the Battle Front With Christ: A Biography of Mordecai F. Ham* (Nashville, Tenn.: Old Kentucky Home Revivalist, 1950), 28.
17. Henry Allen Ironside, *Holiness: The False and the True* (New York: Loizeaux Brothers, n.d.), 12–15, 28–34.
18. Cited by Lawson, *Deeper Experiences*, 197–200.
19. Cited by Smith, *Enduement*, 57, 58.
20. From a statement made in Glasgow, Scotland, cited by Chapman, *Dwight L. Moody*, 412, 413.
21. Phoebe Palmer, *The Way of Holiness*, cited by Lawson, *Deeper Experiences*, 269.
22. Cited by Smith, *Revival*, 42, 43.
23. Adrian Rogers, *The Secret of Supernatural Living* (Nashville, Tenn.: Thomas Nelson Publishers, 1982), 9, 10.
24. Oswald J. Smith, "The Anointing of the Spirit" (Toronto: The Peoples Church, n.d.).
25. Cited by Norman P. Grubb, *C. T. Studd: Athlete and Pioneer* (Grand Rapids, Mich.: Zondervan Publishing House, 1937), 40–44.
26. From a letter to his sister, Mrs. Broomhall, cited by Howard and Geraldine Taylor, *Hudson Taylor's Spiritual Secret* (Chicago: Moody Press, 1932), 158–164.

27. From R. A. Torrey, *The Holy Spirit, Who He Is and What He Does* (New York: Fleming H. Revell Co., 1927), 198–200.

28. From his journal entry for Monday, January 1, 1739, cited by Lawson, *Deeper Experiences*, 120.

INDEX